SOCIAL WORK THEORIES IN CONTEXT

CREATING FRAMEWORKS
FOR PRACTICE

2ND EDITION

KAREN HEALY

First edition 2005
Second edition 2014

First published 2005 by
PALGRAVE MACMILLAN

Palgrave Macmillan in the UK is an imprint of Macmillan Publishers Limited,
registered in England, company number 785998, of Houndmills, Basingstoke,
Hampshire RG21 6XS.

Palgrave Macmillan in the US is a division of St Martin's Press LLC,
175 Fifth Avenue, New York, NY 10010.

Palgrave Macmillan is the global academic imprint of the above companies
and has companies and representatives throughout the world.

Palgrave® and Macmillan® are registered trademarks in the United States,
the United Kingdom, Europe and other countries

ISBN: 978–1–137–02424–4

This book is printed on paper suitable for recycling and made from fully
managed and sustained forest sources. Logging, pulping and manufacturing
processes are expected to conform to the environmental regulations of the
country of origin.

A catalogue record for this book is available from the British Library.

A catalog record for this book is available from the Library of Congress.

Typeset by Aardvark Editorial Limited, Metfield, Suffolk.

Printed and bound in Great Britain by
TJ International, Padstow

CONTENTS

LIST OF FIGURES AND TABLES

Figures

Table

PREFACE

In this second edition of *Social Work Theories in Context*, I have built on the framework in the first edition of the book, which has stood the test of time. However, as I engage in professional practice, research and advocacy for the social work profession and the people our profession serves, I am aware that some aspects of our context and knowledge base are changing. This edition reflects these changes.

First, I have reorganized the book into three parts. Part 1 comprises two chapters in which the key concepts of discourse and theory for practice that underpin the book are introduced, alongside the dynamic framework for practice. Part 2 then focuses on the discourses shaping our practice environments and Part 3 outlines contemporary theories for practice. This reorganization is intended to ensure that from the outset readers are introduced to the key concepts and connections can be more readily made between the discourses shaping our practice contexts in Part 2 and theories for practice in Part 3.

Second, I have further developed the theoretical framework regarding the discourses shaping the institutional contexts of social work practice. In recent years, new public management has influenced diverse terrains and contexts of social work practice, and is discussed in Chapter 3. Today, neuroscience, and its potential and limits, is the subject of much debate, and is also influential in the 'psy' discourses on which social work draws, thus it is considered in Chapter 4. Of great interest too, has been the growth of alternative discourses, particularly the increased demand for voice and influence in the survivor movements in fields such as mental health and child welfare services. I acknowledge the growing influence of religion and spirituality on service contexts and processes by extending the discussion of these discourses in this edition. The increasing interest in the environment and social work is also reflected in discussion of environmental social work discourse in Chapter 5.

Third, this edition better recognizes the significant influence of systems theory on social work practice. I have also extended the range of theories for practice considered this book with discussion of the influence of 'psy' theories, such as motivational interviewing, on problem-solving practice, and more extended discussion of the strengths and solution-oriented approaches.

The reasons I initially wrote the book continue to sustain me in the second edition. I wrote this book to give social work practitioners, students and educators a foothold in the diverse and often perplexing contexts of, and theories for, practice. Throughout my career, first as a student social worker then as a social work practitioner, and now as a researcher, educator and director of a large nongovernmental community service agency, I have held a strong interest in the philosophical foundations of social work practices, particularly how these foundations are expressed and transformed in direct practice. My first book, *Social Work Practices* (Healy, 2000), aimed to expand critical approaches to social work by recognizing the diverse ways social workers go about achieving practice goals associated with empowering and critical practice, such as enhancing service user participation and promoting cooperative action. In short, I argued that there are many ways of being a change agent and that some of the established critical approaches to practice obscured this diversity.

In *Social Work Theories in Context*, I aim to further my project on the philosophical foundations of social work practices by outlining the key ideas underpinning the contemporary organization of, and approaches to, practice. If there is a core message to this book, it is this: by understanding the ideas that underpin our institutional contexts and formal theory base, we can critically use them and, where necessary, change them to achieve the values and goals to which we are committed.

By introducing you to the philosophical foundations and historical and geographical origins of key practice approaches, I hope to enhance your capacity not only to use theory, but also to contribute to formal theory creation. Despite the continuing gulf between theory and practice, I am convinced that many practitioners also seek to understand and develop theories of professional practice. However, many are alienated by the extent to which social work philosophies and theories are separated from, or even pitted against, the institutional contexts of social work practice. The first edition of the book grew, in part, from the 'theory refresher' workshops for practitioners that I began to hold for social workers in 2001. I have continued to develop these workshops to meet the emerging demands, opportunities and challenges of social work practice. The strong interest in these workshops has also strengthened my conviction that social workers do 'do' theory. The practitioners I meet at these workshops are often able to articulate how they have developed theoretical frameworks learned in their professional education for their current domains of practice. Very often, this has involved a careful sifting through elements of theory that are useful or not, and the further development of ideas to respond to the needs of their practice environment. For example, social workers in child protection services can use the strengths perspective as an addition, and perhaps a counter to, the growing use of standardized risk assessments in this field. Social workers in elderly care services may use elements of the critical tradition to challenge ageist assumptions about the capacities of older people.

In this book, I bring together a critical introduction to theories of direct practice and the ideas shaping the institutional contexts of practice – what I term 'discourses'. This is because I regard social work as a contextual activity that varies across practice contexts. By integrating analysis of context and theory, I aim to contribute to increased opportunities for social workers to develop theories in situ. Discussion of social work theories for practice and the contexts of social work practice usually occurs in separate domains, resulting in frustration for those charged with formal theory building and practitioners. One way we can promote dialogue between these two 'worlds' is by recognizing the profound influence of context in the use and development of theories for practice.

I consider that all practising social workers are social work theorists, in that each of us constructs understandings that guide us in identifying who and what should be the focus of our practice and how we should proceed. This book aims to open dialogue between social work practitioners and formal social work theory by outlining the philosophical foundations, historical and geographical origins, practical applications, and strengths and limitations of five contemporary theories of practice.

I also hope that this second edition of *Social Work Theories in Context* will enable students, practitioners and educators to make sense of how social work purpose is created through interaction between institutional contexts, service user needs and capacities, and the formal professional practice base. Social work education programmes often do a great job of introducing students to the formal professional value base of practice. Students also learn basic skills and formal theoretical frameworks for social work practice. But to use this base in practice, we must also have the ability to 'read' our institutional context, particularly its formal and informal goals and practices. I do not mean that social workers should then simply acquiesce to these organizational dictates, but, to be an effective practitioner and an effective change agent, we should understand the institutional context within which we are working. By merely socializing students into the formal professional practice base, without also linking this to a capacity to read their institutional context, we invite social workers to run 'headlong' into and against their practice context. This is a recipe for burnout and cynicism, as practitioners quickly become disillusioned with the formal base of the profession, as being 'okay in theory' but not much help in practice.

Given that most new social workers graduate to junior positions with limited official organizational power, their capacity to read and work within these organizational constraints (even as they seek to achieve institutional change) is a basic survival skill and vital for sustaining and enhancing their capacities for change practices. In recent years, I have worked on research about the transition to practice for newly qualified workers. This has heightened my awareness of the critical role of organizational context in shaping

the opportunities social workers have to engage in progressive change practices, and also the importance of analysing their institutional environments
if they are to be effective at realizing social work values.

In discussing the contextual nature of social work practice with practitioners, my concern has grown about what appears to be the increasingly
constrained environments of social work, yet I am also often pleased to
learn that a great deal of change work is already going on (often quietly and
surreptitiously) within many practice contexts. Much of this change work is
unrecognized by, and unwritten in, formal social work theory. Perhaps it is
not even possible to write it. As a social worker working primarily in an
academic environment, I am aware that our theoretical frames can perhaps
provide a guide to help practitioners articulate and improve their practice,
but we must be cautious in claiming a truth status for any theoretical
perspective. To do so would be to reinforce an authoritarian relationship
between academia and the field that is unhelpful for creating collaborative
approaches to theory building. I respect that social workers actively
construct their frameworks for practice and that formal theories provide a
thread rather than the entire context for practice.

Social workers practise in a broad range of contexts with people experiencing a diversity of concerns and oppressions. Part of the social worker's
brief is to be agents of change with clients, within our organizational
contexts, and within society more generally. I hope this book will further
social workers' capacities to understand, and contribute to, the profession's
capacity to use its institutional contexts and formal theory base to create
change in favour of the vulnerable populations with whom we work.
Creating change of this kind should be our primary and unifying concern.

ACKNOWLEDGEMENTS

I would like to thank the people who supported and inspired me for the first and second editions of this book. I thank my friends and colleagues at the University of Sydney and the University of Queensland for our conversations and debates about the intellectual foundations of social work. I also acknowledge thousands of social work practitioners and students to whom I presented my ideas in classes and theory refresher workshops for over a decade. Their many questions and ideas have helped me to refine this work.

While writing this most recent edition, I was also elected national president of the Australian Association of Social Workers, a challenging and exciting role. I thank my companions on the board and in the association who have stimulated my thinking about social work practices. I would like to acknowledge Colin Peile, who, as my PhD supervisor almost two decades ago, provided such an outstanding and inspirational role model as a social work theorist and educator.

I thank my colleagues involved in social work nationally, particularly Karyn Walsh from Micah Projects who constantly challenges me to think about the links between theory and practice. My thanks to my colleagues in Scandinavia, especially Siv Oltedal, Rolv Lyngstad and Gunn Strand Hutchinson from the University of Nordland in Norway, Tommy Lundström, Marie Sällnas and Pia Tham in Sweden and Synnöve Karvinen from the University of Helsinki in Finland for stimulating discussions about international comparative social work.

Throughout this book, I use practice examples and case studies to illustrate and develop my arguments. I gratefully acknowledge the following social workers for assistance in providing, or developing, these case studies: Pauline Coulton and Lyn Krimmer, Annette Michaux and Karyn Walsh.

I again thank Catherine Gray, commissioning editor, for our continuing professional work together that now spans almost a decade.

Finally, for friendship, love and care, I thank Khloe Healy and Dennis Longstaff.

PART 1

INTRODUCTION

This book is about the ideas that shape the contexts and the professional practices of social work. Social work is a profession that varies enormously by historical, geographical and institutional contexts. Social workers aim to be agents of change with and on behalf of the people with whom they work; to achieve this, it is vital that we, as social workers, understand our practice contexts. Further, our institutional contexts of practice are constantly changing because of social, economic and political changes, while advances in social work theory and knowledge also influence our professional purpose and approaches to practice.

What remains constant is the need for us, as social workers, to negotiate our purpose in practice. All professions negotiate their purpose, but this is more complex for social workers than for many other professions due, in part, to the diverse character of social work practice and the range of contexts in which social work occurs. For example, the work of a social worker in a government child protection authority varies markedly from that of a mental health social worker in private practice or a community health setting.

Social workers usually negotiate their purpose with a range of stake-holders, including service users, service users' families, communities, team members, employing agencies and society at large. In negotiating our professional purpose, we may draw on our formal practice base, which includes our values and the theories for practice developed within the profession. But this is not enough. Because social work practices are profoundly shaped by our practice environments, it is important that we are actively engaged in influencing these contexts as well. For example, social workers should be involved in challenging organizational policies that are discriminatory and interfere with our goals of achieving positive health and welfare outcomes for the people with whom we practise.

Part 1 comprises two chapters. Chapter 1 introduces a discursive approach to understanding our practice context. We argue that an under-standing of practice context is an integral aspect of all social work practice and that our practice context can be understood in terms of competing sets of discourses. The terms 'discourse' and 'discourse analysis' are defined and the three key sets of discourses that shape many contemporary contexts of social work practice are outlined. These are discussed in more detail in Chapters 3–5.

Chapter 2 focuses on a dynamic model of practice, which illuminates how key elements of institutional context, service user and community expectations, our professional practice base and our practice framework interact to construct our professional purpose. This dynamic model of practice underpins the analysis of the discourses shaping our practice contexts (Part 2) and theories for practice (Part 3). In Chapter 2, we also look at three approaches to theory use, with a particular emphasis on a critical reflexive approach, which informs the introduction and analysis of theories for practice in this book.

1

UNDERSTANDING OUR CONTEXT

Our primary purpose in this book is to introduce a contextually informed approach to social work practice. We provide social work practitioners, students and educators with frameworks for understanding the diverse and often perplexing contexts of, and theories for, practice. By understanding the ideas that underpin our practice contexts and formal theory base, we enhance our capacity to achieve the values and goals to which we are committed. In this chapter, we explain the importance of discourse and discourse analysis for thinking about professional practice, and briefly outline the three sets of discourses that are most influential for social work (considered in more detail in Part 2). This will form an important preparation for Chapter 2, where we introduce a dynamic model of practice, which proposes that our professional purpose is constructed through interaction between various components of our institutional contexts, professional practice base, professional purpose and practice framework. Here, three approaches to theory use are introduced, which will be drawn on in the analysis of theories for practice in Part 3.

The Importance of Discourse

In this book, a discursive approach is used to identify and analyse the key philosophies and ideas that shape social work practices within health and welfare institutions. The term 'discourse' refers to 'a system or aggregate of meanings' (Taylor, 2013, p. 14) through which certain social phenomena, such as 'need', 'knowledge' and 'intervention', are constructed. In other words, from a poststructural point of view, discourses are the sets of language practices that shape our thoughts, actions and even our identities. They are, in Parton's words (1994, p. 13), 'frameworks or grids of social organizations that make some actions possible whilst precluding others'. This notion of discourse recognizes language as 'a form of social practice, rather than a purely individual activity or a reflex of situational variables' (Fairclough, 1992, p. 63); and a key assumption on which it relies is that discourses have material effects on our practice. Discourses constitute our understanding of service user needs and shape what is regarded as 'appropriate' ways of understanding and responding to those needs, as well as legitimatizing some kinds of knowledge and practice while devaluing others. For example, as we shall see in Chapter 3, the increasing influence of the new public management discourse in mental health services has contributed to the categorization and valuing of certain kinds of activities, such as 'therapeutic intervention', while making it more difficult to recognize and value the 'grey zones' of practice such as relationship-building activities (see Saario and Stepney, 2009). This can create challenges for social workers in accounting for their practices in these grey zones.

The approach to discourse analysis developed in Chapters 3–5 can be described as 'critical', in that we interrogate how discourses operating in our field of practice construct our contexts, our professional purpose and the relations of power and knowledge in them. Critical discourse analysis is concerned with understanding how language use contributes to the dominance of certain truth claims and the privileging of particular actors within any practice context, and what, if anything, other actors, such as social workers, care providers or service users, can do to disrupt these truth claims to allow for alternative meanings, including different ways of understanding need and responding to 'problems' (Taylor, 2013, p. 14).

The concept of discourse and the method of critical discourse analysis provide important tools for social workers as we seek to understand and create change in, and through, our institutional contexts. Health and welfare contexts are sites of competing discourses, each of which offers different interpretations about the nature of client needs, expert knowledge, the nature of the social work role and, specifically, the kinds of 'help' or interventions that will best address the concerns and issues facing service users. In some health and welfare contexts, there is little overt struggle between different discourses. In these contexts, one discourse, or set of compatible discourses, has gained dominance in determining the official practices of the institution. However, in many contexts, tensions exist between different ways of constructing the practice context, particularly in determining the nature of client needs and the social work role.

The relationship between discourses and social work practice is dynamic, in the sense that discourses profoundly shape social work practice, yet social workers can also actively use and contest the discourses that influence their practice domains. To do so requires that we understand them. At a minimum, discourse analysis can help us to understand, and actively use, the concepts that shape our institutional environments and influence our professional purpose. From a discourse perspective, it is vital that social workers understand and use the language practices that dominate practice contexts if they want to maximize the opportunities for their own and clients' perspectives to be recognized in these contexts. For example, in many health and welfare settings, concerns about cost-effectiveness dominate and so, at a pragmatic level, it is helpful for us to understand and use this concept in presenting our practices and new initiatives with and on behalf of service users.

Social workers can also use discourse analysis to contest established ways of viewing and responding to client needs. Fook (2002, p. 89) asserts that: 'simply choosing not to accept dominant ideas and pointing out contradictions can work to resist, challenge and change these dominant meaning systems'. By understanding the discourses that construct our practice environments, social workers can be involved in opening these contexts to 'alternative framings of reality' (Parton, 2003, p. 9). Using discourses in this way, social workers can work with stakeholders to develop different and more helpful ways of understanding and responding to client 'needs'. For example, in many fields of health and welfare, social workers have an important role to play in highlighting the social and structural contexts of the issues facing service users and encouraging service responses that move beyond 'fixing' the individual's problem to addressing the social and structural origins of these issues.

Part 2 illuminates the discourses shaping our purpose as practice. Three sets of discourses (Figure 1.1) profoundly influence the practice context, people's expectations of social work services and the construction of service user 'need', and the theories underpinning social work practice.

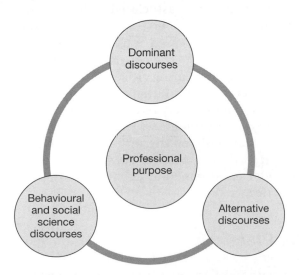

Figure 1.1 Discourses and professional practice purpose

The three sets of discourses shaping professional practice purpose are dominant discourses, social and behavioural science discourses, and alternative discourses. 'Dominant discourses' (Chapter 3) refer to the discourses that are most influential in shaping power and knowledge relations in health and welfare services. They shape the institutional contexts of practice, determining the forms of knowledge that are valued, the types of services and the power/knowledge relations between the service provider and service user.

'Social and behavioural science discourses' (Chapter 4) are those received from the disciplines that have traditionally provided the knowledge and theory base for the social work profession. They are founded primarily in the social and behavioural sciences and while it is possible to identify a wide variety of disciplinary influences on our professional knowledge base, we focus on the 'psy' and sociological discourses. They have been influential and also the site of considerable tension within the professional base of social work, with significant variation internationally and across different fields of practice in the extent to which the profession recognizes and constitutes itself through these discourses. For example, social workers working in mental health and counselling services are more likely to be informed by, and constituted through, 'psy' discourses, while those practising in community and policy practice roles will probably draw more significantly on and constitute their role through sociological discourses.

The 'alternative' discourses exist outside the other two discourses but nonetheless exert a powerful influence on the construction of our purpose and practices as social workers. Chapter 5 considers three sets of discourses – citizen rights, those associated with religion and spirituality, and environmentalism. In the first edition of this book, the term 'consumer rights discourse' was used, but here we refer to a 'citizen rights discourse', which better reflects the construction of the people engaged with social services as rights-bearing citizens rather than as consumers of services. This broader notion of the citizen as rights bearing in all domains of life, rather than merely having the right to consume services, has been central to various progressive social movements in health and welfare services. An analysis of the influence of the environmentalist discourse on social work is new to this edition, and reflects the emerging influence of broader environmental debates on the (re)constitution of professional practice.

Theories for Practice

In Part 3, we concentrate on theories for practice, which are a specific aspect of social workers' professional toolkit. Like discourses, theories for practice contribute to the construction of our professional purpose, but unlike discourses, theories for practice represent particular ways in which our profession has sought to define and enact its professional purpose. In some instances, discourses shaping our context may clash with social work theories for practice, such as the tensions between new public management ideas and anti-oppressive practice, while in other cases discourses may inform our theories for practice, such as the influence of behavioural and social science discourses on our theories for practice.

Consistent with other social work theorists (Howe, 1987, p. 16; Payne, 2005), we use the term 'theories for professional practice', also known as 'social work theories', to refer to formal theories that are intended to guide and explain social work practices. Theories for practice are frameworks developed by social workers that offer specific guidance as to the purpose of social work, the principles for our practice and often imply specific methods of intervention. Part 3 is structured around five groups of theories for practice – systems theories, problem-solving theories, strengths and solution-focused theories, modern critical social work theories, and postmodern social work theories, as illustrated in Figure 1.2. Within each group of theories, key contemporary theories for practice are outlined and analysed.

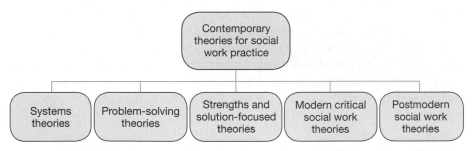

Figure 1.2 Contemporary theories for social work practice

Theories for social work practice are constantly evolving and new theories are also emerging from within these perspectives. Our key focus is on theories developed by social workers for social workers, because they were developed with at least one, and often more, contexts of social work practice in mind and it is vital that we are cognizant of our practice context and professional base. This is important because our theories for practice reflect the value base of our profession and the specific nature of our work, which involves working alongside people who are vulnerable and marginalized. Sheldon and Macdonald (2009, p. 3) assert that:

Social work's disciplinary territory is the poor, troubled, abused or discriminated against, neglected, frail and elderly, mentally ill, learning-disabled, addicted, delinquent, or otherwise socially marginalized up-against-it citizen in his or her social circumstances.

To recognize and champion our own theory base is not to deny important contributions from other disciplines. Hence, where relevant, we have included reference to theories from other disciplines where these extend our understanding of, or capacity to implement, social work theories for practice. For example, Chapter 7 includes an introduction to motivational interviewing in relation to its potential incorporation into problem-solving approaches.

A contextual approach underpins the discussion of theories for social work practice in Part 3. We illuminate the historical, geographical and institutional contexts in which each approach emerged. An understanding of the original contexts and practice purposes for which specific theories were developed can assist us to adapt and transform these theories for practice within our specific practice contexts and with reference to the unique characteristics of every practice interaction. Furthermore, we show that the strengths and limitations of each theory need to be analysed within specific contexts of practice. While many social workers, and academics, have a favoured theory of practice, we seek to introduce a range of approaches rather than promote a specific theory for practice. By providing a critical analysis of the development and application of each theoretical approach, we aim to assist the reader to make their own judgements regarding the utility (or not) of the application of theory to their specific context of practice. For example, even where we accept a theoretical perspective, such as modern critical social work theory, as useful, its application in a statutory child protection context will necessarily be different to its use in a community development context.

Discourses and Theories for Practice: What's the Difference?

Discourses and theories for practice are resources through which our professional purpose and practices are constituted. Yet, theories for practice (Part 3) differ from the discourses discussed in Part 2 in at least two important ways.

First, whereas discourses may privilege the knowledge of a specific group, such as the medical or legal specialist, they are a shared resource developed and maintained by a range of actors and institutional practices, while theories for practice are developed for social workers for social work practice. For example, in institutional contexts where the biomedical discourse is dominant, social workers (and other professionals) are required to develop a capacity to use and, where necessary, translate biomedical concepts (see Opie, 1995). By contrast, while other professionals may utilize concepts from theories for social work practice, such as concepts regarding service users' strengths and resilience, these theories are intended primarily to provide guidance in specific forms of social work practice. Indeed, many theories for social work practice have been developed within particular contexts of social work practice, and their utilization beyond these contexts often requires adaptation of the original concepts to recognize the different requirements of other institutional contexts. For example, the strengths perspective was originally developed for practice with people living with chronic mental health conditions, and adaptation to other fields such as child protection demands consideration of the specific practice obligations of social workers in that context (see Turnell and Edwards, 1999).

Second, whereas discourses shape knowledge and power relations in practice by influencing what counts as true and valid and who is recognized as authoritative, theories for practice are intended to offer a range of options for understanding and responding to particular concerns. In relation to social work practice, this means that within institutional contexts of practice, we may have limited choice over the extent to which we acknowledge or engage with discourses that exist within these contexts. A critical discourse analysis approach helps us to understand, and perhaps also strategically use, the opportunities provided by these discourses to realize our values or goals. For example, the growing influence of a citizen rights discourse in many fields of health and welfare has offered new opportunities for patients and service users to challenge some aspects of professional power/knowledge relations (see Crossley and Crossley, 2001; Shakespeare, 2006; Tilley et al., 2012). By contrast, theories for practice offer different possibilities for interpreting our purpose and options for understanding and responding to client needs. For example, a problem-solving approach (Chapter 7) focuses our attention on achieving a mutual understanding with service users and a step-by-step approach to resolving defined issues, while an anti-oppressive approach (Chapter 9) encourages an overtly political construction of service users' concerns and the utilization of critical awareness and collective strategies for achieving individual and social change.

Why Context Matters

This book brings together a dynamic model of practice with a critical introduction to the ideas shaping the institutional contexts of practice and key theories of direct practice. By integrating the analysis of context and theory, we aim to provide increased opportunities for social workers to use and develop theories in situ. Discussion of social work theories for practice and the contexts of social work practice usually occurs in separate domains, resulting in frustration for those charged with formal theory building and practitioners. One way we can promote dialogue between these two 'worlds' is by recognizing the profound influence of context in the use and development of theories for practice.

The book is intended to be used actively by you, the reader. You are invited to think through the perspectives presented here as they apply to your actual or intended contexts of social work practice. Each chapter provides an introduction to the time and place in which discourses and theories for practice developed and the core assumptions underpinning them. This background is intended to assist you to consider how the contexts in which discourses or perspectives developed, and the assumptions on which they are based, have commonalities or differences with the contexts in which you are likely to practise. For example, most contemporary theories for practice originated within a particular geographical and historical context and often with a specific practice concern in mind, such as counselling practice with people experiencing challenges in everyday living, or, as is the case with a citizen rights discourse, the political empowerment of people using health and welfare services. By understanding these original contexts and the assumptions underpinning them, we enhance our capacity to critically analyse the ideas shaping our practice context and, as appropriate, to adapt and develop theories within our specific contexts of practice. This approach encourages you to engage with the material actively and reflectively to consider the possibilities as well as the limitations of the perspectives for your practice contexts and further challenge or develop these perspectives. Opportunities for engagement with the perspectives are supported by exercises, case studies and questions in each chapter.

Throughout the book, you are invited to consider the implications of the material presented for practice with culturally and linguistically diverse client groups. Traditionally, social work practice with people from non-Anglo-Saxon cultures has tended to be characterized as a specialist area of practice. However, within the profession, there is increasing recognition that, in the aftermath of colonization and in a globalized world, social workers engage with service users from a range of cultural and linguistic groups. For example, in Australia, the USA and Canada, First Nations peoples are overrepresented in many areas of statutory service provision such as child protection and in juvenile and adult detention centres. In addition, globalization has resulted in the mass relocation of populations, especially from Africa, Asia and Eastern Europe, to postindustrial nations, and therefore social workers, even in 'mainstream' settings, can expect to have contact with service users from diverse cultural and linguistic backgrounds. Culturally sensitive practice requires that social workers develop an understanding of the history and cultural practices of the client groups they work with and consider the implications of these for practice. Thus, it is important that you consider the cultural and linguistic backgrounds of the client populations with whom you work and the strengths and limits of these different perspectives presented here for practice with these groups of people.

Conclusion

Social workers practice in a broad range of contexts with people who experience a diversity of concerns and oppressions. Part of the social workers' brief is to be agents of change in direct practice, within our organizational contexts, and within society more generally. I hope this book will further social workers' capacities to understand, and contribute to, the profession's capacity to use its practice contexts and formal theory base to create change in favour of the vulnerable populations with whom we work. Creating change of this kind should be our primary and unifying concern.

Summary Questions

1 What does the term 'discourse' mean?

2 It is claimed that discourses have 'material effects' on social work practice. What does this mean and what kinds of material effects did this chapter identify?

3 Discuss one similarity and one difference between 'discourses' and 'theories for social work practice'.

Recommended Reading

- Candlin, C. and Crichton, J. (eds) (2010) *Discourses of Deficit*. (Basingstoke: Palgrave Macmillan).
  Explores how people at particular sites relevant to health and welfare services are discursively constructed as 'deficient'. Demonstrates how the discursive construction of identities and relationships within sites such as the courts and child protection services materially affects people's life changes and warrants intervention in their personal lives. Particularly helpful for illuminating how language influences power relations in social work practices and the material realities of people's lives.

- Taylor, S. (2013) *What is Discourse Analysis?* (London: Bloomsbury).
  Short, accessible introduction to discourse analysis; helpful for readers seeking to understand the origins, strengths and limits of this approach for analysing practice contexts.

2

A DYNAMIC MODEL OF PRACTICE

In this chapter, we consider the dynamic model of social work practice, which seeks to illuminate the processes through which our professional purpose is constructed in social work practice. The components of the model include institutional contexts, professional practice base, service users' needs and expectations, and our own emerging practice framework. First, we consider how the dynamic model fits with the contextual approach to practice introduced in Chapter 1. We then consider each component of the model. We go on to discuss three approaches to theory use and how the dynamic model can inform our use of theory in practice.

Practice Diversity and the Construction of Purpose

The dynamic model of practice (see Figure 2.1 below) provides a framework for understanding how our professional purpose in constructed in practice. As discussed in Chapter 1, social work is a contextually diverse activity. Our professional purpose and our approaches to practice differ across historical, geographical and institutional contexts of practice. Furthermore, social work is a negotiated activity. Many factors contribute to the negotiation of our professional purpose, including the discourses shaping our institutional context, our formal professional base, service users' expectations, as well as our individual frameworks for practice. Sometimes, these different factors 'line up' and social workers experience consistency between their context, their formal professional base and individual framework for practice. Often, however, they do not and social workers must negotiate the conflicts between their formal professional base and various expectations arising from the institutional context and service user and community perceptions of needs and entitlements. For example, in child protection services, the primary role of the social worker may be constructed by the institution as that of assessing and eliminating risk in the immediate situation, whereas the social worker may take a longer term view of balancing up actions to eliminate risk and their long-term consequences for the attachment of the child to their family and community. In some circumstances, social workers face challenges in achieving legitimacy of purpose in ways that meet the often competing expectations of different stakeholders, including service users, employers and society at large.

Social workers are well aware of the importance of context in service users' lives. Indeed, understanding and responding to the 'person in their environment' is a guiding credo of modern professional social work. However, less attention has been paid to how we might understand and respond to our practice environments as an integral part of direct practice. For example, courses on the institutional contexts of social work, that is, the regulatory, policy and organizational environments, are often taught separately from professional practice, whereas we argue that our institutional contexts must be understood as integral to how we construct our purpose in direct practice.

The meaning and practice of all professional activities – indeed all human activities – vary by context; however, social work is more variable than most for three reasons. First, social work lacks a common knowledge base and agreed ways of building knowledge. This contrasts with established, or elite, professions, such as medicine, law and engineering, each of which has a unitary knowledge base grounded in positivist or scientific ways of knowing. By contrast, social workers are divided over questions about how to create knowledge for practice, with researchers debating the merits and limits of scientific ways of knowing for understanding social work practice. Moreover, many of the concepts social workers use are unique to specific institutional locations. For instance, the knowledge and skill base of a social worker in a statutory child protection authority differs greatly from that of a social worker involved in community development work on a public housing estate. Even the way social workers practically engage with core values, such as 'self-determination' and 'social justice', varies markedly by institutional location. For instance, in a mental health service context, the notion of social justice must be considered in the conflict that sometimes exists between the service user's expressed need and their best interests in terms of protection from self-harm.

Second, in contrast to other human service professions, such as nursing and education, social work does not have a primary institutional base. So, while these other human service professions may also lack a positivist foundation for their practice, the presence of a primary service context – the hospital or the school – provides a unifying foundation for knowledge development and use. By contrast, social workers cannot be said to have a primary field or organization of practice. For example, social workers work in a wide variety of fields, including mainstream health and welfare services as well as citizen advocacy services and community development agencies. Social service agencies vary in a number of ways, including:

- *size:* from no paid employees to institutions with tens of thousands of employees

- *purpose:* including the implementation of statutory law or religious mission to client-directed service provision

- *management structure:* from client managed to corporate structures.

They also vary a great deal by nation even among the postindustrial countries.

Third, the primary task of social work varies by practice context and may include, but is not limited to, any one, or a combination, of the following tasks:

- risk management

- implementation of statutory law

- support and advocacy

- direct service to individuals, families or groups

- casework and case management services

- therapeutic intervention

- community education

- community capacity building

- research

- policy development, implementation and evaluation

- social planning

- social service administration.

As we can see, the core task in one context may be incompatible with the primary activity in another. For example, a primary focus on the implementation of statutory law is likely to be incompatible with a community capacity-building role. In addition, while social workers may have some discretion about how they execute their primary task, they cannot usually determine the nature of the task, which is determined by the institutional context and, more specifically, their role description and employer, service user and community rights and expectations. Thus, when constructing our sense of purpose in social work practice, we must be mindful of the primary tasks assigned to us within our practice contexts.

This contextual nature of social work differentiates it from other professions. Our professional practice foundations – our knowledge, values and skill bases – are substantially constructed in, and through, the environments in which we work. For this reason, enhancing our capacity to understand, analyse and respond to our institutional contexts must be an integral part of our frameworks for professional practice. By understanding our context, we can recognize how our practice is shaped by context and how we might act as agents of change within, and in relation to, our context. As Fook (2002, p. 162) asserts:

> Reframing our practice as contextual ... means we reframe our practice as working *with* environments, rather than working *despite* environments. We see ourselves as part of a context, ourselves responsible for aspects of that context. In this way, we see possibilities for change, for creating *different microclimates within broader contexts*.

In short, we need to take seriously the impact of institutional context for shaping our practice approaches, our knowledge base, our sense of purpose and even ourselves as social workers. Yet we should also recognize that we are active participants in, and creators of, the contexts and frameworks through which we practise.

Constructing Social Work Purpose: A Dynamic Approach

Like other professionals, social workers are involved in purposeful activities. However, in contrast to other professions, the contextual and varied character of social work practices means that, in each practice encounter, we are involved in constructing and negotiating social work practice. The dynamic model of social work is presented in Figure 2.1. The concept of professional purpose is at the centre of the model, which is constructed by interactions among four elements: our institutional contexts, service user/community needs and expectations, our professional base and our emerging frameworks for practice, which develop over time through critical reflection on our professional experiences.

The four elements interact in the construction of our professional purpose:

1 *The institutional contexts of practice:* Refers to the laws, including the laws governing the regulation of professional social work, public and organizational policies, and accepted practices shaping the institutions where social workers are located. The institutional context provides the terms of reference for the social work task; that is, what a social worker is formally employed to do. For instance, a social worker in a mental health authority may be tasked to implement statutory mental health legisla-

tion and build community-based resources, such as housing opportunities and social support networks, to enable people with mental health issues to be supported the community.

2 *The formal professional base of social work:* Developed from a range of philosophical perspectives, theories about and for practice, values and beliefs, and the formal skills of social work. It is disseminated through the formal channels of social work education and academic publications. Professional social work education programmes are primarily concerned with introducing and socializing students to the core values, knowledge and skills of the profession. Theories for practice provide a key intellectual component of the professional base of social work.

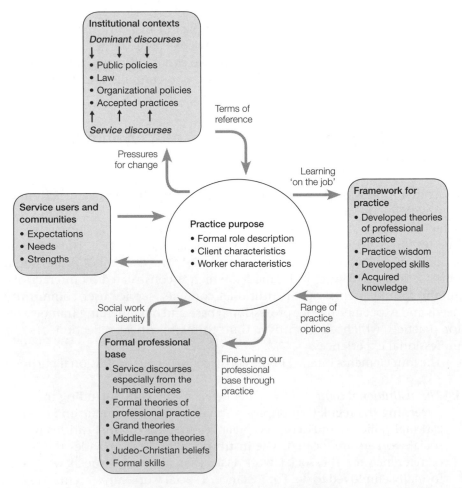

Figure 2.1 Constructing social work practice: a dynamic model

3 *Service users and their communities:* Social workers have recognized the importance of working in partnership with service users and communities. Indeed, the notion of partnership dates back to the work of Mary Richmond and Jane Addams early in the twentieth century and is now evident in all major theories of social work practice. Contemporary social work theories incorporate the idea that the relationship between the social worker and the service user, whether an individual, family or community, is the central vehicle of change. The growth of citizen rights movements in a range of health and welfare fields has also held out challenges to social workers, and other human service professionals, to be accountable in the exercise of professional power and engage service users in decisions that affect them (see Chapter 5).

4 *Framework for practice:* Refers to the mixture of formal knowledge and skills and informal 'on-the-job' knowledge and skills developed by social workers in practice. It includes formal theoretical and substantive knowledge as well as tacit, or difficult to articulate, knowledge that can be built up through repeated exposure to practice situations. For example, an experienced child protection worker may develop a strong capacity to predict situations of high risk by drawing on formal risk assessment tools and practice-based knowledge of the kinds of situations likely to lead to negative outcomes for children.

We now consider the interaction among the elements of the dynamic model of social work (Figure 2.1). The institutional context, particularly laws and public policies, shapes the key obligations borne by social workers and, in some instances, by service users. Yet, as social workers, we can also use our experiences in implementing institutional policies and practices to advocate for change in them. For example, a social worker in mental health services responsible for finding suitable accommodation for service users may also work with policy makers and politicians to improve responses to the housing needs of people with mental health issues.

The regulatory environment is also an important part of our context. Over the past decade, considerable changes have taken place in the regulatory environment of the profession of social work internationally. While the professional regulation of social workers is well established in all states of the USA, provinces of Canada and Israel, in many other countries it is more recent and, in some contexts, minimal. In 2003, the Social Workers Registration Act was introduced in New Zealand, and since 2005, social work has been a registered profession in the UK. In Australia, social work remains a self-regulating unregistered profession, in which the national professional association plays a key role in monitoring professional educational standards and the professional conduct of its members. It is important to note that Australia has a highly deregulated environment, in which many health and human service professions, such as dieticians, speech therapists and social workers (among others), are not registered by government but are self-regulating via their professional associations.

The formal regulation of social work in many countries has brought with it the increased involvement of governments in defining practice standards, with significant implications for establishing the scope and limits of our professional purposes. For example, in England, professional social work education standards are shaped by the National Occupational Standards produced by the Quality Assurance Agency (Spolander et al., 2011). In New Zealand, the Social Workers Registration Board is responsible for assessing the competence of professional social workers in relation to a specified set of social work standards. In the USA, although professional social work standards are established in legislation, the professional association plays a central role in monitoring those standards.

The increasing involvement of governments in regulating the social work profession in some countries undoubtedly has some benefits for the social work profession and, potentially, for the people the profession serves. Government regulation denotes a formal recognition of the role and status of a profession and can also promote public safety by ensuring that practitioners meet defined standards of professional knowledge and skill, as well as providing sanctions for professional misconduct (DeAngelis and Monahan, 2012). However, in addition to concerns about the elitism entailed in professional registration, social workers have also raised concerns about the potential losses entailed in the increased formal regulation of the profession, particularly where regulation fails to recognize the values that drive professional social work. As van Heugten (2011, p. 174) asks: '[will] an emphasis on competency, skills, essentialist ideology, and knowledge for practice in agencies ... squeeze critical social science and social scientists out of the social work academy?'

Regardless of the level and nature (or absence) of formal regulation of social workers, it would seem important that all social workers stay involved in debates about professional regulations. As a profession, we can benefit from the views and contributions of regulatory authorities, particularly in terms of the standards needed to secure public safety. Yet, the profession also has an important role to play in defining the nature of professional knowledge, skill and purpose. In short, all social workers need to understand the impact of external regulatory authorities in shaping the professional base and, at an everyday level, shaping their professional purpose.

Turning to the professional practice base, this includes theories for practice, values and methods and skills that provide the foundation for social work practice. For many social workers, the formal base of the profession is a major contributor to the way they construct their professional purpose.

The formal professional base, especially shared values, can also help forge a common identification among social workers despite the enormous diversity of practice contexts. For example, Sarah Banks (2012) identifies four first-order principles, widely endorsed in many national professional codes and in the practice literature – respect for and promotion of an individual's right to self-determination, promotion of welfare or wellbeing, equality, and distributive justice. However, the formal professional base is not only something that is transmitted to social workers from the formal institutions of social work research and education, but also something that social workers can challenge and transform from their practice experience. The capacity of practising social workers to contribute to the formal base of social work has been limited, in part because of the differences between the relatively informal ways knowledge is built and transmitted in practice and the formal requirements for knowledge production demanded by academic and professional institutions. Practice research centres and research partnerships between universities and service provider institutions or individual service providers can promote dialogue between academia and research institutions – where knowledge is further developed. Further initiatives of these types are required to promote dialogue between the formal professional base and the diverse range of social work practices and ensure that theories of professional practice are relevant and useful for explaining and guiding practice.

Another significant contributor to our practice purpose is service users' expectations, needs, strengths and capacities. The notion of partnership, central to contemporary social work theories for practice, means that service users' interests should be recognized as distinct from our professional practice base and our institutional contexts. It means that, in practice, we need to focus our efforts on understanding service users' viewpoints, needs and capacities, as well as engaging them in an understanding of the nature of our role (see Trotter, 2004, 2013; Cree and Davis, 2006).

These elements of professional practice base, institutional context and service user perspectives influence how we construct, and experience, our practice purpose. For some, this is often an area of tension and conflict in social work practice. Some (lucky) social workers practise in environments where their frameworks and their contexts are consistent. For example, a social worker who is strongly committed to anti-oppressive theory is likely to find that employment in an advocacy agency is consistent with their professional framework, but that employment in a statutory authority presents considerably more challenges for them. Most of us are likely to experience some tension between the sense of purpose constructed by our practice context and our professional base. In part this is because, as this book shows, the sets of ideas dominating most mainstream health and welfare agencies are markedly different to the discourses underpinning human service professions in social work. However, if we can understand these differences, they can be a source of creative tension and inspiration for change in many practice contexts.

The final element of the model is the professional framework for practice. This is the professional framework that social workers develop through practice and construct from information and directions gained from the other three elements, including the formal professional base, but not limited to them. As social workers become more advanced in their practice, they are often able to draw on a richer framework for practice than is possible for novices. This strong and, to some extent, intuitive understanding of the practice context allows the advanced professional to handle complex and uncertain situations with confidence and competence (Fook et al., 2000, p. 148). Advanced practitioners can use their unique professional framework to expand their sense of purpose beyond that which might be immediately apparent either from the formal professional knowledge base or within their organizational context (see Fook et al., 2000).

A Dynamic Approach to Theory Use

Social work theory for practice is an important element of the dynamic process through which our purpose is constructed. Here, I discuss various approaches to theory use and outline how a critical reflexive approach is most consistent with the dynamic model of social work practice. Three ways of using and developing theories for practice are discussed – evidence-based practice, reflective practice, and reflexive practice.

Debates about Theory Use in Practice

Theories for practice are frameworks developed by social workers to guide social work practice. These theories vary in terms of who and what they identify as the focus of social work interventions. For instance, problem-solving theories focus on individuals' problems, while the strengths perspective prioritizes people's strengths. Furthermore, while they can incorporate a range of methods, some are more oriented to work with individuals, while others are more likely to lead to the incorporation of social change practices. These theories also vary in relation to their agreement or not with the 'scientific' method or evidence-based practice. For example, the task-centred approach, a form of problem-solving practice, is aligned with the scientific method, as illustrated in its development through randomized controlled trials and the onus it places on the social worker to continue gathering and analysing evidence of practice outcomes. In contrast, the strengths perspective and solution-focused brief therapy adopt a sceptical view of the scientific method of the subjective nature of all knowledge building, and the responsibility of the practitioner is to explore and develop rich interpretations of service users' situations, rather than aim for a singular truth.

The relationship between formal theory and practice in social work is a vexed one, as it is in many human service professions (see Schön, 1983). Social workers often express an ambivalent attitude towards theory (Howe, 1987, p. 15; Fook et al., 2000). For many social workers, theory is, at best, a luxury to think about when the 'real' work of social work is done, at worst it is rejected as authoritarian and irrelevant to practice (Healy, 2000, p. 1).

The commonly encountered criticisms of formalized theories of professional practice in social work can be attributed, in part, to the processes of theory development. Traditional forms of theory building have separated theory development from its application. Often, social workers have been reluctant to engage with theories developed in the 'ivory towers' of academia, far away from the complexities – and mundane aspects – of social work practices. In addition, some social work researchers have treated social workers and service users as objects of study, rather than co-participants in knowledge production. Again, the separation of the researcher and the researched, as well as theorist and practitioner and/or service user, has created barriers to social workers' use of theory in practice. The diversification of research for practice methods, including research/practice partnerships, and increased attention to methods that allow for knowledge synthesis are creating some avenues for collaborative theory development and translation of knowledge to practice (see Baldwin, 2012; Shardland, 2012).

In addition, practising social workers have objected to the kinds of theories developed through traditional research methods. Eileen Munro (1998, p. 2) observes that:

> There have been long-standing debates about how to integrate theory and practice, to use heart and head, and to combine clear, logical reasoning and a caring and humane style ... The dominant scientific model, until recently, has been a behavioural/positivist one which, to many, has seemed irreconcilable with their existing wisdom.

The critical reflexive approach to theory use and development adopted in this book asserts that a conflict between theory and practice can be resolved by recognizing that as social workers use theory, *we are also creating theory* in practice. In this way, we do not simply apply formal theory, such as the theories we consider in Part 3, but we can use them as a basis for making knowledge in practice.

The increasing influence of new public management in the organization of social work services has also led some social workers to question the role of theory of practice. Theories of professional practice are intended to enable social workers to enact practice as a thoughtful, analytic and creative activity. In the changing contexts of social work practice, in which practice is becoming increasingly fragmented, the opportunities for practising in this way may be increasingly constrained (Healy and Meagher, 2004; Saario and Stepney, 2009). Only through collaborative effort, both within the profession and across other human service occupational and service user groups, can social workers promote the cultural valuation of social services work as a professional activity (see Healy and Meagher, 2004). Clarity about the theoretical foundations of our practice can help us to seize and extend opportunities for our practice

Why Theory Matters

Social workers often find it difficult to name the theoretical frameworks they use in practice (Howe, 1987, p. 17; see also Fook et al., 2000). We may even encounter social workers who profess to have abandoned theory once they finished their formal education. Yet all social workers base their practice on theoretical assumptions, whether they are aware of them or not (Munro, 1998, p. 6). Our theoretical framework guides us in deciding who or what should be the focus of assessment or intervention and, as we shall see, different frameworks offer varying ideas about the focus, objectives and processes of social work practices. Although research has repeatedly shown that few social workers use theories in a formal, explicit way (Munro, 1998, p. 46; Fook et al., 2000, p. 189), there are a number of reasons why we should develop our capacity to identify, use and develop formal social work theory in our practice.

The first reason is accountability to service users, employers and funding agencies. Drawing on research about service users' experiences of social work practice, Howe (1987, p. 164) reports that service users preferred 'social workers who appeared clear about what they were doing and why they were doing it, and social workers who say where they were going and how they were going to get there' (see also Trotter, 2006). New managerial reforms of the social services sector have led to pressure on social workers to articulate the basis of, and rationale for, their practices. In this climate of distrust of professionals and expectations of transparency in practice processes, social workers will need to be able to clearly articulate what they do and their rationale for it. A sound grasp of theory for practice and knowledge for practice is essential to this task.

Improving service quality provides a second reason for developing our capacity to identify, use and build theory in practice. Theory allows us to critically examine commonsense ways of seeing and doing things (Thompson, 2006). Thus, theory can enable us to critically review assumptions and accepted ways of doing things that work to disadvantage service users. In this way, theory can enhance our capacity to explore a broader range of practice options than would be evident from a commonsense viewpoint. For example, the strengths perspective (see Chapter 8) helps us to see clients' strengths and capacities that might otherwise be invisible to us, other service providers, or others in the service users' personal and community networks. In addition, by creating a dialogue between the formal theories of social work and our own sense of social work purpose, as we have constructed it, we can expand our capacities for creative responses to the problems and issues we face in practice (Fook et al., 2000, p. 188). By understanding a broad range of theoretical frameworks, we are in a good position to develop practice strategies that build on the strengths and opportunities provided by different theoretical frameworks. For example, in one practice encounter, we may draw on aspects of problem-solving, strengths and critical social work theories in order to analyse and respond to the local and structural contexts of the issues facing the service user.

The capacity to articulate the theoretical bases of our practice is fundamental to assessing and enhancing the quality of the services we provide. Social work theories provide sets of principles that can be examined in practice and against which our practice can be evaluated. The introduction of managerial reforms to the social services sector has led to increased scrutiny of social work effectiveness. Many social workers, particularly those working within the critical tradition, regard the concept of service effectiveness with some suspicion because of its relationship to managerial control of service delivery processes (Trinder, 2000, p. 143). Yet, the notion of effectiveness is also relevant to the core social work values of social justice and professional integrity. Writing on social work in probation services, Trinder (2000, p. 149) reminds us that:

> Social workers and probation officers work with some of the most vulnerable as well as the more dangerous members of society, and have an ethical duty to offer the most effective help.

A further reason for engaging with the formal theoretical base of the profession is that we all share responsibility for developing this base. All professions, including social work, rely on formal theoretical frameworks for practice. As Rojek et al. (1988, p. 174) assert: 'general, transferable knowledge is indispensable. Without it, social workers would be forced to invent social work from scratch every time they started work with a new client.' Yet, in social work, the discussion about theory development and use is often seen as the realm of academics. The non-participation of practitioners in debates about, and the development of, formal theory means that the profession is denied insights from a broad range of practice perspectives. Practitioners do use and create knowledge in practice but, by and large, this knowledge work occurs informally and remains in the heads of individual practitioners or, at best, is transferred orally through supervision. The informal and individual-istic character of this knowledge means that it is unavailable to the social work profession more broadly and can only be used in limited ways in educa-tional processes. Kirk and Reid (2002, p. 203) criticize social workers' oral tradition of knowledge development and dissemination on the grounds that:

> as long as observations are communicated only informally, verbally, and among a few colleagues, they remain apart from the profession's established knowledge. Adding to the knowledge base involves making thoughtful, written contribu-tions to the literature.

In addition, while informal knowledge remains inside our heads, we fail to subject it the external scrutiny required to further our understanding of its strengths and limits within our practice contexts and across other sites of service provision. In other words, informal knowledge-building processes allow us a great deal of freedom, but they can also foster delusion about our effectiveness in achieving our practice purposes.

Creating and Using Theory in Practice: Debates about Evidence and Reflection

While many social work commentators agree that theory is vital to profes-sional social work practice, social workers continue to debate how best to develop and use theory in practice. Any consideration of how theory can be used in practice needs to take into account the longstanding debates about the nature of knowledge production in social work. While there are a variety of views about knowledge production, two dominant voices have been those of the empirical practice movement and the reflective tradition. In the social work literature, these two schools are often polarized, yet in prac-tice many social work theorists and practitioners draw on both schools of thought. For this reason, the distinctions between the two schools are better understood as a continuum rather than two entirely separate camps. At their most extreme, these schools foster entirely different ways of devel-oping and using knowledge in practice. It is these distinctions that we draw out here.

Reid (1994) uses the term 'empirical practice movement' to describe the commitment among some researchers, practitioners and other stakeholders, such as employers, to insist that social workers embrace scientific knowledge-building methods in social work. Advocates of empirical practice, also known as 'evidence-based practice', argue that social work should be grounded in rational knowledge validated through scientific methods (Reid, 1994, p. 166). The burgeoning interest in evidence-based practice can be attributed to growing demands by employing organizations, members of the profession and the general public that service providers should be accountable for ensuring best use of public money and best outcomes for service users.

During the 1960s and 70s, a series of high-profile evaluation studies on US social work practice studies raised serious questions about the effectiveness of social work intervention (Trinder, 2000, p. 143; Kirk and Reid, 2002, p. 38). This alarmed many in a profession that has prided itself on responsiveness to service users, and led to the establishment of evidence-based social work projects aimed at providing a scientifically grounded social work practice. William Reid and Laura Epstein's task-centred practice approach (1972) is one of the best-known examples of this (see Chapter 7). Today, while social workers continue to debate the merits of evidence-based practice, the movement continues to gain strength in some fields of practice, particularly in areas of high-risk decision-making, such as child protection (see Munro, 1998), and in institutions that value evidence-based approaches, such as many arenas of health service delivery (Plath, 2006).

While the empirical practice movement is a relatively recent arrival to the social work field, the quest for a scientific base for practice is not. The leaders of the Charity Organisation Society (COS), founded in London in 1869, were keen to develop a scientific basis for practice, and envisioned that, ideally: 'Charity would be, like science, an orderly systematic process in which practitioners gathered facts, made hypotheses, and revised them in the light of the additional facts from each case' (Evans, cited in Kirk and Reid, 2002, p. 27). Mary Richmond (1917), a social work pioneer (1861–1928), described social diagnosis as 'the product of a scientific process. Facts are gathered to serve as the basis for hypotheses, which are then tested by obtaining relevant evidence' (Reid, 1994, p. 166). While Richmond and her colleagues sought to develop a systematic framework for practice, their research was limited to single case studies. By contrast, members of the empirical practice movement seek to use more robust scientific methods, preferably experimental designs, for designing and testing social work approaches.

Today, social workers continue to face growing pressure from funding bodies and the general public to demonstrate their effectiveness 'as concern about the effects of social provision on recipients and the public purse has deepened' (Taylor and White, 2000, p. 181). In this context of increasing external pressure, leaders of the empirical practice movement continue to agitate for change from within the social work field. They are often highly critical of social work theory development and use, charging it with failing scientific standards of knowledge development. Kirk and Reid (2002, p. 20) argue that: 'The knowledge base of social work is ill defined and difficult to identify, delimit, or organize. Moreover, most of it is not the product of rigorous scientific testing.' Advocates of the empirical practice movement argue that social workers should become more research literate, that is, they should use research findings in practice and scientific methods to evaluate their own effectiveness. According to Munro (1998, p. 23): 'This movement encourages social workers to use empirically tested methods of helping to formulate their reasoning, and to evaluate their own work rigorously.' One of the key strengths of this movement is that it provides a framework for social workers to critically review the sources and forms of the information they use in decision-making. According to Munro (1996, 1998), attention to the sources and processes of decision-making can enable us to avoid 'avoidable' mistakes – especially important for decision-making in high-risk situations in fields such as child protection and mental health.

Notwithstanding the attractions of an evidence-based approach to practice, social workers need to be cautious in adopting this framework for theory building and knowledge use. In many fields of social work, the research base for particular approaches is underdeveloped or in dispute (Plath, 2006). In other words, in the 'grey zones' where social workers practise, theory and knowledge are far from clear cut. Also, an evidence-based approach can lead to a 'top-down' approach to theory development and use and the alienation of social workers from theory and knowledge building in practice. In this top-down approach, the social work researcher develops and tests social work theory that the practitioner then applies in practice (Taylor and White, 2000, p. 184). Theory and knowledge development are separated from their use on the grounds that practitioners do not have the time or the scientific tools to develop robust theories of practice (see Kirk and Reid, 2002). The principles of scientific neutrality, on which evidence-based social work is founded, also call into question the capacity of practising social workers to objectively evaluate their own practices. The separation of theory development and use in the evidence-based tradition gives practitioners little scope for questioning how the theory is developed or how it might be challenged in practice.

Another problem is how the social worker is to make sense of the large volume of research, some of which may be contested, in many fields of social work. Systematic reviews, which involve the rigorous search for, evaluation and synthesis of research knowledge within specific practice domains, offer some potential for translation of knowledge for practice. However, as noted by Sharland (2012, p. 483), the meta-analysis of social work research is limited by the diverse range of variables, such as client characteristics and service contexts, affecting the outcomes in social work practice. Systematic reviews can enhance rather than replace local experience as we seek to use theory and knowledge in practice.

In contrast to proponents of the empirical practice movement, social workers within the reflective tradition argue for the recognition of practitioners' lived experience of practice as a basis for making and using knowledge in practice. Again, like the empirical practice movement, elements of reflective knowledge building are well established in our profession. Jane Addams (1938) sought to develop a theoretical base for her work at Hull House in Chicago (which she co-founded with Ellen Starr) through regular reflective analysis of the activities in which she and community members were involved. The social experimentation approach described by Addams (1938) is akin to action research strategies associated with the pragmatist philosopher John Dewey, who was a professional associate and friend of Addams and visitor to Hull House.

In a similar vein, Donald Schön (1983, 1995), a leading scholar on reflective knowledge use and development in human services professions, argues against what he describes as the 'technical rationalist' approach underpinning the evidence-based approaches to knowledge development. In the technical rationalist approach, professional knowledge is derived from a scientific knowledge base and applied to clearly defined, well-bounded scientific problems (Thompson, 1995). For example, a civil engineer could use a technical rationalist approach to design a bridge, but this approach would be of more limited use to resolve public concern about where the bridge is to be built. Schön (1995, p. 34) critiques the application of a technical rationalist approach to human services work on the grounds that:

> By defining rigor in terms of technical rationality alone, we exclude, as *non*rigorous, much of what competent practitioners actually do in the indeterminate zones of practice where they confront problematic situations, unique cases, and conflicts of values or objectives – we exclude the artistry they sometimes bring to technical problem solving and the judgments on which it depends.

In this excerpt, Schön does not entirely dismiss technical rationality, that is, evidence-based knowledge, rather he insists that this sort of knowledge alone cannot provide the basis for knowledge development and use in human services. In part, this is because the evidence available in social work decision-making, which usually involves perceptions and feelings as well as material facts, is often ambiguous. In addition, many of the problems we deal with in social work are 'messy' and 'indeterminate' and 'cannot be "solved" in any clear, measurable or calculative way' (Parton, 2000, p. 452; see also Trinder, 2000, p. 149). For example, when we are directed to assess whether a family is neglecting their baby, we may see some signs of neglect, such as the baby's bottle filled with curdled milk, and other signs of care, such as the parents' and extended family members' physical affection for the child. In making our decision about intervention, we should prioritize the safety of the baby, and we might also take into account structural factors, such as the effects of structural disadvantage on the family, institutional factors, such as balancing the potential benefits and harm arising from child protection and family support intervention, and local factors, such as whether we can work with the family and local support services to assess, and ensure, that the baby's care needs are met.

In contrast to the evidence-based tradition, Schön (1995) proposes a reflective approach to knowledge development and use, which comprises 'knowing in action' and 'reflection in action'. 'Knowing in action' refers to the process of developing knowledge in practice, rather than applying pre-existing theories to it (Schön, 1995, p. 39). In contrast to evidence-based practitioners, advocates of reflective practice view intuitive and tacit knowledge as an essential dimension of effective practice (Fook et al., 2000, p. 222). Schön (1995, p. 40) uses the term 'reflection in action' to refer to the processes of refining knowledge in action so as to promote new ways of responding to the problems we encounter in practice. The capacity to reflect in action is important for responding to non-routine events in practice. For example, practitioners working in the field of palliative care will usually develop a repertoire of processes for helping service users deal with grief and loss. In practice, they are likely to find that in each case this repertoire must be adapted to respond to the service user's unique circumstances. The capacity to reflect in action is central to using our knowledge and skills flexibly in response to the specific characteristics of the service user and our institutional contexts.

The reflective approach places the practitioner, rather than the academic or researcher, centre stage in knowledge development and use. A key strength of this approach is that it recognizes and values social work practitioners as active creators and users of theory and other forms of knowledge. Taylor and White (2000, p. 196) contend that: 'By introducing subjectivity, reflective writing brings us much closer to practice than objectivist accounts.' It also promotes open-ended approaches to practice that allow for the local complexities of defining issues and responding to them. In endorsing a reflective approach, Parton (2000, p. 452) argues: 'Uncertainty, confusion and doubt should form an essential part of any theoretical approaches which are serious about being useable in practice.'

Yet, this emphasis on practitioners' reflections as the basis for knowledge creation and use is problematic in a number of ways. The emphasis on intuitive and tacit knowledge means that the bases of our knowledge claims remain inaccessible to other stakeholders, such as service users, employers or funding agencies (Taylor and White, 2000, p. 193). Also, by holding practitioners' reflections to be a true account of social work practice, this approach leaves no room to critically interrogate the knowledge claims made by the practitioner. As Taylor and White (2000, p. 200) warn:

> Whilst critical reflective practice opens up the possibility of a more uncertain, ambiguous and complex world, it tends to close much of this down again by obscuring clients' perspectives and freezing practitioners' confessional accounts as true representations of what happened.

The intuitive knowledge valued in reflective practice is also difficult to use for formal educational purposes. As, according to Schön, our knowledge is developed in and through action, our capacity to transfer this knowledge outside specific practice contexts is limited. Furthermore, in some contexts of practice involving safety critical or legally binding decision-making, a primary reliance on intuitive and tacit knowledge may increase the risk of incorrect decisions. It may also lead to the production of knowledge that is not recognized by formal decision-making institutions such as courts. For example, if we are to present our case at court for, say, taking a child or an apparently suicidal person into the care of the state, we need to able to articulate the basis of our professional judgement in terms of the current state of 'scientific' and professional knowledge in our field, especially if we are called on to act as expert witnesses.

Finally, by focusing primarily on inductive knowledge building, that is, building knowledge from our practice experiences, we may fail to fully utilize formalized theories for practice as a basis for creating theory and knowledge in practice. We are in danger of expending energy on constantly 'reinventing the wheel' rather than developing and extending existing theory and our own knowledge base. In short, this approach does not establish a dialogue between the practitioner's intuitive knowledge and the formal theories for social work practice, but instead prioritizes the practitioner's experiential knowledge over all else. Similarly, by focusing on uncertainty and complexity, the reflective approach may lead practitioners to ignore those aspects of social work where some degree of certainty is possible and necessary. For instance, a great deal of empirical work has established effective strategies for working with involuntary clients and some of these approaches run counter to established practices within the profession. For example, Trotter (2004, 2006) identifies that the demonstration of high levels of empathy without a simultaneous focus on prosocial perspectives can lead to poorer outcomes for clients in child protection and criminal justice contexts. Information of this type, that is, empirically developed knowledge of a field, is important for novice practitioners whose lack of substantive knowledge of the specific practice domain may act as a barrier to purposeful reflection on their practice situation.

Approaching Theory Reflexively: Creating Theory in Practice

We turn now to reflexive practice, a notion that draws on discourse analysis techniques and the critical reflective tradition. Carolyn Taylor and Susan White (2000) used the term practising 'reflexively' to refer to an approach that seeks to encourage social workers (and other health professionals) to interrogate their knowledge production practices. Whereas the evidence-based approach separates knowledge development from practice knowledge, reflexive practice recognizes that social workers are always making knowledge in practice. Yet, although the reflective tradition, as outlined in Schön's work, recognizes that social workers construct knowledge, it prioritizes practitioners' experiential and tacit knowledge over other formal knowledge, including formal theories. In so doing, the reflective tradition can diminish the role of formal practice theories as a basis for critical reflection on our practice and it does not adequately scrutinize practitioners' accounts of the truths of their practice. The reflexive approach demands that:

> practitioners begin listening to themselves more carefully, attending to their rhetoric of persuasion and their constituting practice – that is listening with a critical ear to their sense- and knowledge-making practices. (White, 2009, p. 169)

White and her colleagues use a range of discourse analytic techniques to assist social workers to achieve critical insight into their practices.

In this book, we recognize the value of the reflexive approach developed by Taylor and White (2000; see also Hall et al., 2006; White, 2009; Hall and Slembrouck, 2010). There is much to be gained by enhancing the opportunities for social workers to think more critically about how they construct their practice and how our practices are constructed in the institutions where we practise. Consistent with the aim of reflexive practice to make the 'familiar strange' (White, 2009, p. 170), this book examines the key discourses shaping the institutional contexts of practice with the intention of assisting the reader to analyse the contexts within which their practices are embedded. In Part 3, the origins, assumptions, strengths and limitations of major theories for practice are outlined, in order to assist you to critically reflect on the contexts in which you are practising and critically assess and develop the practice approaches in which you are engaged.

Conclusion

Social workers are active participants in, and subjects of, the practice contexts in which we work. We construct our sense of purpose with service users through negotiation between expectations arising from our institutional context, our formal professional base, and our frameworks for practice. In this chapter, we examined the elements that constitute social work practices, while recognizing that our practices are constantly renegotiated in each practice interaction. We considered three approaches to theory use in practice and suggested that a critical reflexive approach is most consistent with the dynamic model of practice introduced in this chapter. In Part 2, we turn to analysis of the discourses through which our professional purpose is negotiated, and in Part 3 we analyse the theories for practice that inform our professional purpose and approach to practice.

Summary Questions

1 What are the components of the dynamic model of social work practice outlined in this chapter?

2 Why is it important to recognize the dynamic construction of professional purpose in social work practice?

3 What is theory for social work practice?

4 What are the barriers to theory use in practice?

5 What does a critical and reflexive approach to theory use involve?

Recommended Reading

- Banks, S. (2012) *Ethics and Values in Social Work*, 4th edn. (Basingstoke: Palgrave Macmillan).
  Excellent reader-friendly overview of values and ethics in social work.

- Cree, V. and Davis, A. (2006) *Social Work: Voices from the Inside*. (New York: Routledge).
  Presents the voices of people using a range of social work services, including users of child welfare and family support, mental health, disability and aged care services. Powerful articulation of how service users perceive our purpose and our potential to do better. Drawing on the voices of service users, draws together common themes about improving practice.

- Healy, K. (2011) *Social Work Methods and Skills: The Essential Foundations of Practice*. (Basingstoke: Palgrave Macmillan).
  Introduction to the methods and skills in social work practice, including work with individuals, families, groups, communities and in policy contexts. Companion to this book, in that it incorporates the theoretical concepts outlined here, within the practices of social work.

- Kirk, S. and Reid, W. (2002) *Science and Social Work: A Critical Appraisal*. (New York: Columbia University Press).
  Critical appraisal of the strategies and methods that have been used to develop knowledge for social work practice. Identifies how social workers draw on scientific knowledge and techniques and critically evaluates the evidence-based tradition and social workers' engagement with this tradition.

- Schön, D. (1983) *The Reflective Practitioner.* (New York: Basic Books).
  Seminal text that defines this approach and outlines its value for human service professions such as teaching, nursing and social work. Excellent introduction to the drivers for an evidence-based approach to practice.

- Sheldon, B. and Macdonald, G. (2010) *A Textbook of Social Work.* (New York: Taylor & Francis).
  Informative introduction to the history and current context of social work. The lead authors are internationally renowned for their work on evidence-based practice. Important contemporary guide to social work context and practice debates today.

- Taylor, C. and White, S. (2000) *Practising Reflexivity in Health and Welfare: Making Knowledge.* (Buckingham: Open University Press).
  Ground-breaking work outlining the theory and practice of reflexivity in health and welfare practices. Provides practical strategies for social workers to interrogate knowledge production practice in which they are engaged.

- White, S., Fook, J. and Gardiner, F. (eds) (2006) *Critical Reflection in Health and Social Care.* (Buckingham: Open University Press).
  Excellent introduction to theory and practice of critical reflection and reflexivity in health and social care fields. Outlines key concepts and methods that can be used to enhance practice through effective critical reflection. Incorporates discussion of the relevance and use of critical reflection in a range of contexts, including direct practice, research and social work education.

Recommended Websites

- **www.ifsw.org**
  The International Federation of Social Workers

- **www.scie.org.uk**
  UK-based Social Care Institute for Excellence (SCIE), which gathers and analyses knowledge for practice and provides practical resources for evidence informed practice in social work and related services.

- **www.cochrane.org**
  Cochrane Collaboration, an independent organization focused on developing knowledge for practice in healthcare and related fields.

Practice Exercise **Values and social work**

Examine the IFSW's definition of social work, given on its website, and consider these questions in relation to that statement.

- How does the statement fit with your sense of purpose in social work?

- What challenges does this definition present social workers working in health and welfare services today?

PART 2
DISCOURSES SHAPING PRACTICE CONTEXTS

Social workers work in a wide variety of practice contexts. In many of these contexts, the knowledge claims of certain kinds of professional experts, such as medical, legal or financial, dominate the construction of service user needs and interventions. Analysis of the discourses operating in our practice contexts can provide us with insights for understanding, improving and, in some situations, disrupting existing practice conditions. The purpose of such analysis must always be towards the realization of improved circumstances for the people who use our services.

In Chapter 1, the concept of discourses was introduced. The term discourse was defined as 'a system or aggregate of meanings' (Taylor, 2013, p. 14) through which certain social phenomena such as 'need', 'knowledge' and 'intervention' are constructed. This book draws on the key assumption from poststructural theory that discourses have material effects. In other words, the language practices that occur within our practice contexts actively create our professional purpose, identities, power relations and intervention options (Rojek et al., 1988; Parton, 1994; Opie, 1995; Krumer-Nevo et al., 2011). In Chapter 2, we considered a dynamic model of practice to outline how our professional purpose is constructed through interaction between our contexts, service user and community expectations, our professional practice base and our emerging frameworks for practice.

In Part 2, we critically analyse three sets of discourses operating in a variety of health and welfare service contexts and through which social work practices are constituted. In this critical approach to discourse analysis, the assumptions and operations of the three sets of discourses considered in Chapters 3–5 are interrogated. The three sets of discourses are dominant discourses (biomedicine, law, neoclassical economics, and new public management), social and behavioural science discourses ('psy' and socio-logical discourses) and alternative discourses (citizen rights, religion and spirituality, and environmental social work).

Through analysis of the discourses through which social work is consti-tuted, we draw attention to 'the conditional, changeable character of social work' (Rojek et al., 1988, p. 131). The purpose of this critical analysis is not only to better understand how our purposes and practices are discursively constituted, but also to inform action arising from the ongoing critical awareness of the constraints and opportunities provided by the discourses operating in our practice contexts.

3

DOMINANT DISCOURSES IN HEALTH AND WELFARE
Medicine, Law, Economics and New Public Management

Social work has grown and has been shaped by discourses of the health and welfare organizations where social workers are often numerically in the minority and the position of social workers is contested and marginal. For more than three decades, health and welfare organizations have been the site of struggle as the discourses linked to the elite professions, particularly medicine and law, have been challenged by neoclassical economics and new public management (NPM) discourses.

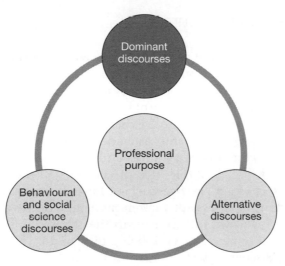

Figure 3.1 Discourses in interaction: emphasizing dominant discourses

In this chapter, we begin with a discussion of the discourses of biomedicine and law, which have traditionally dominated many of the health and welfare institutions where social workers practice. We then examine the increasingly dominant discourses of NPM and neoclassical economics.

As represented in Figure 3.1, the dominant discourse of biomedicine, law, neoclassical economics and NPM stand apart from, yet also interact with, other discourses, such as the 'psy' and sociological and alternative discourses discussed in Chapters 4 and 5.

We propose that the discourses of biomedicine, law, neoclassical economics and NPM have a dominant influence on the construction of service users' needs and the responses to them in practice contexts. Yet, while these discourses are often debated, their core assumptions are rarely outlined. It is frequently assumed that we all know what these terms mean, even though the speakers and writers themselves may differ in their defini-tion of the terms. In this chapter, we aim to remedy this by outlining the features and practical implications of these ideas and to invite you, the reader, to consider their application to your practice.

We turn now to an examination of the dominant discourses shaping contemporary health and welfare institutions. We first consider the features of each discourse and their practical effects for social workers and service users. We then analyse the uses and limitations of each of these discourses for achieving our purposes, as we construct them, within specific sites of social work practice.

The Biomedical Discourse

Traditionally, the biomedical discourse has been one of the most powerful discourses shaping practice contexts, particularly in health services, such as hospitals, rehabilitation services, and mental health services (Dziegielewski, 2013). It also influences a wide range of social service contexts, such as child protection practice, where medical experts often play a pivotal role in defining and assessing what counts as evidence of risk of harm and abuse. As a result of biotechnological advances and the dominance of biomedical industries (Gomory et al., 2011), this discourse is extending further into many areas of socio-legal practice, such as forensic investigations in child protection and criminal assault matters and the controversial terrain of genetic testing. Yet, as we will see later in the chapter, this discourse faces challenges and, in some contexts, is being displaced by NPM and neoclas-sical economic discourses in the organization and delivery of health and welfare services.

Social workers have a well-established interest in the 'medical model' as a framework for practice. Mary Richmond's social diagnosis approach (1917) shows the early ambitions of the social work profession to mirror the discourse of medicine through the adoption of notions of systemic diagnosis and intervention. During the 1970s, radical social workers critiqued the medical model of service delivery as ignoring the underlying structural causes of service users' problems (Decker and Redhorse, 1979). In many fields of health and welfare services, social workers continue to argue against a medical model of service delivery on the grounds that it leads us to focus on 'modifying the person, assuming that any difficulties lie in the individual's deviation from "normal" rather than in the lack of accommodation within the environment' (Quinn, 1998, p. xix; see also Gomory et al., 2011).

The term 'biomedicine' is widely used in the biological, medical and social sciences to refer to the dominant contemporary approaches to medicine that derive from the biological sciences. We adopt the term 'biomedical discourse' from the field of medical sociology, where it is used to refer to a specific set of ideas and practices associated with a biological approach to medicine. According to Mishler (1989; see also Williams, 2003, p. 12), these are some of the key concepts of the biomedical discourse:

- *Diseases and other 'malaises', such as disabilities, are deviations from normal biological functioning:* Biomedical assessment and intervention focus on addressing deviations and correcting them, rather than adapting the environment to accommodate differences.

- *Various malaises are caused by specific biological agents or processes, that is, the doctrine of specific aetiology:* Biological explanations of diseases are privileged over understanding the social patterning of a range of phenomena from diseases through to challenging behaviours (Kenen, 1996, p. 1545; Gomory et al., 2011). For example, Gomory et al. (2011, pp. 151–2) observe that in child welfare services, the biomedical discourse has contributed to 'a thoroughly medicalized approach to family poverty, disorganization and distress, to the detriment of the unfortunate children involved'.

- *The universal nature of diseases, regardless of culture, time and place:* For example, 'diseases' such as schizophrenia occur across cultures and have been present throughout history. However, the biomedical discourse fails to acknowledge the enormous cultural and historical variations that affect every aspect of people's understanding and experiences of this 'disease', as well as varying social responses to it (Jenkins and Barrett, 2004).

- *Medicine is a scientifically neutral enterprise:* The knowledge prized in the biomedical discourse is that which is, ostensibly, unbiased by the prejudices of the scientist or medical practitioner and grounded in evidence obtained by scientific means (Gomory et al., 2011). The evidence-based tradition in medicine, which has more recently influenced social work, is founded on this ideal.

How the Biomedical Discourse Shapes Practice

The biomedical discourse profoundly influences service delivery in many health and welfare contexts. First, it determines who is seen as knowledgeable or expert and who is not. Expertise is associated with knowledge of the biological basis of health and illness. In practice, this confers power on the biomedical experts, particularly medical scientists and practitioners, for defining and leading intervention efforts (Dziegielewski, 2013). This does not mean, however, that biomedical experts only use biomedical knowledge in their decision-making. For example, a doctor in a palliative care unit may encourage the family of a terminally ill patient to resist further biomedical intervention. Rather, it is suggested that in contexts where the biomedical discourse dominates, a truth status is attached to biomedical knowledge even though other discourses will also be operating in these environments. Indeed, in environments where this discourse is strong, such as mainstream hospitals, economic, legal and religious discourses can also shape decision-making.

Another practical effect of biomedicine's dominance in many health and welfare environments is that social workers must understand and use biomedical terminology in order to communicate effectively in these practice domains (Dziegielewski, 2013). Moreover, we may have a role in translating biomedical terminology for service users as we assist them to negotiate health and welfare systems.

Advances in genetic research and related technologies have also led to assessments in health services moving beyond a focus on existing conditions to incorporate consideration of future possible health outcomes (Taylor, 2001, p. 4). Information gained via the new genetic technologies is used in a variety of ways, many of which are highly controversial. Genetic information can be used to implement preventive measures to avert or delay disease development (Taylor, 2001, p. 3). For instance, some women carry a gene that places them at elevated risk of developing breast cancer (Rosenberg and Rosenberg, 2012). Armed with this knowledge, some women may choose to seek regular screening for cancer, or reduce their risks through pharmacological and surgical interventions, including prophylactic mastectomy. Genetic information can also help prepare individuals for the onset of diseases for which there is currently no cure. One example of this is Huntington's disease, an inherited and fatal brain degeneration condition that does not appear until mid-adulthood; it can be predicted but cannot be cured. Individuals may find information about their genetic status useful for decision-making in relation to their own lives by, for example, making preparations for the onset of increasing disability.

Predictive genetic testing for fetal 'abnormalities', such as Down syndrome, is an especially controversial terrain. Advocates of testing for fetal abnormalities argue that this allows the parents to make an informed choice about whether to continue with or terminate a pregnancy involving a fetus with a disease or disabling condition. If parents continue with the pregnancy, although the evidence suggests that few do once an abnormality is detected (France et al., 2012), they can prepare themselves and their families to care for a baby with a disease or disability. There are many opponents of genetic testing for fetal abnormalities. Many religious groups associate these tests with the denial of the unborn child's right to life. Some disability rights advocates argue that predictive testing extends society's discrimination against people with disabilities to the womb, leading us to focus on the 'problem' of disability, rather than on society's intolerance of differently abled people (for further discussion, see Chapter 5).

As a result of advances in biomedical technologies, the biomedical discourse has extended further into many areas of health and welfare. This has many implications for social work practice, one being that social workers, especially those working in healthcare contexts, are involved in assisting service users in decision-making around an increasing range of possible health outcomes. Social workers have expressed concerns about the social justice implications of the new biomedical technologies (see Taylor et al., 2008), and raised critical questions about their deployment. Do service user groups receive fair and equitable access to these technologies? Do they receive too little access? Are their rights to self-determination assured? What about confidentiality considerations? The following case study is intended to assist you to think through some of the dilemmas these new technologies may raise in social work practice. We will discuss these issues later in the chapter.

Case Study **Genetic testing**

Imagine you are a social worker in the women's health service of a large metropolitan hospital. Laura is referred to you by one of the gynaecological specialists at the hospital to assist in her decision-making about whether to seek genetic screening for a breast cancer gene. Laura is 35 years old, married and has two children under five years. She has a family history of breast cancer; her mother and grandmother died of the disease in their mid-forties and one of Laura's older sisters, who is 41, is being treated for breast cancer. Her eldest sister, who is 43, shows no signs of the disease and does not plan to be tested. Laura is unsure about whether to seek the test or not and says she is afraid of finding out that she carries the gene.

- What do you see as your purpose in this situation?

- What principles and values would be important in working with Laura?

Imagine instead that Laura is considered at risk of Huntington's disease. There is no cure or treatment for this fatal condition and so the primary purpose of genetic testing would

▶

be to reveal whether or not Laura will develop the disease, rather than to prevent or treat the condition.

- What do you see as your purpose in this situation?
- In what ways it is similar or different to the previous situation?
- In what ways, if any, would these differences alter your approach to the situation?

Biomedical Discourse: Uses, Issues and Problems

The uses and limitations of the biomedical discourse are the subject of heated debate, particularly within the social sciences and some fields of social work practice (see Sparrow, 2005; Dziegielewski, 2013). On the positive side, the practical impact of the biomedical discourse on people's lives in postindustrial countries is irrefutable. Biological understanding of the nature of infection and disease has contributed to the development of a range of preventive measures, such as mass vaccinations and screening, that have contributed to substantial declines in illness and death from a range of diseases. For example, the mass introduction of cervical screening has contributed to a sharp decline in the number of deaths from cervical cancer in postindustrial societies, while the recent development of a cervical cancer vaccine is also likely to contribute to a further decline in deaths from cervical cancer.

In addition, advances in biomedical interventions, such as surgical and pharmacological treatments, have contributed to substantial improvements in the management and treatment of a range of illnesses and potentially life-threatening conditions. Kelly and Field (cited in Williams, 2003, p. 20) point out that many modern medical procedures, such as coronary artery bypass, renal dialysis, hip replacement, and the pharmacology of pain relief have significantly improved or restored the quality of life of many of those suffering from chronic illnesses. Similarly, proponents of the new genetic technologies argue that these offer opportunities for further advancement in the prevention and treatment of a broad range of conditions (Rosenberg and Rosenberg, 2012). In relation to Laura's case, we can see that genetic technologies can provide Laura with information about her susceptibility to breast cancer. This information could be used to implement strategies for prevention and early intervention, thus enhancing Laura's chances of avoiding or surviving the disease, if she is found to be susceptible. In the second part of the case study, genetic testing would provide solid evidence of whether or not Laura will develop Huntington's disease. While there is currently no treatment or cure for Huntington's disease, Laura could use this information to prepare herself and her family for the onset of the illness.

Much of the time, many of us have no quarrel with biomedical discourse. Faced with a serious illness or injury, most of us would submit to biomedical expertise and we would encourage service users to do the same. In many practice contexts, however, we are likely to experience tensions between our formal professional base, particularly our values, and the assumptions and uses of the biomedical discourse. One area of concern is the biological reductionism of the biomedical discourse. By focusing on a disease or an injured organ, the biomedical discourse is in conflict with the holistic and systemic approaches to practice championed by social workers (see Bland et al., 2009; Gomory et al., 2011). A holistic approach seeks to understand the person in their social context and promote an optimal state of physical, mental and social wellbeing, not merely the absence of disease (Daly et al., 2001, p. xiii).

Another concern relates to the impact of the biomedical discourse on the allocation of public resources for health and welfare interventions. Gomory et al. (2011, p. 151) note that the biomedical industry's championing of biomedical interventions has contributed to an 'enormous transfer of public funds to the pharmaceutical companies', which has occurred despite a lack of evidence of a biological basis for some of the forms of human distress experienced by clients of mental health services, particularly the distress arising from poverty and marginalization.

In contexts where the biomedical discourse dominates, social workers have an important role to play in highlighting service users' interests and needs beyond their medical diagnosis. A holistic approach to assisting Laura in her decision-making would not deny the potential benefits of genetic testing but would require us to promote Laura's capacity to be self-determining. One way we could do this is by exploring with Laura her interpretations of the meanings of the family history of cancer, the meanings of the genetic tests for her, and identifying options for care and support whether or not she undergoes the tests (see McGrath, 1997; Dziegielewski, 2013). In short, we would seek to engage with her as a whole person and not primarily in terms of her patient status. Similarly, a holistic approach might lead us to question with Laura the relevance of genetic testing for promoting her quality of life. We might explore with her how she would manage a result showing that she carried the gene for Huntington's in the absence of any treatment for the condition (Taylor et al., 2008).

Another concern is that the biomedical discourse leads to the medicalization of more and more areas of our lives. Hunter et al. (1997, p. 1542) assert that 'medicalization occurs when a behaviour or problem is defined in medical terms and when medical treatments are seen as the appropriate solutions'. 'Medicalization' means that medical explanations are attached to a range of problems or issues that might otherwise be seen as either non-medical in nature or part of the 'normal' range of human behaviour. Medicalization reflects, and contributes to, the increasing dominance of biomedical discourses and institutions in Western societies (Lupton, cited in Williams, 2003, p. 16). Medicalization also contributes to the devaluing of non-medical responses to the problems and issues facing service users – when a problem is understood in primarily biomedical terms, the only rational response becomes a biomedical one.

Returning to Laura's case, consistent with the principle of self-determination, we could explore what pressure, if any, she feels to undertake the genetic tests, that is, to do what is technologically possible. We could explore with Laura options for resisting the biomedical interventions offered to her, what pressures she feels from others, such as medical staff or family members, and we could rehearse how she would explain to them a decision not to undergo the tests. Through this, we can help to make resistance of the biomedical model a realistic option for her, if she so chooses.

A further concern is the potential for biomedical knowledge to contribute to social oppression. Although biomedical knowledge is understood, within the terms of the biomedical discourse, to be scientifically neutral, the ends this knowledge can serve are far from impartial. As discussed earlier, disability rights activists have argued that new genetic technologies can extend disability oppression to the womb (see Chapter 5). In addition, genetic information may contribute to discrimination towards individuals identified at risk of illness or disability. Taylor et al. (2008, p. 20) define genetic discrimination as 'the differential treatment of asymptomatic individuals or their relatives on the basis of actual or presumed genetic differences or characteristics'. This discrimination can include financial discrimination, such as denial of insurance or employment opportunities, through to unfavourable social treatment, such as hurtful remarks about relationship or reproductive options.

Consistent with the principle of social justice, we need to be critically aware of the potential for biomedical information to lead to discrimination towards Laura. It is important for us to establish whether Laura is required by any external agency to undertake these tests, the extent to which the test results are confidential, and what avenues of complaint or redress are available to Laura with regard to the discriminatory outcomes associated with the disclosure of genetic information (Taylor et al., 2008).

Review Question

Thinking of your area of practice, or an area of practice that interests you, such as mental health services, discuss how, if at all, the biomedical discourse shapes the construction of service users' needs and social work practices in this context.

Legal Discourse

The legal discourse has, like the biomedical discourse, powerfully shaped many of the contexts where social workers practice. Here, we consider the main impacts of the legal discourse on social work practices. We then turn to an examination of key concepts in the legal discourse and the uses of, and concerns about, this discourse as a vehicle for achieving our purpose in social work practice.

Social Work and the Law

Ball (1996, p. 3) defines the law as 'the body of rules whereby a civilized society maintains order and regulates its internal affairs as between one individual and another, and between individuals and the state'. Many authors also emphasize the social control dimensions of law. For instance, Austin (cited in Coleman and Leiter, 1996, p. 244) defines law as 'the order of a "sovereign" backed by the threat of sanction in the event of noncompliance'. Two main types of law impact on social work practice:

1 *Statutory law:* A law that has been passed by Parliament, also known as 'Acts of Parliament' (Brayne and Carr, 2010, Ch. 1). Statutory laws exist in many areas of social services work and shape the role and obligations of social workers in these contexts.

2 *Case law (or judicial precedent):* Law established by previous case reasoning and case findings; used to define and refine existing laws and may be used to make new law (Ball, 1996, p. 4). Case law can impact on the way statutory legislation is interpreted, which can affect our use of statutory law in direct practice.

In addition, social workers may be required to abide by specific codes of practice associated with their institutional contexts (see Ball, 1996, p. 4). These institutional codes are public declarations of what service users can expect from the agency, such as confidential service delivery. Social workers who fail to respect them may be the subject of complaint to a higher authority, such as the ombudsperson or other complaints tribunal, and may find their failure to abide by the code counts against them in court action (Ball, 1996, p. 4).

Law as a Discourse

Law, like biomedicine and economics, is a contested domain, that is, there are many strands of legal thought. Here, we focus on the dominant discourse of law, formally known as 'legal positivism'. According to Anleu (2000, p. 6): 'Legal positivists view the law as a formal, logical system of legal rules … Positivism has been the dominant philosophy of law since the nineteenth century.' The discourse of legal positivism, as the dominant discourse of law, shapes the commonsense understandings widely held by lawyers and the general public about the purpose and processes of law.

The discourse of legal positivism holds that the law is objective and rational, and represents the law as 'impermeable to personal values or individual manipulation' (Anleu, 2000, p. 6; see also Bourdieu, 1987). This commitment to objectivity is expressed in the ways legal processes are described and performed. For example, Bourdieu (1987, p. 830) observes that judicial language 'bears all the marks of a rhetoric of impersonality and neutrality'. Through these language practices, judges and magistrates represent their decision-making as objective, dependent on legal fact and reasoning, rather than on personal views (Anleu, 2000, p. 4).

Also, legal positivism requires that social processes comply with distinct legal categories if they are to be recognized in formal legal process. These categories construct our identities and actions as static entities that contrast markedly with the fluidity we often experience in our lives (Bourdieu, 1987, p. 832). For example, in the legal discourse, one is constructed as either a 'plaintiff' or a 'defendant', 'victim' or 'non-victim', 'guilty' or 'not guilty', 'sane' or 'insane', 'liable' or 'not liable' and so on (Bourdieu, 1987, p. 832). Yet the realities of clients' lives, and indeed our own, often defy these categorizations. For example, from the available evidence about the childhood experiences of many violent offenders, we know that perpetrators of abuse have often experienced abuse themselves, particularly as children.

Finally, the discourse of legal positivism assumes that the law is authoritative. The discourse of law is based on the assumption that citizens recognize the law as the supreme arbiter of truth and thus they will comply, whether voluntarily or by coercion. Further, the legal discourse holds that our responsibilities before the law should override all other considerations. For example, in most jurisdictions, social workers can be compelled by law to share confidential information in some situations such as acting in the interests of the client or the public (Brayne and Carr, 2010, p. 112).

Consistent with our value of professional integrity, it is vital that we are aware of, and communicate to service users, how the law may shape our relationships and, in particular, how it shapes how we may deal with information provided by clients to us.

Legal Discourse in Social Work Practice

Social workers need to understand the legal discourse, in part, because the law often defines our key responsibilities to employing agencies and service users. Slater and Finck (2011, p. ix) point to the constitutive power of legal discourse:

> Regulations create, effect, and shape the organizations where you work, how you identify who are your clients, what activities you may perform, what obligations you have to clients and in some cases, what limits you set on how long you may work with a client.

The constitutive power of the legal discourse is particularly evident in statutory contexts where social workers have an explicit responsibility to implement statutory law. The statutory responsibilities carried by social workers are delegated to them via their employing organization. This means that social workers are empowered to use statutory law not through their professional training or registration, but through their context of employment. This is an important distinction to make, as the types of statutory obligations we bear are very much tied to our site of employment and some social workers do not hold statutory obligations.

Notwithstanding the coercive dimensions of statutory power, this form of law can also have protective and empowering functions. Despite extensive critique of the statutory role of child protection social workers, in some circumstances this legislation can be used to advocate children's right to be free of exploitation and abuse (K. Healy, 1998). Indeed, social workers have argued that the *absence* of statutory law in some contexts, such as care of the elderly, limits their capacity to protect some vulnerable service users from abuse and exploitation (Braye and Preston-Shoot, 1997, p. 10).

Social workers should have an understanding of the law because the law impacts on service users' lives in myriad ways. Many service users' problems and concerns have legal dimensions and social workers should be able to identify legal concerns and facilitate service users' access to legal representation (Brayne and Carr, 2010). This knowledge should include understanding of:

- the statutory laws in your area of practice
- human rights and anti-discrimination legislation
- the operation of the legal system and how to access legal representation in your area of concern
- case law relevant to your area of practice.

In recent years, interest has emerged in the concept of 'therapeutic juris-prudence', which refers to the use of law 'to contribute to the psychological and physical wellbeing of individuals' (Slater and Finck, 2011, p. 18). This concept has given rise to a range of socio-legal studies and reform efforts of the law especially for marginalized or silent populations. Alongside other interested parties, social workers have contributed to changes in the law related to a range of human welfare concerns, including child protection, domestic violence, and the recognition of the human rights of people with disabilities, children and young people.

Another reason for understanding legal discourse is that we can use it to support and advocate for the protection of service users' rights (Swain, 2002, p. 266). For example, human rights legislation and anti-discrimination laws are intended to provide all citizens with basic human rights such as freedom from discrimination and procedural fairness in administrative matters. Social workers can use this legislation to improve the accountability of social service agencies for providing appropriate and accessible responses to service users (Swain, 2002, p. 266).

Practice Exercise **Using the law**

Imagine you are a social worker working in a nongovernmental family support service for vulnerable families. One of your clients is Chelsea, a 35-year-old single mother of three children, Jack (10), Penny (8) and Sarah (3). Chelsea suffers from bipolar disorder and occasionally requires hospitalization for her condition. Kath, Chelsea's mother, is 56 years old and lives nearby. Kath often looks after the children when Chelsea is unwell and has a good relationship with the children. Jim, Chelsea's ex-partner and father of the three children, is also supportive but lives two hours' drive away.

This afternoon, you were contacted by the local authority child protection service, informing you that Chelsea had a serious episode overnight and had to be hospital-ized. The local authority has been unable to contact either Kath or Jim and so the children have been taken into temporary custody of the authority. The children reported to the local authority that their grandmother was away on a week's holiday. Chelsea is currently in hospital under sedation. In her phone call to you, the child protection authority social worker expresses concern about the long-term wellbeing of the children, noting that this is the second time in six months that Chelsea has been hospitalized and one issue appears to be noncompliance with the medication regime prescribed by the treating psychiatrist. The child protection worker states that Chelsea's condition is long term and negatively impacts on her ability to care for her children, and that she is considering taking an extended order for the children for one month so that they can remain with the foster carer with whom she has placed them and their situation be fully assessed.

▶

You are concerned about this plan in relation to its disruption for the children and because you believe that the children are generally well cared for by the extended family network and have a strong attachment to their mother.

Drawing on the discussion of the uses of legal discourse in social work practice, identify:

- your legal responsibilities as a social worker in this context

- legal issues arising in this case

- how you would address these legal concerns.

In reflecting on Chelsea's case, let's first consider our possible legal responsibilities as social workers. As a social worker working in a family support service, you may have legal responsibilities, and you certainly have ethical responsibilities, to ensure that the children are well cared for and are not at risk of harm. One legal issue concerns discrimination against Chelsea on the basis of her mental health status. The fact that Chelsea has been diagnosed with bipolar disorder is not, of itself, a barrier to being a caring parent and there are important questions here about whether Chelsea is being viewed unfavourably as a parent because of her mental health status. If this is so, human rights and anti-discrimination legislation are likely to be relevant. A further concern is the possible contravention of the relevant child protection legislation, particularly in relation to provisions to support vulnerable families and to remove children only as a last resort, where no reasonable possibility exists for caring for the children within their family or kinship network.

Non-legal options for responding to Chelsea's case include seeking a family group meeting with Kath and Jack to work out the next steps in providing support to the Chelsea and her children. Legal options include seeking legal representation for Chelsea particularly to address the matters of discrimination and rights to support the least intrusive intervention by child protection authorities.

Legal Discourse: Issues and Concerns

As we have seen, legal discourse shapes social work practice and, in some contexts, can be used to promote social work values, such as self-determination and social justice. Swain (2002, p. 267) argues that social workers should 'acknowledge the points at which legal interventions and remedies can prove effective, and to seek to exploit these for the betterment of all'. Yet commentators in the legal and social service fields also raise a number of concerns about the legal discourse, many of which challenge claims that the law is an objective and rational process.

Commentators argue that legal assumptions and processes are value laden (Bourdieu, 1987, p. 826). Critical analysts argue that what appears as objective reasoning by the judiciary reflects their class, gender and race status, which can, in turn, make the practices of people of a different class, gender and ethnic status appear deviant, abnormal and pathological (Bourdieu, 1987, p. 847). Critical commentators point out that the law can contribute to the production of social inequality by, for example, limiting access to participation in the legal process to those deemed to be legal experts (Bourdieu, 1987, p. 818). Thus, rather than an instrument for achieving justice, the law is experienced by many service users as 'remote, incomprehensible, expensive or irrelevant' (Swain, 2002, p. 267).

Another way the law contributes to the reproduction of social inequality is when statutes and legal decision-making neglect the social and economic contexts of issues before the law. Research on the social effects of law has demonstrated that the law can be an instrument of social control (Anleu, 2000, p. 230). Critical analyses show that laws in a range of fields disproportionately affect the most disadvantaged and marginalized groups in society (Bourdieu, 1987, p. 817). For example, in child protection services, statutory law can be used as a vehicle to impose Eurocentric and middle-class norms on working-class and non-European families (Bessarab and Crawford, 2013). Social workers have an important role to play in identifying and contesting legal discourse where that discourse places disproportionate burdens on the people with whom we practise.

Finally, although the law offers some ways of remedying social concerns, it can limit change possibilities (Bourdieu, 1987, p. 816). Anleu (2000, p. 234) contends: 'The legal arena also constrains social action as it requires social problems and complaints to be translated or transformed into legal concepts and legal remedies.' In this process of translation, structural causes are erased as sites of legal concern as legal action must be directed towards specific parties, such as governments, companies or individuals. The law can be a useful tool for individual and group advocacy, but other forms of action, such as policy and attitudinal change, are also important for addressing the challenges facing the people with whom we practise.

Discourses of Neoclassical Economics and New Public Management (NPM)

It is hard to overstate the profound influence of the discourses of neoclassical economics and NPM on the organization and delivery of health and welfare services over the past two decades (Kirkpatrick et al., 2005; Levy, 2010). Despite drawing on many common concepts, these two discourses have varying origins and are primarily directed at different domains. The neoclassical economic discourse focuses on economic activities, while NPM is concerned with how public services are organized and delivered (McDonald, 2006, p. 70). Proponents of NPM often draw on neoclassical economic concepts in their proposals for public service reforms. These discourses provide support for:

- the introduction of free-market ideas into the organization of social work services

- a focus on economic efficiency, workforce flexibility and service delivery

- a concern with performance measurement.

Here, we describe the features and importance of these discourses for shaping social work practice today.

As we shall see, economics, particularly the neoclassical economic discourse, influences social work practice in a variety of ways. As a discipline, economics is concerned with the allocation of scarce resources for maximum benefit (Sandler, 2001; Edwards, 2007). Economics is not, however, a single or unified discourse and economists vary in their views of how their core concerns are to be addressed. Neoclassical economics is also referred to as 'neoliberal economics' (see Friedman, 1982) or 'economic rationalism', although, technically, economic rationalism is 'a simplification of a sub-school' of neoclassical economics (Edwards, 2007, p. 36). We focus on neoclassical economics because since the mid-1970s, this discourse has become the dominant framework in economics and public policy decision-making in many postindustrial countries (Stillwell, 1996).

If social workers are to be active participants in determining the allocation of social service resources, it is vital that we understand the terms of this dominant discourse so that we can challenge it on its own terms (Edwards, 2007). As we shall see, even neoclassical economists concede that there are limits to this discourse and we can use this knowledge to ensure that these limits are respected in our practice contexts. First, we consider the key features of this discourse and then analyse its effects in social work practice contexts.

Neoclassical Economic Discourse: Key Concepts

Whether or not we agree with neoclassical economics (and most social workers do not), it is important for social workers to understand the key assumptions of this increasingly influential discourse.

The free market occupies a central, even sacred, place in neoclassical economic discourse. Sandler (2001, p. 20), an economist, states that: 'markets can be a thing of beauty when they function properly'. According to this discourse, the invisible hand of the market ensures the efficient allocation of resources for the maximum benefit, that is, maximum wealth creation. Through the free market, the interests of buyers and sellers are coordinated to ensure the production of goods and services that are valued most by consumers at the best price. In addition, free markets encourage competition between sellers, which also contributes to the efficient allocation of resources. Neoclassical economists argue that free-market competition provides a vital mechanism for driving down costs and weeding out ineffective and inappropriate uses of scarce resources.

Across many postindustrial countries, governments have introduced markets to health and social services on the premise that 'the market can deliver better and cheaper services than government' (J. Healy, 1998, p. 32). In the market model, governments become purchasers, rather than primary providers, of these services, and governments purchase services from the nongovernmental sector, in which agencies compete with each other for service contracts. The neoclassical economic discourse infers that increased competition among social service providers will ensure that governments, taxpayers and service users receive better value for their money.

Markets in social services are referred to as 'quasi-markets' because they differ from traditional commercial markets. One of the key differences is that, in the social services, the entity purchasing the service, usually the government or insurance company, is not the entity receiving the service, that is, the service user. In part, this is because consumers of social services often have a limited capacity to pay for services. Another difference is that 'consumers' do not necessarily choose the services, such as child protection, that are delivered to them. These services are part of the social surveillance role of the state and thus fall outside the usual understanding of consumer goods and services within the neoclassical economic discourse.

The neoclassical economic discourse holds that individuals are self-interested, rational actors. It is assumed that individuals act in ways that reflect and promote their individual self-interest and, in so doing, contribute to the 'betterment of everyone' (Sandler, 2001, p. 10). The neoclassical economic discourse promotes criticism of all forms of third-party intervention, that is, forms of intervention that the recipient did not request and for which they do not cover the costs. For example, from a neoclassical economic perspective, family support services to vulnerable families may be questioned on the grounds that the families themselves rarely request such services and are not usually in a position to pay for them. Advocates of the neoclassical economic discourse argue that third-party directed forms of intervention are paternalistic and can interfere with our capacities to act in our own self-interest. Also, because recipients do not pay for third-party interventions, they can lead to the ineffective allocation of resources as goods and services that consumers neither want nor value. Applying these arguments to community care provision, we would assert that individuals choosing their own services will act in their own self-interest to ensure that they get the best service at the best price and, furthermore, if they pay for these services, they will value them more highly than if a third party had met the costs.

Another important concept in this discourse is freedom of choice. Milton Friedman (1982, p. 195), a winner of the Nobel Prize for economics and key exponent of neoliberal economic philosophy, contends that:

> The heart of the liberal philosophy is a belief in the dignity of the individual, in his [sic] freedom to make the most of his [sic] capacities and opportunities according to his [sic] own lights, subject only to the proviso that he [sic] not interfere with the freedom of other individuals to do the same.

Neoclassical economists argue that the freedom to choose is a fundamental human right to be protected as long as it does not interfere with others' freedom. Proponents of this principle oppose most forms of welfare and social service provision on the grounds that it imposes a tax burden on others, thus impeding their freedom of choice. In this discourse, freedom of choice is also linked to economic efficiency as, it is asserted, people make rational choices consistent with their individual self-interest. By ensuring individuals have, wherever possible, the freedom to choose what kinds of goods and services they will consume, we achieve the 'highest possible standard of living' from a 'finite pot of resources' (Edwards, 2002, p. 38). Returning to our illustration of community care, the argument is that when individuals are able to choose their service provider, they will choose the most effective and efficient community care services and, in so doing, will weed out operators who lack these qualities.

Neoclassical economists favour minimal government intervention or small government. Proponents of neoclassical economics are concerned about distorting the operation of free markets and argue that large government programmes often lead to the redirection of public money towards 'feathering the nests of the few at the cost of the many' (Edwards, 2007, p. 65). The assumptions arising from this discourse are that if governments provide social services such as community care services, they will inhibit the capacity of private providers to compete for this 'business' and limit the development of efficient and effective services because ineffective and inefficient services will remain.

In this discourse, the role of government is constrained to three core responsibilities. The first is that government should promote conditions to maximize the free operation of the market. One way governments do this is through legislation to protect private property rights. According to this discourse, governments have a responsibility to ensure that nongovernmental service providers can compete for public funding for the provision of health and welfare services (Gibelman and Demone, 2002). A second responsibility of government is to provide public goods, that is, goods and services that benefit all citizens but which individuals are unable or unwilling to pay for individually. For neoclassical economists, public goods include items such as national defence systems, anti-terrorist capabilities, protection of the environment, and public works (Sandler, 2001). Interestingly, neoclassical economists do not generally regard the provision of health or social services as public goods despite the importance of people's wellbeing to an effective economy. Rather, health and social service provision are seen as the personal responsibility of service users.

A third responsibility of government is to provide goods and services when the market has failed and it is established that government involvement would do no further harm to the capacity of the market to respond (Edwards, 2007). As governments are still experimenting with quasi-markets in human services in many countries, policy makers in the fields of health and welfare policy have a responsibility to monitor services for market failure and to step in where these occur.

NPM: Shifting Social Work to a Business Frame

There are many similarities between the NPM discourse and neoclassical economics. In particular, proponents of NPM incorporate neoclassical economic concepts regarding the valorization of the market and, related to this, a minimalist role for the state in the delivery of health and welfare services (Ellison, 2007). However, while the neoclassical economic discourse has influenced economic policy, NPM is focused primarily on how public services are organized and delivered, with implications for health and welfare services.

Based on the assumption that free markets increase service efficiency, quality and choice, the NPM discourse promotes an increased use of market mechanisms in the organization of health and welfare services. Clarke (2004, p. 36) describes the link between neoliberal economic theory and NPM: 'managerialism embodies this [neoliberal] decision-making calculus in its commitment to a rational, ruthless, business-like view of organizational and policy choices'. Proponents of NPM argue for a decreased role for governments in service delivery, seeing the role of government as one of 'steering not rowing' (Osborne and Gaebler, 1993). In the NPM discourse, governments outsource service delivery functions as far as possible to nongovernmental service agencies. These agencies compete for government and other forms of funding, such as philanthropic and fee-for-services, which leads to economic efficiency and services that are responsive to consumers' interests.

A second theme in the NPM discourse is flexibility at every level of service organization, from the way services are managed to how the workforce is organized. NPM views centralized bureaucracy as antithetical to locally responsive and accountable services, and so seeks to decentralize decision-making. The traditional divisions between management and service provision are challenged by the NPM discourse, as middle and front-line services are reconfigured as business units. Middle managers and front-line workers are expected to take responsibility for ensuring economic efficiencies and managing risk (Berg et al., 2008).

A related theme is the focus on the management of practice process and outputs. Consistent with the neoclassical economic view of individuals as essentially self-interested actors, proponents of NPM expect all actors in the practice process – policy makers, social workers and service users – to act from self-interest rather than in the interest of the general good. For this reason, proponents of NPM seek to depoliticize the policy and practice process by appealing to notions of evidence-based decision-making and management of practice outputs (Clarke, 2004). This gives rise to an 'audit' culture, in which a service's worth is measured by quantitative outputs, with those outputs defined by governments rather than by those involved in delivering or receiving services (Saario and Stepney, 2009, p. 41).

Implications for Social Work of Neoclassical Economics and NPM

Having considered the themes underpinning the dominant discourses of neoclassical economics and NPM, we turn now to their implications for social work practices. First, proponents of neoclassical economics argue for reduced government involvement in the provision of health and welfare services. Proponents of the neoclassical economic discourse argue against most forms of state welfare and social support to individuals on the grounds that it imposes a burden on the entire community to address the needs of relatively few (see Friedman and Friedman, 1980; Sandler, 2001). For the most part, the neoclassical economic discourse portrays people drawing on state benefits as unproductive citizens and a 'fiscal burden' on the state (Leonard, 1997, p. 114). In this discourse, the unproductive citizen has few, if any, rights to make a claim on the state or society for support. In many postindustrial countries, this discourse has been used to justify increasing constraints on welfare provision to disadvantaged individuals.

Similarly, advocates of neoclassical perspectives argue that the provision of social services by a third party is paternalistic and provides perverse incentives for individuals to remain dependent on social service providers

(Freidman, 1982, p. 34). One upshot is the view that individuals should be required, wherever possible, to pay part or all of the costs of the services they use. For more than two decades, this concept of user payment has been introduced into a growing range of social services (J. Healy, 1998). In its most extreme form, the concept of 'user pays' means that service users can be required to contribute to the costs of services they did not request and may even resist, such as prison services.

Nonetheless, most proponents of neoclassical economic discourses accept, perhaps begrudgingly, that government does have a role to protect vulnerable citizens and, in limited instances, to be a social service provider of last resort. These include circumstances where the market has failed to provide adequate services. Government involvement may also be justified where the individual whose welfare is at stake is not a 'responsible adult' (Friedman, 1982, p. 195). For example, Friedman (1982) accepts that the state has a responsibility towards children at risk of abuse or adults suffering serious psychiatric or intellectual ability that inhibits their capacity for freedom of choice. A further condition for government intervention in welfare provision is where large-scale coordinated action is required to address a problem. For example, government involvement may be required to introduce national policy initiatives such as 'welfare to work' programmes. Even in these circumstances, government intervention is only warranted when such intervention will not do further harm to the market and the individual's right to freedom of choice.

In contrast to neoclassical economics, the NPM discourse is focused on how public services should be organized and delivered, and this has impli-cations for social work practices that are, to a large extent, reliant on public sector funding. The influence of this discourse on health and welfare services is visible in an increased focus on the management of risk and the achievement of predefined quantitative outputs. The narrowing of our practice focus threatens to render invisible or invalid the relationship-based, holistic and values orientation that is the core of professional social work (see Bland et al., 2009). Moreover, the focus on auditing practice inevitably diverts attention and resources from direct service work with service users to a focus on paperwork through which performance is assessed and managed (Saario and Stepney, 2009, p. 51).

NPM is associated with the deprofessionalization of the workforce in some fields of health and welfare service delivery. Deprofessionalization of the social work workforce is evident in the declining preference for the employ-ment of professionally qualified social workers in fields of practice where such qualifications were previously considered preferable if not mandatory (Healy, 2009). The NPM discourse contributes to the deprofessionalization of the social work workforce as practitioners' roles are more narrowly defined and employers seek increased flexibility and competition among human service providers. In addition, proponents of NPM seek to challenge professional boundaries on the grounds that they serve to protect the self-interest of professionals while denying opportunities for competition, flexibility and cost-containment in the human services workforce. The NPM discourse has contributed to a questioning of professional qualifications in many traditional fields of social work practice, such as child protection, leading to concerns about service quality and workforce capacity (Healy, 2009, p. 403).

NPM is also associated with decreased participation of service providers and service users in the creation of policy or social service programmes. Both the NPM and neoclassical economic discourse see individuals – whether policy makers, service providers or service users – as self-interested actors. Accordingly, proponents of NPM are sceptical of participatory policy processes on the grounds that they 'not only failed to reflect the public good, but also seriously distorted public policy' by focusing disproportionately on special interests rather than the public good (Fawcett et al., 2010, p. 35). Furthermore, policy and practice development are seen as the responsibility of experts, whose role it is to apply principles of rationality and efficiency in the design of policy and programmes in health and welfare settings. The role of those directly engaged in service delivery, or in receipt of services, is limited because 'service delivery is seen as *output* of policy, rather than social policy in action' (Fawcett et al., 2010, p. 37). The lived experience of the service user and the practice wisdom of the practitioner are marginalized in the policy process.

Uses and Limits of Neoclassical Economic and NPM Discourses

Social work commentators rarely support neoclassical economic or NPM discourses. Most consider them to be inconsistent with core social work values, particularly social justice (see Leonard, 1997; Heffernan, 2006). Yet, as neoclassical economics increasingly dominates many areas of health and welfare provision, some argue that social workers must understand and learn to use its basic concepts (see Gibelman and Demone, 2002). Indeed, Stoesz (2000, p. 621) argues that our failure to understand the terms of this discourse 'only assures political irrelevance and programmatic decline'.

While it is difficult to think of any consistencies between the core concepts of neoclassical economics or NPM and social workers' purposes and values, we can identify some such consistencies in the *effects* of these discourses. Some studies have suggested that the NPM and neoclassical economic discourses have created unexpected spaces for service user or service provider empowerment. Notions of 'choice', so central to neoclassical theory, may create spaces for increased service user choice in some domains of service provision, such as the introduction of direct payments to people with disabilities to enable them to purchase their own care services. For many years, members of consumer rights groups in the disability services sector have agitated for increased consumer control over service provision to them. Ironically, the introduction of the neoclassical economic principles of free markets and individual choice into the public policy domain has helped to create an environment favourable to the introduction of direct payments to service users (Carmichael and Brown, 2002, p. 797). Studies on direct payment programmes have shown that increased consumer choice about service provision and control over payments lead to greater satisfaction than when these services are organized and paid for by others (Carmichael and Brown, 2002).

In the NPM discourse, opportunities for social worker empowerment may be associated with the decentralization of leadership and management within the reorganization of services. NPM reforms have required most social workers to develop managerial expertise such as that associated with managing budgets and ensuring financial and legal accountability of service provision. A comparative study of social workers in England and Sweden found that this local accountability increased the development and recognition of management skills among frontline social workers and, as such, was associated with increased employment opportunities and mobility. As Berg et al. (2008, p. 125) observe:

> This new situation, with its focus on management and leadership in the public sector under pressure from New Public Management reforms, has opened up job opportunities for women in social work where they are numerically dominant at lower and middle levels. It looks as if earlier ideas that recognize stability and the building of knowledge and experience within an organization are being replaced with an ideology constructed through a new managerial and leadership discourse where generalized management and leadership knowledge is negotiable, even marketable, in a flexible labour market.

Berg et al.'s research suggests that NPM may serve to destabilize aspects of the gender divide in social work in which male social workers are disproportionately represented in centralized service management roles, while female social workers are concentrated in less powerful and less well-remunerated service roles. The danger is that as direct service work becomes reconstituted as a managerial role, the nature of direct social work as involving values of social justice and an orientation towards change is also under threat (Healy, 2009).

Neoclassical economics and NPM discourses have also facilitated an increased role for the nongovernmental sector in the provision of services. From the perspective of these discourses, not-for-profit services are consistent with an appropriate division of labour, as governments lead and nongovernmental agencies deliver services (Osborne and Gaebler, 1993). Also, the nongovernmental sector is seen to provide better value for money than government services, partly because nongovernmental services often bring extra benefits that complement the formal services they provide (Harris et al., 2003). Economists refer to these extra 'unpaid for' benefits as 'externalities' (J. Healy, 1998, p. 34). For example, nongovernmental services are often able to draw on public goodwill in the form of donations of time and money. This increased reliance on nongovernmental, particularly not-for-profit agencies may also have benefits for service users, particularly where community-based services are in a position to provide more locally responsive services and where service users may feel more able to engage with services that are perceived to be outside the state.

A further effect is that neoclassical economics and NPM discourses challenge social workers to critically evaluate established practices and practice proposals. The principle of freedom of choice encourages us to critically examine paternalism in our practices. Consistent with this principle, we must constantly ask who has determined our involvement in service users' lives and we must also respect service users' rights to choose the focus and form of interventions, as far as possible within the dictates of our practice context. We are also challenged to recognize the economic implications of our practice proposals; this discipline is often missing as, for example, social workers are urged to 'develop provisions for meeting people's needs rather than rationing resources' (Dominelli, 1988, p. 161). Even with a dramatic increase in public funding for health and welfare services, a proposition that seems unlikely in the near future, service provider organizations will have to make decisions about resource allocation. The clear message of neoclassical economics and NPM is that there is no magic bullet and the decision to place resources of time, money and personnel to one end limits the *opportunities* to commit these resources to another end. Thus, in presenting our case for resource allocation to one set of ends, such as the establishment of a new youth accommodation programme, we must show not only why this is a useful end in itself, but also why this particular allocation is preferable to the competing possibilities for resource allocation.

Issues and Concerns of Neoclassical Economic and NPM Discourses

Social work and policy commentators have extensively critiqued the neoclassical economics and NPM discourses. The primary thrust of these concerns is that while the principles of these discourses may, or may not, work in traditional commercial contexts, they are entirely inappropriate for social service provision. Key concerns include, first, that these discourses undermine public support for the health and welfare services. Social services expenditure is represented as a drain on the economy, rather than as a public responsibility and investment in society (Leonard, 1997, p. 113). In this way, these discourses allow governments to distance themselves from their responsibilities for a more just society.

Critics also argue that service quality, specifically service comprehensiveness and accessibility, is compromised by increased competition in the social services sector. Competition provides incentives for service provider agencies to offer services at the lowest possible costs to the funding body. The incentive to cut corners in service delivery is exacerbated by the fact that service users have little 'buying power' and thus little say in negotiating service contracts. In the social services sector, there are few options for cutting service costs and all these measures compromise service quality. For instance, one way of cutting expenditure is by slicing labour costs. This can be achieved by replacing professional labour with volunteer and non-professional labour, with the consequence that service users have reduced access to professional services. Another way services maintain their competitive edge is by focusing on service users who are most amenable to fast and demonstrable outcomes (Gibelman and Demone, 2002). J. Healy (1998, p. 38) warns that 'selection inequities are already common in social services, but the profit motive offers yet another incentive for avoiding troublesome consumers'. Furthermore, evidence from the USA suggests that the growth of for-profit enterprises in the social services sector can contribute to the further erosion of service quality. Gibelman and Demone (2002, p. 392) point out that the primary goal of the for-profit agency, maximizing profit maximization to shareholders, is in conflict with quality service delivery.

The further concern is that increased competition, over time, can lead to reduced diversity of service provider agencies. In the short term, privatization leads to an increase in the range of service provider organizations as nongovernmental service providers replace state-run service departments. However, in the longer run, privatization in the social services sector can lead to the replacement of large state bureaucracies with large private monopolies (see Gibelman and Demone, 2002; Healy, 2002). This is because large social service organizations experience significant advantages in a competitive environment. Smaller organizations and, more specifically, consumer-run organizations are at a competitive disadvantage because they have much less capacity to dedicate resources to the competitive effort (Healy, 2002).

Finally, the concept of individual choice is not necessarily consistent with the value of self-determination. Within the terms of these discourses, the capacity to choose is constrained by one's capacity to pay. By returning all responsibility to the individual, these discourses obscure the systemic and structural influences on people's 'free choices' as well as the broader impediments to people living a life of their choosing.

Conclusion

In this chapter, we have considered the assumptions and implications of four discourses that have a dominant influence on many practice contexts. Often, these discourses coexist and may even compete in defining the role of social workers, and other professionals, as well as the needs and interests of service users. By understanding these discourses, we enhance our capacities to use them and, where necessary, challenge their influence on social work practices.

Summary Questions

1 What tensions exist between the social work value of promoting self-determination and the biomedical discourse?

2 What are the core assumptions of the discourse of legal positivism and to what extent can this discourse be used to promote social justice for service users?

3 What are the uses and limits of the neoclassical economics discourse for promoting the wellbeing of service users?

4 What opportunities and tensions might social workers experience in contexts where the new public management discourse is influential?

Recommended Reading

Biomedicine

- Dziegielewski, S. (2013) *The Changing Face of Health Care Social Work: Opportunities and Challenges for Professional Practice.* (New York: Springer).
  Comprehensive introduction to the changing context of healthcare social work. Discusses the challenges and possibilities for bringing social work perspectives, particularly the understanding of the person in their environment and social work values, to practice in settings where biomedical and economic rationalist perspectives prevail. Practical guide to practice excellence in healthcare.

- Rosenberg, L. and Rosenberg, D. (2012) *Human Genes and Genomes: Science, Health and Society.* (Amsterdam: Academic Press).
  Overview of the core concepts in genetic science and their relationship to a range of health and psychosocial issues. Includes a detailed introduction to the influence of genes on patterns of illness as well as on personal traits. Provides an important basis for the bioscience knowledge needed to practise in many health service contexts; also offers a useful grounding in genetics for social workers in a range of practice contexts.

Law

- Brayne, H. and Carr, H. (2010) *Law for Social Workers*, 11th edn. (Oxford: Oxford University Press).
  Handbook compiled by two lawyers. Contains detailed and accessible information about a range of social welfare laws in Britain and social workers' roles and responsibilities under the law. Emphasizes social workers' role in statutory law and also in advice and advocacy roles. Although written in a British context, is relevant to social workers in any context where legal systems impact on the social work role.

- Slater, L. and Finck, K. (2011) *Social Work Practice and the Law.* (New York: Springer).
  Collaboration between a social worker and a lawyer. Outlines the nature and constitutive power of the law. Well-written, practical guide to the myriad contexts in which the law shapes social work practices. Especially recommended for readers in North America.

Neoclassical Economics

- Edwards, L. (2007) *How to Argue with an Economist: Reopening Political Debate in Australia*, 2nd edn. (Cambridge: Cambridge University Press).
  Reader-friendly introduction to core concepts in neoclassical economics and the ideology of economic rationalism. Shows how to strategically use economic rational arguments and challenge aspects of neoclassical economics that limit our capacity to achieve humane and just outcomes for service users. Uses contemporary policy examples to illustrate the arguments.

- Friedman, M. and Friedman, R. (1980) *Free to Choose: A Personal Statement.* (Melbourne: Macmillan).
  Outlines the core concepts of and arguments for neoclassical economics.

New Public Management

- Kirkpatrick, I., Ackroyd, S. and Walker, R. (2005) *The New Managerialism and Public Service Professions.* (Basingstoke: Palgrave Macmillan).
  Comprehensive introduction to NPM ideas and how they have shaped services in several fields of health and welfare practice in the UK.

- Osborne, D. and Gaebler, T. (1993) *Reinventing Government: How the Entrepreneurial Spirit is Transforming the Public Sector.* (New York: Plume).
  Classic text on NPM, outlining the argument for smaller government and the introduction of free-market principles into the public sector.

Recommended Websites

- **http://web.ornl.gov/sci/techresources/Human_Genome/**
  US Department of Energy Human Genome Project provides an overview of the history and achievements of the human genome project. Includes extensive discussion of the biomedical implications of the human genome project, particularly for predictive testing and gene therapy.

- **http://cancer.gov**
  National Cancer Institute provides information on cancer types, genetic testing for predicting susceptibility to some forms of cancer, prevention and treatment of a wide range of cancers.

- **www.socialworkfuture.org**
  Social Work Action Network (SWAN), an international network based in the UK. The SWAN manifesto is based on a critique of NPM. SWAN seeks to bring together social workers, activists and service user communities in opposing managerialism and promoting new collective movements for an alternative, better world. Includes resources and networking opportunities for those seeking to join SWAN's action for change.

4

BEHAVIOURAL AND SOCIAL SCIENCE DISCOURSES
'Psy' and Sociological Ideas in Social Work

The formal professional base of social work relies on received ideas, especially from the behavioural and social sciences. Social work is an applied social science discipline (Rosenman et al., 1998, p. 215). Pearman and Stewart (1973, p. 12) describe behavioural and social sciences as the 'attempt to describe the characteristics and products of human behaviour as they occur within social configurations'. Notwithstanding the range of behavioural and social science ideas that influence the knowledge base of social workers, this chapter focuses on discourses within the disciplines of psychology and sociology because of the substantial body of evidence pointing to the central influence of these ideas on the formal base of social work practice.

The struggle between ideas from the disciplines of psychology and sociology has been at the forefront of tensions in the knowledge base of social work, with each discipline playing an influential role at different times in the profession's history, in various practice contexts and in different geographical contexts. Even today, in different contexts, psychological and sociological discourses are influential in shaping the professional knowledge base. This chapter provides you, the reader, with an understanding of the historical and contemporary influence of psychological and sociological discourses on the formal knowledge base of social work.

Figure 4.1 highlights the social science discourses we focus on in this chapter, positioned below, but interacting with, the dominant discourses discussed in Chapter 3. This represents the subordinate position of social science discourses in many practice contexts compared to the dominant discourses. While the professional base of social work is primarily constructed through these social science discourses, in practice, social workers also have to understand and actively engage with the dominant discourses that shape their practice. Sometimes, differences in the ways these discourses construct client needs and the social work role contribute to substantial conflict for workers. As we are shaped by, and negotiate, these conflicting perspectives, it is important that we are able to critically reflect on the social science discourses underpinning our professional base.

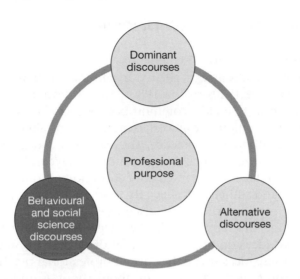

Figure 4.1 Discourses in interaction: behavioural and social science discourses

The social science disciplines of psychology and sociology are sites of enormous internal diversity. Through much of the profession's history, social workers have tended to draw on discourses within these disciplines that share a 'humanistic' orientation, that is, an orientation towards the realization of human potential, autonomy and self-determination (see Johnson, 1994, p. 6). This humanistic orientation has a complex relationship with Enlightenment ideas of individualism, rationality, objectivity and progress on which the dominant discourses depend. On the one hand, many social science disciplines were founded on the recognition of, and sought to value, the unique worth of the individual. On the other hand, these disciplines have also presented critiques of the contradictions of Enlightenment ideals and, in particular, the capacity of human service professions such as social work to realize these ideals, given the tense and often contradictory position we occupy between the state and service users (Garrett, 2009). Recently, 'psy' discourses that are less humanistic in orientation and more focused on the scientific understanding and management of human problems have also become influential.

In this chapter, we discuss the historical and contemporary influence of the psychological and sociological disciplines on the development of the formal knowledge base of social work. We turn first to the influence of psychological discourses.

Social Work and the 'Psy' Disciplines

Historically, the social work discipline has been closely aligned with the professions of psychology and psychiatry. In a formative phase of professional social work, from the 1920s to the 1950s, the profession drew heavily on psychodynamic ideas to build a common base of social work practice. Today in the popular imagination, social work continues to be aligned with psychological expertise, although in practice, the nature and degree of affiliation with the 'psy' knowledge varies by geographical context and fields of practice. While many of the taken-for-granted concepts underpinning direct practice, such as empathy and authenticity, have their origins in 'psy' discourses, social workers debate the relevance of these discourses in practice.

First, we define the term 'psy' knowledge and consider the historical influence of 'psy' ideas on the development of social work and the various ways in which these ideas shape the base of professional practice today. We then consider some of the key debates about the uses and limits of 'psy' ideas for direct social work practice.

A Historical Overview of 'Psy' in Social Work

The term 'psy' was coined by social scientists to refer to 'heterogeneous knowledges' developed from the psychological sciences, such as psychology, psychiatry and the behavioural sciences, which provide practical techniques for understanding, diagnosing and promoting change within the individual (see Rose, 1999, p. vii). According to social workers Parton and O'Byrne (2001, p. 38):

> The 'psy complex' refers to the network of ideas about the nature of human beings, their perfectibility, the reasons for their behaviour and the way they may be classified, selected and controlled. It aimed to manage and improve individuals by manipulation of their qualities and attributes and was dependent upon scientific knowledge and professional interventions and expertise. Human qualities were seen as measurable and calculable and thereby could be changed, improved and rehabilitated.

A core assumption of 'psy' disciplines is that many problems facing service users can be classified and treated at the level of individual psychological or even physiological processes. Undeniably, 'psy' ideas have had a profound influence on the development of the social work profession. Indeed, many of the concepts widely accepted by professional social workers can be traced to the influence of the 'psy' disciplines, especially psychoanalytic theory. Yet the social work profession has an ambivalent relationship to these disciplines and the use of 'psy' ideas varies historically and geographically.

Modern professional social work was founded in the religious charity movements of the late nineteenth century. However, the pioneers of professional education in the first decades of the twentieth century sought to distance the profession from its religious origins and to found a scientific base for social work practice. The first professional social work educators, notably Mary Richmond (1917), turned to the social sciences, particularly sociology and economics, rather than the 'psy' disciplines, as the core knowledge foundation for the profession (Shoemaker, 1998; Cree, 2010).

During the 1920s, the social work profession increasingly turned from socioeconomic theories towards psychological theories, especially psychodynamic perspectives, as its primary knowledge base for direct practice (Stein, 1958, p. 226; see also Hamilton, 1958, p. 13). In part, this was a response to disillusionment with the emerging sociological theories, specifically Mary Richmond's social diagnosis approach, which, although strong on analysis of service users' problems, appeared to offer little direction for social casework intervention (Hamilton, 1958, p. 24). Leading social work schools in the USA turned to the 'psy' disciplines, especially the work of Freud, to develop intervention approaches for social casework (Hamilton, 1958). This direction was to have considerable influence on the emerging social work profession.

From the 1920s to the 1950s, psychodynamic theory became a dominant and unifying framework in social casework (see Hamilton, 1958, p. 18). In the USA, psychiatric specialities were established in a number of schools of social work, drawing primarily on Freudian psychodynamic theories (see Woods and Hollis, 1990, p. 13; Borden, 2000). In 1946, the Tavistock Clinic was established in London and its training programmes in psychodynamic therapy with children and families influenced the scope and focus of professional social work. The Tavistock Clinic drew on ideas from a second generation of psychoanalytic theorists, particularly Donald Winnicott and John Bowlby, whose work focused on child development and maternal attachment. This work provided an intellectual base for social workers to extend their practice domain into psychotherapeutic work with children and families (Rose, 1999, p. 173).

The increasing influence of 'psy' discourses on social work, especially in the postwar period, can also be attributed to the diversification of the 'psy' sciences themselves. Psychiatrists treating soldiers suffering post-traumatic stress disorder began to question the psychoanalytic assumptions about the enduring effects of early personality development and came to support a more dynamic and malleable view of psychological processes (Rose, 1999, p. 21). This changing conception of human personality led psychiatrists to diversify their practice approaches from long-term psychodynamic practice to experiments with brief intervention models. The crisis intervention approach, developed by American psychiatrists Caplan and Lindemann, was one of the new models to emerge out of this period of experimentation and drew on the view that crises provided opportunities for human growth (Kanel, 2003, pp. 14–15). Crisis intervention was introduced to social work in the 1960s and maintains currency today as a contemporary model of practice (see Chapter 7).

The changing view of human psychology also led to an increased emphasis on personal growth and preventive intervention. In the postwar period, according to Rose (1999, p. 21):

> Madness was now thought of in terms of social hygiene. Mental health could be maintained by proper adjustment of the conditions of life and work; poor mental hygiene and stress could promote neurosis in large numbers of people.

In some practice contexts, social workers' interventions were directed away from a primary focus on the treatment of chronic conditions towards the prevention of mental health problems and the promotion of personal growth. In the USA, this appears to have opened up a niche market for social workers in personal development for, as Woods and Hollis (1990, pp. 4–5) note: 'Probably more than ever, caseworkers concern themselves with the development of conditions and capacities for health rather than only the ameliorization of pathology.' By contrast, in countries such as Australia, New Zealand and the UK, where opportunities for private psychotherapeutic practice are severely constrained by the lack of third-party funding arrangements for social workers, personal growth therapy has remained a marginal area of professional practice.

The Retreat from Psychodynamic Theory

During the 1950s, many social workers began to question the profession's embrace of psychodynamic theories. Social workers shared many of the concerns raised by psychiatry and psychology about the lack of a scientific base and evidence of the effectiveness of psychodynamic therapies. This concern intensified over the next two decades, as various experiments on long-term psychodynamic casework failed to demonstrate any greater effectiveness than short-term, problem-focused interventions (Reid and Shyne, 1969; see also Rose, 1999, p. 237).

But social workers' concerns about 'psy' ideas went beyond a concern with effectiveness to a growing discomfort about the limited capacities of these discourses to acknowledge the social dimensions of service users' concerns. From the late 1950s, social workers, particularly from within the re-emerging systemic and radical traditions, expressed a growing interest in putting the 'social' back into social work theory (Stein, 1958, p. 227). During the 1960s, the profession threatened to split between those who aligned to 'psy' perspectives and those aligned to the social science disciplines and the new social movements of the period. During the 1960s, numerous practice approaches were developed to reintegrate 'psy' and social perspectives towards a common base for social work practice. Among the most celebrated and enduring of these is the 'psychosocial' approach to casework developed, initially, by Florence Hollis, an American casework theorist (Woods and Hollis, 1990, p. 14). According to Woods and Hollis (1990, p. 16), psychosocial casework is 'a blend of concepts derived from psychiatry, psychology, and the social sciences, with a substantial body of empirical knowledge derived from within casework itself'. Psychosocial approaches remain popular in social casework today because of their emphasis on understanding and responding to the person in their social environment.

Since the 1960s, social workers' critique of the 'psy' foundations of social work has grown substantially, although an alignment between 'psy' discourses and our profession remains strong. Critical social workers have canvassed their concerns about the failure of 'psy'-based approaches to adequately acknowledge, let alone address, the structural challenges facing service users (see Leonard, 1966; Lees, 1972, Ch. 1). In response to these criticisms, during the 1980s and 90s, many critical social work theorists sought to integrate radical and social action perspectives with the psychosocial model of casework practice. Jan Fook's (1993) model of radical casework, anti-oppressive casework approaches, and various feminist developments of casework practice are illustrations of this movement (Bricker-Jenkins et al., 1991). These initiatives have enabled social workers to integrate the analysis of structural and cultural injustices into social casework, which remains a key method of social work practice (see Maidment and Egan, 2004).

'Psy' Ideas Today

Today, 'psy' disciplines continue to form a substantial part of the professional base of social work, especially with respect to skills for direct practice with individuals. Nicolson et al. (2006, p. 9) assert that psychological knowledge is relevant to 'every interpersonal encounter in the practice of social work'. The 'psy' discourse has been especially influential in informing social work in relation to human development, human adaption to change, interpersonal relationships, psychological trauma, mental health, the assessment and amelioration of risk, and, more recently in relation to debates about the contribution of neuroscience to understanding issues such as harm, addiction treatment and individual resilience. Many social work education programmes require students to complete core units in psychology, and many schools of social work, particularly in the USA, Canada and New Zealand, incorporate training in the psychiatric classifications of the Diagnostic and Statistical Manual of Mental Disorders (DSM).

Psychodynamic ideas in social work continue to endure as one set of a suite of 'psy' ideas used in medium- and long-term psychotherapeutic work (see Borden, 2000; Nicolson et al., 2006). However, social workers' involvement in psychotherapeutic work of this nature varies substantially by geographical context. For example, in many states of the USA, licensed social workers are eligible for third-party reimbursement, which has given rise to significant opportunities for social workers to provide psychotherapeutic services in private practice contexts (Woods and Hollis, 1990, p. 5; see also Gibelman, 1995, Ch. 8). In other countries, such as the UK, where social workers are primarily employed in government authorities or nongovernmental community services where psychotherapy is not a core social work task, psychodynamic ideas are less central to the professional knowledge base. In Australia, the relatively recent emergence of government reimbursement for accredited mental health social workers in private practice has contributed to an increasing number of social workers involved in psychotherapeutic work.

Yet, even in contexts where social workers are not involved in psychotherapeutic work, psychodynamic ideas have an implicit, although often unrecognized influence on the formal base of social work. Indeed, some psychodynamic concepts have become mainstream ideas in social work and an implicit part of the knowledge base of the profession. One illustration of this is the importance most social workers place on the relationship between worker and service user as a vehicle of change *in itself*. This reflects the psychodynamic discourse emphasis on the importance of 'empathic attunement', self-understanding, strengthening coping capacities, and worker/service user 'fit' (Borden, 2000, p. 368; see also Woods and Hollis, 1990, p. 25). As we shall see in Part 3, the importance of a helping relationship characterized by empathy, authenticity and mutuality is widely accepted as central to effective practice across the majority of contemporary models of practice, from problem-solving to anti-oppressive approaches (see also Hamilton, 1951, p. 52; Woods and Hollis, 1990, p. 26; Maidment and Egan, 2004).

'Self-knowledge' on the part of the worker is another psychodynamic concept that is widely endorsed within the formal base of social work. The psychodynamic model introduced the notion to social work that 'self-awareness' is an essential component of effective practice (see Hamilton, 1958, p. 34). For example, Hamilton (1951, p. 40), a leading thinker in psychodynamic social work, insisted that:

> the worker must first be able to understand himself [sic] and his [sic] own emotional drives and impulses before he [sic] can truly accept the 'bad' feelings, aggression, or even love and gratitude in others.

Today, the notion of self-awareness is no longer solely aligned to therapeutic modalities, and has instead become part of a range of practice approaches. Indeed, the anti-oppressive model, which eschews many 'psy' concepts, maintains that workers must understand how their own biography, in this case their membership of various social groupings, affects their capacity to develop an effective working relationship with service users (see Chapter 9). The emphasis on self-knowledge has also come to the fore in the models of reflective practice that have recently risen to prominence (see Napier and Fook, 2000; White et al., 2006). These approaches emphasize the importance of reflection on personal biography and personal responses to the service user and their situation as an integral part of knowledge use in practice.

'Psy' Discourses and the Scientific Management of Human Problems

Apart from the enduring, and sometimes unrecognized, influence of the psychotherapeutic discourse in social work, in recent decades, other 'psy' discourses have gained ascendancy in many health and welfare services and in some parts of the social work profession. These increasingly influential 'psy' discourses, which include cognitive behavioural therapy and neuroscience, are associated with a 'scientific' approach to the understanding and management of human problems.

Cognitive behavioural therapy (CBT) has become a dominant treatment approach in some fields of health and welfare, particularly those that involve the management of emotional and behavioural problems. Proponents of CBT assert that this approach is consistent with a scientific, evidence-based approach to practice and distant from the more 'emotional', value-laden approaches to practice that have often characterized social work interventions (see Sheldon, 2000). On the other hand, critics argue that the narrow focus of CBT interventions neglects the structural factors contributing to phenomena such as offending behaviour and the importance of cultural sensitivities in developing appropriate responses (see Gorman, 2001). Indeed, in their critique of CBT approaches to probation work, Smith and Vanstone (2002, p. 819) argue that: 'A standardized, routine one-track approach based on an ideology rooted in the pathologizing of people who offend is likely to sustain structures inimical to social justice.'

Over the past two decades, neuroscience has also emerged as an important field in relation to the scientific management of human problems in many fields of health and welfare. Neuroscience refers to the 'study of the brain and nervous system' (The Royal Society, 2011, p. 1). The burgeoning field of social neuroscience, which examines 'the relations between biological and social processes', is of particular relevance and controversy for social workers (see Matto and Strolin-Golzman, 2010, p. 147). The concept of 'neuroplasticity', the notion that the brain changes physically in response to social conditions, is central in the neuroscience discourse. Research on neuroplasticity has generated a great deal of interest in diverse fields, including mental health, child protection, youth justice and addictions (see Matto and Strolin-Golzman, 2010; Royal Society, 2011; Wastell and White, 2012). For example, child protection advocates argue that evidence regarding the adaptability of the brain demonstrates the need for early and, if necessary, highly intrusive measures to prevent the lasting structural brain damage assumed to be corre-lated with early exposure to adverse life events (see Perry, 2002, 2009). The notion that the infant brain is both adaptable and vulnerable has informed policy initiatives, such as early intervention programmes for vulnerable chil-dren, including the Brighter Futures programme in New South Wales, Australia and the Sure Start programme in the UK.

Heated debate abounds about the potential contribution of the neuro-science discourse to social work and social policy fields. Some proponents argue that social workers have 'a unique obligation to participate in and contribute to neuroscientific research' (Matto and Strolin-Goltzman, 2010, p. 150; see also Perry, 2009; Matto et al., 2014). They contend that neurosci-ence allows for more objective and insightful measures about the nature of harm and risk and also for the evaluation of service outcomes. Matto and Strolin-Goltzman (2010) suggest that brain imaging technology can be used to evaluate changes to the brain arising from effective biopsychosocial interventions. Others criticize what they see as an overly enthusiastic embrace of a scientific field still in its infancy and far from 'policy ready' (Wastell and White, 2012, p. 411). Critics points to the contradictory and exaggerated claims about the potential for neuroscience research to gain insight into matters such as child protection risk and the timing of inter-vention measures. For example, Bruer (1999) argues that the concept of neuroplasticity illuminates the capacity of the brain to adapt and recover throughout life, and, as such, does not justify the primary focus on early childhood intervention proposed by some child welfare advocates. Among their many concerns, Wastell and White (2012, p. 399) argue that the uncritical embrace of the neuroscience discourse in child welfare suppresses 'vital *moral* debates regarding the shape of the state intervention in the lives of children and families'.

Review Question

What psychological ideas are prevalent in your current or intended area of practice? How do these concepts extend, or limit, our capacity as social workers to achieve social justice in practice?

Strengths and Limits of the 'Psy' Discourse

Most social workers use 'psy' ideas in social casework practice with service users. These ideas are not the preserve of the 'psy' professions, as they also circulate within the dominant cultures of postindustrial societies (Rose, 1999). Thus, 'psy' terminology, such as 'self-awareness', the 'unconscious' and 'self-control', is likely to be used in a range of organizational contexts and among professional and service user groups. Even so, commentators remain divided over the relevance of 'psy' ideas to social work practice.

Proponents of 'psy' ideas argue that these concepts provide us with a language and practical strategies for realizing the humanistic values and goals that underpin modern social work (see Borden, 2000). Certainly, 'psy' ideas can reinforce social workers' focus on valuing individual needs and aspirations as the basic guide to intervention. The enduring influence of many 'psy'-based concepts, such as the centrality of the helping relationship, attests to their relevance to the humanistic ethos of contemporary social work.

Some social workers also advocate the use of 'psy'-based risk assessment tools in areas of high-risk social work practice (see Summers, 2003). These risk assessment tools can provide social workers with an overview of the psychological factors associated with elevated risk, many of which may not be immediately apparent in our interactions with service users. While many academic commentators are critical of the increased emphasis on risk management in welfare practice, it is also the case that a comprehensive understanding of risk factors is a professional and legal obligation of social workers in some practice contexts. 'Psy'-based risk assessment tools can make important contributions to the assessment of risk, especially for novice social workers. Contexts in which 'psy'-based risk assessment tools are likely to be helpful include those where there is:

- A significant risk of harm or death for service users, such as child protection and mental health, or to others, as may be the case in work with offenders.

- Significant turnover of frontline staff, as is the case in some statutory authorities. In these situations, it is likely that many direct service providers have little direct practice wisdom to draw on that is relevant to assessment, especially in high-risk situations.

- An expectation by employer agencies or client groups that social workers will be primarily responsible for assessing the risk of harm and that, in some circumstances, they may be required to do so 'on the spot', with little assistance from other professionals. For example, a social worker in a statutory health authority is required by law to assess their clients' risk of harm to themselves or others and, in some circumstances, where the client poses a high risk of this nature, the social worker may have to make an immediate decision to schedule the patient for involuntary inpatient mental health care.

- An expectation that social workers' assessments will contribute to formal decision-making, where the implications of decisions may have profound and enduring consequences for service users. For example, some social workers are required by the courts to make decisions about the removal of children from their families and the institutionalization of people suffering severe mental illnesses. It is our ethical responsibility to ensure that these decisions are made from a comprehensive and rigorous knowledge base and 'psy'-based risk assessment tools can form an important part of this base.

In these situations, it may be unreasonable to expect practitioners to rely on the notions of reflective knowledge building and practice wisdom that have become increasingly popular within the discipline of social work. For example, in practice contexts where there is a high turnover of frontline staff, practitioners do not necessarily have sufficient experience to draw on practice wisdom. Indeed, intuitive knowledge built on life experience, as opposed to direct practice experience in a specific context, may be especially unreliable in dealing with highly emotive and unusual situations involving high risks to service users (Killen, 1996; Shlonsky and Wagner, 2005).

In addition, in high-risk environments, the costs of getting decisions wrong are unacceptably high for clients, so it social workers' duty to draw on a broad range of evidence with the lowest risk margins possible (Shlonsky and Wagner, 2005). Many of the formal 'psy'-based risk assessment tools have been developed by statistical analysis of risk factors in large numbers of child protection cases or through expert review of risk factors, and so provide the worker with an understanding of risk factors that may not be apparent in their immediate interactions with service users. For example, we may have worked with a parent who managed heavy drug dependency while meeting their responsibility to keep their child safe and well; but this should not blind us to the general association between heavy parental drug use and an elevated risk of child abuse and neglect (Semidei et al., 2001). Finally, in formal decision-making contexts, such as courts and biomedical contexts, social workers are often required to demonstrate the principles on which their assessments are made. 'Psy'-based risk assessment tools provide an evidence foundation for decision-making that can be used in collaboration with other knowledge sources, such as our relationship with the service user, to develop comprehensive and defensible assessments in these contexts.

Despite the extensive role of the 'psy' discourse in the formal base of social work, 'psy' discourses are also the subject of extensive critique within the profession. Social workers often work with highly marginalized people, and the adequacy of 'psy' ideas for understanding and responding to clients in their social, political and cultural contexts of oppression is widely questioned. For example, social workers have criticized the rise of CBT as the dominant treatment model, on the grounds of its failure to acknowledge the broader structural and cultural contexts of service users' needs (Smith and Vanstone, 2002).

Critical sociologists, especially Rose (1999) and Donzelot (1997), have highlighted the role of 'psy' discourses in enabling government to judge and regulate the behaviour of individuals, children and families (see also Wastell and White, 2012). The 'psy' disciplines have established categories for diagnosing and categorizing 'normal' and 'abnormal' child development and family functioning. They have been used to 'treat' and improve individual and family functioning, but, at the same time, have allowed governments and human service experts to wield power at the most intimate levels of service users' lives (Rose, 1999, pp. 133–4).

There is concern about the potential for 'psy' ideas to do harm to service users when applied to practice contexts divergent from the psychotherapeutic contexts for which they were originally intended (see Healy, 1998; see also Smith, 2001). The emphasis on concepts such as 'empathy' and 'mutuality' can be misleading and confusing for service users in contexts where social workers have statutory responsibilities, such as child protection, criminal justice and some mental health roles (Trotter, 2004, 2006). Referring to child and family welfare practice, Smith (2001, p. 289), a British social work commentator, reminds us that:

> In their daily work with children and families social workers are constrained by a panoply of regulation, guidance and procedure ... Their interactions with children, parents and foster carers are governed not by trust, but by formal and often written agreements.

In short, the concept of the 'helping relationship' as the vehicle for change is problematic in contexts where the social work role is not only about helping, as in statutory social work.

A further problem is the potential for the concepts of 'empathy' and 'mutuality', originally drawn from the 'psy' discourse, to limit workers' capacity to undertake responsibilities associated with decision-making in high-risk situations. An empathic approach demands that we put ourselves in the shoes of the other, but in contexts such as child protection practice, it is critical that workers are also able to maintain sufficient emotional distance to enact their protective role (see Killen, 1996). Furthermore, Trotter's (2004, 2006) research in the fields of child protection, juvenile justice and adult probation services has established that the worker's demonstration of empathy without equal emphasis on challenging antisocial attitudes and behaviours is associated with poor outcomes for clients. In other words, unless the worker moderates the demonstration of empathy with a prosocial attitude, the service user may inadvertently interpret that the worker endorses the continuation of harmful situations and behaviours. Even in non-statutory contexts, the ideals of empathy and mutuality have the potential to do harm by misleading service users about the nature of the social work role. Research with young parents found that the most marginalized service users were confused and often disappointed by what they understood to be offers of unconditional support and friendship, which appeared to be implicit in service providers' emphasis on mutuality (see Healy and Young Mothers for Young Women, 1996). These service users stated that it was important to them for social workers to be explicit about the professional boundaries to their relationship.

Finally, attention must be paid to the importance of critical engagement with 'psy' discourses particularly in relation to those where knowledge development is embryonic and contested. This is especially so in relation to the neuroscience discourse, where many of its core knowledge claims are 'far from settled' (White and Wastell, 2013, p. 1). The influence of 'psy' discourses in many institutional contexts of practice can create tensions between our obligations to engage with emerging knowledge and maintain our values, particularly our professional integrity. As neuroscience becomes increasingly influential, social workers will need to continue to critically evaluate the uses and limits of this discourse for our practice.

Sociological Discourses

The influence of sociology on professional social work has been no less profound than that of the 'psy' disciplines. In a variety of ways, sociological discourses seek to explain the *social* origins and consequences of human behaviour. They provide 'a range of perspectives, commentaries and interpretations of social life and experience' (Cree, 2010, p. 201). In turn, social workers often use these ideas to explain the phenomena they encounter in practice and guide their responses to them.

As discussed earlier, the first social work education programmes drew mainly on ideas from the social rather than the psychological sciences. In the late nineteenth century, according to Cree (2010, p. 3; see also Bloom, 2000), the projects of sociology and social work were linked to the

> promise of the "modern age": that through scientific discovery and rational investigation, the "truth" might be uncovered, which would lead to an improvement in the workings of society and in the lives of individuals.

The shared knowledge base of social work and sociology is evident in the work of Jane Addams (1860–1935), who held leadership positions in professional associations in the burgeoning fields of social work and sociology in the early part of the twentieth century. Moreover, in her work on 20 years in the Hull House movement, first published in 1910, Addams described her approach as a form of social experimentation, in which knowledge about social change was built through engagement with such change activities (see Addams, 1938).

However, following the First World War, social workers retreated significantly from sociological perspectives, and the 'psy' disciplines were the primary source of received ideas for social work. By the late 1950s, the pendulum had swung back towards the social sciences, especially sociology, with a series of ground-breaking publications on this topic, such as Peter Leonard's (1966) widely cited *Sociology in Social Work*. The changing political context of this period led to the emergence of a suite of new social and social service programmes, including community development, poverty alleviation initiatives, and community health services. To be credible and effective in these new settings, social workers had to reorient their knowledge base from an individualistic psychoanalytic frame to perspectives that recognized the social contexts of service users' lives. The following decades saw continued debate within social work about the application of sociological ideas to the analysis of the problems facing service users, the social work profession and the organization of social services (see Pearman, 1973; Brewster and Whiteford, 1976; Day, 1987; Sullivan, 1987). Nonetheless, today, sociological discourses continue to inform social work theory building, particularly in relation to modern critical and postmodern practice approaches (see Gray and Webb, 2009). Social workers' engagement with social science theory is not limited to sociological discourses; however, their influence remains more significant and far-reaching than any other discipline other than the 'psy' disciplines.

Today, the place of sociological discourses in social work is not without contest. Indeed, as neoclassical economics ideas and 'psy' discourses have (re) gained prominence, social workers are likely to face increasing pressure to return to a focus on individual responsibility and individual change (Cree, 2010, p. 95). Even so, social science perspectives, particularly sociology, continue to feature in social work educational programmes throughout the postindustrial world (Hutchinson et al., 2001). Furthermore, growing public expectations of quality in service delivery and demands from consumer organizations for more holistic, preventive and democratic approaches to practice make social science perspectives as important as ever for social workers. We turn now to the key ways in which sociological discourses inform the contemporary professional base of social work practice.

The sociological discourse asserts that humans are profoundly social beings, and challenges individualistic explanations of social and personal problems by drawing attention to the social practices and social structures that sustain these problems (Stein, 2003; Cree, 2010). For example, sociologists Davis and George (1993, p. 22) criticize the biomedical discourse's failure to recognize 'the ways in which disease and health are intimately linked to the social organization of the population in which they occur'. In other words, a sociological discourse suggests that many things we experience as individuals, such as illness, are also socially organized and produced.

The sociological discourse also highlights the way in which socioeconomic status shapes one's life experiences and life chances. Social science research has repeatedly demonstrated the impact of socioeconomic disadvantage on a range of health and wellbeing indicators. This research has established that the most disadvantaged citizens experience significantly higher rates of chronic physical and mental health problems and premature death than more advantaged citizens (McLeod and Bywaters, 2000). By exposing the impact of socioeconomic status on our life opportunities, sociological discourses challenge the concepts of individual choice and individual responsibility that are central to the neoclassical economics discourse (see Chapter 3).

In addition, a sociological discourse draws attention to the social construction of social 'reality' and, in so doing, calls into the question the idea of 'objective reality', on which the dominant discourses depend. It also encourages us to question the individualistic orientation of the 'psy' perspectives outlined earlier. Critical social science investigations have exposed the historical and cultural variations in common understandings of entities such as health, illness, normality, madness and crime. Moreover, the sociological discourse also raises questions about how social reality is determined and whose constructions prevail over others. Cree (2010, p. 199) urges us to examine the 'vested interests that seek to forefront specific kinds of meanings, definitions and evidence'.

Finally, the sociological sciences focus on professions, like medicine and social work, as well as health and welfare institutions as objects of inquiry. In various ways, these research projects have destabilized the commonsense view of professional expertise and health and welfare institutions as caring and benign, showing them to be vehicles for the exercise of oppressive forms of power. In the realm of social work, sociological insight has challenged the occupational self-image of social work as a caring profession by exposing 'the primacy of its control functions over its caring functions' (Dominelli, 1997, p. 20). These critical investigations can enable social workers to adopt a more self-reflective and critical stance about the purposes and effects of their practice.

Case Study **Comparing 'psy' and sociological discourses**

Imagine you are a social worker in a nongovernmental community support organization. A worker from an employment agency referred Michael, a 45-year-old Chinese man, to you for counselling. The worker says Michael is very depressed due to his family situation, and that this depression is impacting on Michael's ability to find work.

When you meet Michael, he is neatly dressed and carrying a briefcase as if he is going to work. He speaks quietly and often bows to you. Michael tells you he has been married for 20 years and has a 15-year-old son and a 12-year-old daughter. It was an arranged marriage and they migrated to Australia shortly afterwards. Their family are all overseas. He is an accountant and used to have his own successful business.

Michael says that about 10 years ago his wife began acting aggressively towards him, physically and emotionally abusing him. She harassed and abused his clients, making it difficult for his business to continue. Michael says her aggression has been a lot worse over the past few months. He describes her following him in the street and abusing him, physically attacking him when he is asleep and threatening him with knives. His son is also starting to verbally abuse and threaten him at home. Michael's business has failed and he is now reliant on welfare payments as his primary income.

Michael wonders if his wife has a mental illness but she refuses to see her doctor. Michael's mother-in-law has hinted at mental health problems when his wife was a teenager. He contacted the mental health crisis team once after she had been very violent but they stated they could do nothing unless his wife was willing to see them.

Michael believes he must have done something wrong to cause his wife to be upset but is unable to work out what this is. He wonders if he is being punished for something he did in a previous life. Michael says it is his duty to stay with his wife and children, but feels ashamed that they are so unhappy and says he in not worthy to be called a man.

Michael is unwilling to talk to their family doctor, as it will expose the family's shame, but he is unable to sleep, is tense, anxious and depressed. Michael feels helpless and is fearful for himself and his family and sees no positive solutions, but wants to work so he can pay the mortgage and support his family. He would like help to regain some self-confidence and to develop strategies to help him cope with his family situation.

In guiding your considerations, it may be useful to consider:

● What information and issues would the 'psy' discourses highlight?

● What information and issues would the sociological discourses highlight?

● What ideas from both discourses would influence how you would intervene with Michael?

Responding to the Case Study

The 'psy' and sociological discourses incorporate humanistic orientations, which encourage us, as social workers, to seek to understand Michael's view of his situation and promote his self-determination. The case study also raises issues about Michael's safety and that of his wife, given her use of knives to threaten Michael. Our legal obligations around mental health and criminal code legislation to report matters of this nature to the relevant authorities may cut across our use of the 'psy' and sociological discourses to analyse and respond to this case study. Nonetheless, these discourses would lead us to approach the case study in quite different ways.

Looking through a 'psy' lens, we would be likely to focus on:

● *An investigation of Michael and his wife's psychological conditions with a view to diagnosis:* The information we have is suggestive of possible psychological disorders. Michael is showing some symptoms of depression and possibly other psychological disorders such as anxiety. His description of his wife also suggests that she may be suffering a severe psychiatric disorder.

● *An assessment of psychological risk factors:* The information suggests that Michael may face serious risk either to himself, as a person possibly suffering from a depressive illness, and also from his wife, especially in relation to his assertion she has threatened him with knives.

● *Sources of resilience:* Michael has faced considerable challenges in his life – migration and adaptation to a foreign culture and, more recently, the loss of status associated with his failed business. From a 'psy' perspective, we would explore sources of resilience that Michael has used in facing these challenges.

From this analysis, one likely course of action is the referral of Michael and his wife to mental health specialists for psychiatric assessment and possible psychiatric intervention, such as pharmacological interventions. 'Psy' professionals may also offer treatments such as CBT, which have been found useful for alleviating depression. Using insights from 'psy' discourses, the social worker could also continue to offer supportive casework intervention, to help him with his feelings of helplessness and isolation, while Michael undergoes psychiatric assessment.

By contrast, using a sociological approach, we would highlight:

- *The social organization of family life and gender roles:* For example, we might examine the cultural expectation that, as a husband and father, Michael should be the breadwinner and consider, with him, how this contributes to his depression.

- *Cultural constructions of mental health and illness:* We may question the referring worker's construction of Michael's problem as one of 'depression' as a way of categorizing his concerns. We might seek to understand Michael's response as less one of individual psychopathology, as the label 'depression' implies, and instead view it as a response to conditions of structural injustice. We would also explore Michael's view of his experiences with his wife to explore a range of explanations, not only the one of mental illness hinted at in the case study. We could also explore whether Michael is a victim of domestic violence and, if so, how we can provide the appropriate supports and options for him to escape the situation.

- *A focus on structural and social injustices:* A sociological lens would encourage us to see Michael's problem in structural and social contexts. In many postindustrial societies, there is a growing body of middle-aged men in white-collar occupations facing unemployment, partly as a result of globalization and partly changing technologies in the workplace. Michael's situation is not simply one of his 'depression' impacting on his ability to find work, but also one where as a middle-aged, white-collar worker he is structurally disadvantaged in the marketplace. It is also possible that, as a member of a cultural minority, Michael faces racial and cultural discrimination in his attempts to find employment. From a sociological perspective, we would explore these concerns with him.

From this analysis, our likely course of action would be, first, to reduce Michael's sense of 'helplessness' by identifying the broader conditions that contribute to his situation and assisting him to focus on these rather than the personal explanation of his situation. We would encourage him to critically reflect on the social expectations he carries about being in paid work in order to be a 'man'. We would aim to build social support that may enable him to achieve socially and culturally meaningful roles. For example, we may focus on how he can use his accounting and business knowledge within his own community to support Chinese agencies or help young people develop skills in this field.

Review Question
_____

Now that we've considered the key themes of social science discourses and their application to a case study, discuss what you see as the key strengths and limitations of
sociological discourse in an area of social work practice that interests you.

The Uses and Limits of Sociological Discourses for Social Work

Sociological discourses have much to offer social work practitioners. They enable us to understand and articulate service users' problems within their social contexts (Stein, 2003, p. 105). Many social work texts explicitly draw on sociological concepts, such as socioeconomic disadvantage, status and stigma, in analysing service users' problems and developing social work and social policy responses (see Dominelli, 1997; McLeod and Bywaters, 2000; Cree, 2010). Cree (2010, p. 6) asserts that without this critical understanding of social context, social workers are likely to pathologize and blame individuals and families for the problems they face and, in so doing, 'perpetuate the oppression and discrimination that characterize the lives of users of social work services'.

Sociological analysis can also help us to think critically about our own practices and the health and welfare institutions in which we work. For instance, a sociological approach can enable us to critically examine how health and welfare institutions and professional practices contradict our values, such as respect and self-determination, and our practice goals, such as empowerment (McLeod and Bywaters, 2000, p. 12). Critical analysis can lead to the development of new kinds of responses to consumer needs, such as citizen-led institutions (McLeod and Bywaters, 2000, p. 12; see also Crossley and Crossley, 2001). For example, in the case of Michael, a sociological approach would lead us to question 'psy' labels, such as depression, and focus instead on assisting Michael to achieve socially and culturally meaningful roles in his cultural community.

Despite the uses of sociological discourse for contemporary social work practice, there are also many issues and limitations of this discourse. First, significant tensions exist between the core purpose and focus of sociology (and the social sciences more generally), that is, to systemically build knowledge about society, and the primary action orientation of social work (Bloom, 2000). Davies (cited in Cree, 2010, p. 6) asserts that 'sociologists ask questions; social workers must act as though they have answers'. The different scale of the problems typically dealt with by social workers and sociologists further exacerbates these tensions. In particular, when approaching welfare concerns, many sociological analyses seek to systematically analyse whole social systems, such as the organization of prisons, child welfare systems or even whole societies, such as postindustrial societies. By contrast, social work intervention is typically on a smaller scale, focusing on individuals, families, groups or communities. The vastly different foci of social science investigations, particularly sociological studies, and social work interventions demand caution in the transfer of ideas from one field to the other, lest the complexities inherent in each are overlooked (Leonard, 1966, p. 97). For example, it is one thing for a sociologist to analyse the social origins of delinquency, it is quite another for a social worker to work with a young person in trouble with the law and face, with them, the consequences of their actions for their family, peers and, in some instances, the victims of their actions.

Also, social workers and sociologists often adopt different processes of knowledge development and application. The action orientation of social work leads social workers to focus on sociological knowledge that is directly useful for practice, such as 'facts' and theories concerning the particular phenomena – mental illness, child abuse and so on – with which they work. This material is often disconnected from the wider gestalt of social science research from which it was originally produced. Thus, according to Leonard (1966, p. 97), the action orientation of the social worker may lead them to 'endow [sociological] knowledge with greater certainty and with greater simplicity, than would the sociologist'.

Furthermore, despite a long history of association between social work and sociology, the relationship between these disciplines is often characterized by a lack of mutual respect and exchange. For example, some social workers criticize sociologists and other social scientists for their lack of practical nous, while some social scientists stand in judgement on social workers for a perceived lack of theoretical sophistication in their articulation of their practices. The mutual hostility generated by caricaturing each 'side' of the social worker/social scientist divide has been most unhelpful for a thorough exploration of the uses and limits of sociological discourses in social work.

Finally, the truths of sociological discourses, like all discourses, can be used to devalue other perspectives. In some sociological analyses, the truths of other discourses, such as biomedicine, are critiqued as social constructions and 'mere territorializations' of social life (Williams, 2003, pp. 16–19).

Yet these constructions can also offer useful ways for understanding and responding to client concerns. For example, in our case study, a sociological discourse, on its own, may lead us to overlook the possible contribution of biology to Michael's depression and the relevance of a biomedical response to his condition. Social workers work in environments where there are often competing definitions of problems and service users' problems demand responses that may require us to draw on the resources of these competing discourses. For instance, Michael may be assisted by a combination of biomedical and social interventions. Thus, in social work, we cannot afford to privilege sociological discourses over other discourses present within the practice context. As Leonard (1966, p. 98) warns:

> Sociological propositions similarly need to be treated with caution, to be questioned as to the evidence which supports them, and to be placed within a framework that takes into account the whole man [sic], biological, psychological, and social.

Conclusion

The formal base of social work draws on a range of received ideas. As our profession has developed, it has drawn on a range of discourses from a variety of disciplines, but mainly from psychology and sociology. Today, there remains considerable contestation among these discourses, and the extent to which they construct modern professional social work varies by geographical and practice contexts. Given the foundational role these discourses play in constructing us as social workers and our practice purposes, it is important that we are able to critically reflect on their uses and limitations for achieving our goals and values within our specific social work practice contexts.

Summary Questions

1   What ideas from psychoanalytic discourses continue to influence social work practice today?

2   How might knowledge from 'psy' discourses assist or limit social workers' capacity to promote service user self-determination?

3   What do social work commentators identify as the opportunities and concerns arising from the increasing influence of neuroscience in health and welfare service contexts?

4 What are the strengths and limits of sociological discourses for helping social workers to realize the value of social justice in practice?

Recommended Reading

'Psy' Discourse

- Matto, H. and Strolin-Golzman, J. (2010) Integrating social neuroscience and social work: innovations for advancing practice-based research. *Social Work*, 55(2), 147–56.
  Makes the case that social workers should actively incorporate neuroscience research into their practice. Focuses on the field of addictions where, it is argued, neuroscience has illuminated the neurological basis of addiction and it is possible to use brain imaging technology to assess the effectiveness of biopsychosocial interventions. Argues that neuroscience has considerable potential for advancing social work practice. In 2014, together with Michelle Ballan, Matto and Strolin-Golzman produced *Neuroscience for Social Work: Current Research and Practice* (New York: Springer), providing further useful reading on this topic.

- Nicolson, P., Bayne, R. and Owen, J. (2006) *Applied Psychology for Social Workers*, 3rd edn. (Basingstoke: Palgrave Macmillan)
  Excellent, succinct overview of the range of psychological perspectives that impact on social work practice. Detailed discussion of the history of psychodynamic theory as it applies to social work, illuminating the continuing influence of these ideas today. Addresses the influence and potential for psychological ideas to inform social work practice across the life course and in a range of interpersonal and macro-practice settings.

- Rose, N. (1999) *Governing the Soul: The Shaping of the Private Self*, 2nd edn. (London: Free Association Books).
  Widely cited work providing a sociological history of the rise and impact of psychological sciences. Includes well-researched material on the influence of 'psy' ideas in the social sciences. Critical of the role of 'psy' sciences in the government of individuals and takes a critical position towards social workers' and other human service professionals' engagement with these ideas.

- The Royal Society (2011) *Brain Waves, Module 1: Neuroscience, Society and Policy*. (London: The Royal Society).
  Excellent comprehensive primer for the layperson. Neuroscience researchers and policy analysts outline key concepts in neuroscience and provide considered debate about the potential uses and limits, including ethical concerns, of neuroscience to a range of social and public policy domains.

- Wastell, D. and White, S. (2012) Blinded by neuroscience: social policy, the family and the infant brain. *Families, Relationships and Societies*, 1(3), 397–414.
  Critical analysis of the actual and proposed application of neuroscience in the child welfare field. Argues for caution in the uptake of the neuroscience discourse, given that the knowledge in this field is not policy ready and many important ethical and practical considerations remain unresolved.

- Woods, M.E. and Hollis, F. (1990) *Casework: A Psychosocial Therapy*, 4th edn. (New York: McGraw-Hill).
  Classic text providing an excellent introduction to the psychosocial model of practice, which attempts to integrate psychodynamic and ecosystems perspectives into social casework.

Sociological Discourses

- Cree, V. (2010) *Sociology for Social Workers and Probation Officers*, 2nd edn. (London: Routledge).
  Reader-friendly introduction to sociological perspectives and their application to a variety of social service contexts.

- Gray, M. and Webb, S. (eds) (2013) *Social Work Theories and Methods*, 2nd edn. (London: Sage).
  Comprehensive introduction to how the ideas of major thinkers in the fields of social sciences, humanities and cultural studies inform social work today.

5

ALTERNATIVE DISCOURSES
Citizen Rights, Religion and Spirituality, and Environmental Social Work

In this chapter, we turn to another set of discourses that have a (re)emerging influence in many contemporary practice contexts. They are citizen rights, those associated with religion and spirituality, and environmental social work. Although these discourses, particularly citizen rights and religious discourses, are increasingly incorporated into mainstream health and welfare provision in many contexts, here, we refer to them as 'alternative discourses' because, like the human science discourses discussed in Chapter 4, they are concerned with providing holistic responses to human need, but dispute aspects of the human science discourses that social workers have relied on in constructing their knowledge base for practice. Alternative discourses offer much more than ways of constituting health and welfare services, even so the focus here is on how these discourses construct core concepts, like client needs and capacities, and the provision of health and welfare services, including the role of the social worker. Figure 5.1 highlights the discourses we focus on this chapter.

Figure 5.1 positions alternative discourses below dominant discourses to demonstrate that, like the human and social science discourses outlined in Chapter 4, these alternative discourses are also subordinate to the dominant discourses of biomedicine, law and new public management that shape modern health and welfare institutions. The positioning of alternative discourses across from the human science discourses, from which the formal knowledge base of social work has historically drawn, shows the strong interaction between the two sets of discourses.

Many discourses outside the human sciences shape how client needs and social work practices are constituted. Other relevant discourses such as human rights and communitarian discourses also inform some aspects of the reformation and critique of service provision and social work practice. We focus on citizen rights and discourses associated with religion and spirituality, as alternative discourses, because of their growing influence in determining client needs and service provision processes in mainstream health and welfare contexts, such as hospitals, statutory authorities, and large nongovernmental community service organizations. We also discuss environmental social work because of the growing concern and influence of environmental movements on social work practice.

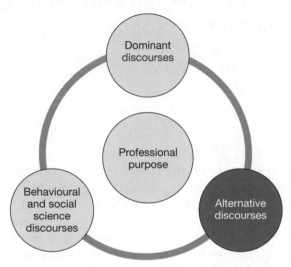

Figure 5.1 Discourses in interaction: highlighting alternative service discourses

Although these discourses are referred to as 'alternative' because they neither dominate the majority of service institutions where social workers practise nor are they recognized as central to the profession as whole, their influence is nonetheless profound and growing.

For more than four decades, citizen rights movements have challenged the dominant constructions of service users as passive recipients, instead promoting recognition of them as active participants in determining their own service needs and responses to those needs. Also, for at least two decades, religious and spiritual discourses have re-emerged as powerful practices in health and welfare services, although religious institutions played a profound role in the establishment of the profession and in the sites where social work is practised in many countries. While religious institutions have been an important part of the social welfare landscape, particularly in the provision of children's homes during the twentieth century, today the renewed influence of religious discourses can be attributed to some modern forces, including the privatization of services in the context of new public management. In addition, the growing influence of spiritual discourses in health and welfare services can be attributed to agitation from service providers and service users who have argued that recognition of spiritual needs is critical to holistic and culturally sensitive health and welfare service delivery. Over the past 10 years, social workers have engaged in a growing debate about environmental matters, recognizing that a focus on the physical environment is a necessary extension of the ecosystems approach to which social workers commonly refer (Dominelli, 2012).

These alternative discourses contest the ways in which the dominant discourses (Chapter 3) and the human sciences discourses (Chapter 4) constitute client needs and health and welfare provision. In different ways, they contest the notions of individualism, rationality, objectivity and linear notions of progress underpinning the dominant discourses of biomedicine, neoclassical economics and law. For instance, citizen rights movements have challenged the status of biomedical interventions as progressive, showing that these interventions can also serve to deny service users other options for achieving their own welfare and wellbeing (Sparrow, 2005). These alternative discourses also contest the human science discourses on which the social work profession has historically relied. For example, discourses associated with spirituality can challenge the humanist ethos, central to modern social work, which focuses on humans as the agents of achieving personal and social change and, in so doing, has denied the place of spiritual authority and meaning in some service users' lives.

Alternative discourses also share some common assumptions with the human science discourses on which the social work profession has traditionally drawn. For example, the citizen rights discourse and critical sociological discourses recognize that relations of power and conflict shape the relationships and service in health and welfare institutions. Similarly, environmental social work recognizes the systems approach central to social work and seeks to extend it to incorporate the physical environment (Mary, 2008). In addition, while these alternative discourses challenge the formal base of social work, they can also offer new opportunities for achieving the kinds of values, such as the promotion of self-determination, social justice and global social change, to which social workers are committed.

Despite their potential for new insights, it is important to approach these discourses critically and cautiously. While they may offer useful alternative constructions of service users' needs and service roles, they are also contested. Within the social work literature, there is an emerging critique of the growing influence of religious themes in some areas of service practice and we will consider these critiques as well as criticisms of citizen rights and environmental social work discourses in health and welfare service provision. In short, we argue that social workers must adopt a critical stance towards these discourses, recognizing their limitations for achieving the emancipatory ends often claimed by their advocates. First, we turn to an analysis of the features and influence of the citizen rights discourse in health and welfare services.

Citizen Rights Discourse

The citizen rights discourse presents service users as rights-bearing citizens who have the right and the capacities to fully participate in determining their health and welfare needs. This construction of the rights-bearing citizen is contrasted with the tendency of the dominant and human science discourses to constitute service users as passive objects of health and welfare interventions (see Crossley and Crossley, 2001). The citizen rights discourse aims to destabilize the dominant constructions of the 'normal' and 'abnormal' and, in so doing, create opportunities for those formerly deemed 'abnormal' to gain increased opportunities to live full and productive lives of their choosing. We are 'different' but 'equal' is the guiding credo of many of the citizen rights movements from which this discourse has emerged.

Citizen Rights Movements in Health and Welfare

The emergence of citizen rights movements can traced to the 1970s, at which time activists within a variety of health and welfare fields began to make links between service users' experiences and the civil rights movement (Campbell and Oliver, 1996, p. 49; Crossley and Crossley, 2001; Shakespeare, 2006). Over the past four decades, a range of movements have emerged within various health and welfare fields, including 'the recovery movement' (Carpenter, 2002, p. 86) and the 'rehabilitation movement' (Bland et al., 2009, p. 43). Today, citizen rights movements have emerged across the spectrum of health and welfare fields and cover a wide range of concerns, including breast cancer, sexual health, HIV/AIDS, organ donation, mental health, disability and ageing.

Members of citizen rights movements in health and welfare fields seek to challenge the pathologizing labels often ascribed to them by health and welfare professionals on the grounds that these labels denigrate service users' lived experiences and capacities. For example, the term 'differently abled' is preferable to 'disabled' on the grounds that the former recognizes the capacities gained through disability. Similarly, the term 'survivor' conveys the strengths of individuals who have survived ill-treatment in human service systems or who have survived various health challenges.

Citizen rights movements are often associated with the development of communities of people with specific lived experiences. One aim of these communities is to build alternative services, through which the capacities and life choices of the citizen can be recognized and enhanced. In contrast to dominant modes of health and welfare delivery that rely on professional experts, these services seek to engage service users in decision-making at all levels of service delivery (see Bland et al., 2009, pp. 48–58).

Often, citizen rights advocates view the law as a vehicle for promoting and protecting service users' rights (see Barnes, 1996; Shakespeare, 2006). In particular, the 1975 United Nations Declaration on the Rights of Disabled Persons is widely seen within disability rights movements as a turning point in affirming the social participation rights of people with disabilities (Campbell and Oliver, 1996, p. 19). Using a human rights framework, citizen rights groups have reconceptualized some of the apparently personal decisions affecting oppressed health and welfare minorities as human rights issues. For example, some citizen rights advocates argue that apparently personal issues such as the management of contraception and menstruation for young women with severe intellectual disabilities should be understood as human rights issues, rather than as personal decisions for family members and carers (for a discussion, see Carlson and Wilson, 1998; McCarthy, 2009).

Like other civil rights movements, citizen rights discourses promote the use of critical thinking and collective action. In particular, critical conscious-ness raising is used by proponents of citizen rights discourses to develop community and service user awareness of the social forces that contribute to the discrimination and disadvantage experienced by people with disabili-ties or mental health challenges. For example, reflecting on the mental health recovery movement, Carpenter (2002, p. 89) observes that the empowerment process is as much about 'recovery from the societal reaction to the disability as it is about recovery from the disability itself'. Public protest can be used to draw attention to the social norms and practices that serve to systematically exclude some citizens. For instance, people with disabilities have engaged in public demonstrations against public transport and building authorities for failing to ensure disability access to community utilities (Campbell and Oliver, 1996, pp. 152–3; see also Shakespeare, 2006). Not only have these actions achieved practical change, such as improved access to public spaces, they have also challenged cultural stereotypes by showing people with disabilities to be active agents of change.

Key Themes in Citizen Rights Discourse

Citizen rights movements in health and welfare are diverse. Here, we focus on a citizen rights discourse that is associated with new social movements. These movements draw on critical social science theories and the progres-sive political values and stances, such as collectivism and redistributive justice, broadly associated with the political Left (see Campbell and Oliver, 1996, pp. 100–1; Oliver, 2001).

A core theme of the citizen rights discourse is a focus on the social structures and cultural problems as the original causes of the problems and barriers facing service users. Tom Shakespeare (2003, p. 199), a disability studies scholar, argues that 'Clearly, the problem of disability is more to do with social and cultural processes than it is to do with biology' (see also Sparrow, 2005, p. 137). Members of citizen rights movements in many fields of disability are highly critical of the focus on individual biology and personal pathology that dominates health and welfare institutions' construction of client need and service provision process. In contrast to the biomedical discourse, which focuses on the diagnosis and amelioration of biological pathology, the citizen rights discourse presents a social model of health and wellness that focuses on 'the removal or amelioration of social and environmental barriers to full social, physical, career, and religious participation' (Quinn, 1998, p. xix; see also Campbell and Oliver, 1996; Oliver, 2001; Shakespeare, 2003). This construction of client need from one of personal change to social change has led to the formation of alternative services for and the opening up of mainstream services to differently abled people.

A further theme is the emphasis on capacity. This can occur in at least two ways. The first is a rejection of the focus on pathology to concentrate instead on recognizing service users' capacities borne of the lived experiences of surviving health challenges and/or human service institutions. Reflecting on the influence of the recovery movement in mental health services, Carpenter (2002, p. 87) states: 'the most fundamental premise of the recovery movement is that people with psychiatric disabilities can and do recover'. The citizen rights discourse invites us to see beyond the pathologizing labels that may pervade health and welfare services.

Another way capacity can be recognized is in terms of a positive valuation of differences in capacities and experiences. A citizen rights discourse challenges the opposition between 'normal' and 'abnormal' that dominates many health and welfare discourses, such as 'psy' and biomedical discourses, to argue that the needs of differently abled people should be recognized as part of the broad spectrum of human experiences and capacities. This discourse challenges health and welfare institutions to open themselves to the diversity of client needs rather than to treat specific client groups, such as 'survivors' of mental illnesses, as 'special' cases who place an extra burden on these institutions.

The citizen rights discourse presents the needs of service users as the need for 'community' rather than for 'cure'. This discourse shows that many 'advances', particularly medical practices and helping practices, such as supportive casework and welfare provision, do little to promote the social inclusion of service users. What is needed is support for alternative communities, in which services users' needs can be recognized in dialogue with the service user and responded to in a holistic, rather than a fragmented and individualistic, fashion. Indeed, some members of citizen rights movements have pointed out that the 'helping' practices of health and welfare professions can further the oppression of service users by failing to recognize and support socially inclusive responses to service users' concerns (Crossley and Crossley, 2001, p. 1484; Oliver, 2001, p. 158). For example, some members of the deaf community argue that new technologies that offer 'hope' of hearing also reflect the profound intolerance of the hearing society towards deaf people (Hyde and Power, 2000).

The citizen rights discourse encourages us all to be critical of the power differentials in health and welfare services, and in society generally, that serve to disempower and marginalize service users (Carpenter, 2002). This discourse highlights the ways in which service users' interests are constructed through powerful professional groups within these institutions and argues that in order to meet their own needs, service user groups must first take decision-making power from powerful groups within these institutions. As Mike Oliver (2001, p. 158) asserts: 'Independent living is ... about nothing more or less than rescuing the [disabled] body from the hands of medics, other professionals and welfare administrators.' Through processes of recovering and valuing their lived knowledge as members of oppressed communities, members of citizen rights movements assert their expertise in their own lives and, more specifically, in defining their health and welfare needs. A citizen rights discourse also calls into question professionals' claim to knowledge that is objective, rational and true (Crossley and Crossley, 2001, p. 1484; Oliver, 2001, p. 158). Instead, the accounts of professional experts become a truth, rather than the truth, about service users' lives.

Finally, according to the citizen rights discourse, service users need to develop a critical self-awareness of their oppression before they can act in their own best interests. For some members of disability rights movements, this process of critical self-awareness involves challenging the dominant cultural narrative of disability as personal tragedy and to recognize, instead, the structural and cultural bases of the difficulties facing people with disabilities. In addition, the development of collective identification is vital to overcoming oppression. For example, one is no longer primarily a person with schizophrenia, instead one is recognized as a member of an oppressed health minority, in this case, those labelled as 'mentally ill'. This process is described by Crossley and Crossley (2001, p. 1484), who, in their review of citizen rights movements in mental health services, observe that the:

> use of collective pronouns such as 'we' and 'us' alongside such typifications as 'survivor' or user, is highly significant ... No longer are they purely individual experiences of a solitary ego. They are the experiences of a group; collective and shared experiences.

We turn now to consider a practice example of how the citizen rights discourse might conflict with a dominant construction of client need and service provision.

Practice Exercise **Sexual health and people living with intellectual disability**

Imagine you work in a disability support service within a government authority. Your role is to support young people living with intellectual disabilities. You are working with Elena, a 17-year-old woman with a moderate intellectual disability. Elena has a supportive family, with whom she lives and is likely to continue living with into the future. In addition to your work with Elena, you often meet Tricia (57), who is Elena's mother and primary support person. Elena's father, Peter (58) is also supportive of Elena but is usually at work when you visit the home. Elena is focused on meeting young men, whom she refers to as her 'boyfriends' and has revealed to you and her mother that she has many sexual partners. It appears that she meets her sexual partners primarily though acquaintances including friends on Facebook. Sometimes, the meetings with men have ended badly. Recently, Elena told you that a young man she had met on Facebook, with whom she had sex, later called her ugly names and made her cry.

Trisha has arranged for Elena to take the contraceptive pill, but is aware that sometimes Elena fails to take it unless supervised by Trisha. Elena is unconcerned about the prospect of becoming pregnant, although you and Trisha are anxious about her capacity to parent a child, particularly at this life stage. Trisha and Peter are sick with worry about the possibility of Elena becoming pregnant and would like you to arrange for Elena to have long-term contraceptive injections from the health clinic at your service. They are even considering exploring the option of sterilization for Elena, which would involve applying to the courts for a review of Elena's situation.

You have raised this idea of taking long-lasting contraceptives via injection with Elena and she has indicated that she doesn't want the injections.

- What do you see as the key issues from your perspective as a social worker?

- What principles would inform your practice here?

- How would you assist Elena and her family with their decision-making?

Elena's case illuminates some possible tensions in the ways in which the citizen rights, legal and biomedical discourses construct client needs and service responses. Consistent with our value base, the social worker needs to work towards the 'best interests' of the service user, but in this situation, this is complicated by the constraints on Elena's capacity to understand the consequences of possible outcomes, such as a pregnancy, and the evidence of harmful outcomes for her in some of her encounters with the men she meets through friends.

A citizen rights discourse emphasizes Elena's right to self-determination, and while the concerns of Elena's mother are also important, they are secondary to Elena's rights to choose to the maximum extent possible (Tilley et al., 2012). For example, writing from a citizen rights perspective, McCarthy (2009, p. 205) cites the desire of family members and professionals to prevent women with significant learning disabilities from bearing children as a legacy of 'past eugenics ideologies'. From a citizen rights perspective, our work with Elena should focus primarily on maximizing her involvement in decisions and in providing support for her to achieve healthy and respectful relationships (Stansfield et al., 2007).

The biomedical discourse highlights the 'opportunities' that biomedical advances provide for achieving Elena's wish for sexual expression along with her parents' desire for Elena not to become pregnant. However, proponents of the citizen rights discourse urge us to recognize that these apparent biomedical advances are not politically neutral and may further the oppression of marginalized groups such as women living with disability. For example, within the biomedical discourse, certain choices appear preferable or inevitable, such as women living with intellectual disability will be subject to contraceptive medicine or surgery, while other options, such as these women may choose to parent, are invalidated (see McCarthy, 2009; Tilley et al., 2012).

In a further contrast to the citizen rights discourse, the contemporary legal discourse seeks to balance a recognition of Elena's human rights to participate in decisions with those of her family, as her guardian and carers, to shape decisions, particularly given that Elena's capacity to independently determine her best interests may be compromised by her intellectual disability. As Stansfield et al. (2007, p. 577) observe: 'Common law guidance states that substitute decisions for those lacking capacity must be in that person's best interests and the least restrictive option.' In this context, guidance would need to be sought from sexual health specialists regarding the least intrusive and best option in the family context. The least intrusive option is unlikely to be sterilization, an option raised by Tricia, although in the context of Elena's ambivalence about her current contraception, a more long-acting contraceptive option (such as injectable hormonal contraceptives) may need to be considered by Elena and her family. In terms of Elena's best interests, this also requires that she and her carers are informed about the possible consequences of any alternative proposed contraception (McCarthy, 2009).

In this situation, the concept of 'best interests' is differently interpreted within the terms of a citizen rights discourse, which aims to maximize the individual's right to choose, with the legal discourse, which aims to recognize the rights of different parties, including parties with authority as guardians and carers. In this context, a focus on informed decision-making is also useful in our work with Elena and her family. The principle of informed decision-making means that the individuals involved 'should not be hindered in his or her understanding, reasoning or decision-making and should be able to make a decision in a context free from constraint or undue influence' (Hyde and Power, 2000, p. 120). We can promote informed decision-making by ensuring that Elena and her family are more fully informed about the opportunities available to them to manage Elena's wish for sexual expression and the family's concerns that she is able to express herself in a safe environment while minimizing the risk of pregnancy.

Consistent with the principle of informed decision-making, we should be sensitive to how the information is provided to Elena and her family. We would need to make sure that the information offered by health professionals is provided in a context that is sensitive to the rights and needs of people living with an intellectual disability and respectful of the responsibilities borne by Tricia and Peter as Elena's guardians and long-term carers. One danger of a purely citizen rights view in this case is that it can lead us to downplay the views of carers and guardians as 'exaggerated or unwarranted' (McCarthy, 2009, cited in Tilley et al., 2012, p. 422).

Critical Analysis of the Citizen Rights Discourse

The citizen rights discourse is consistent with key social work values, built as it is on values of empowerment, self-determination and social justice and offering practical strategies for citizens to participate in determining their needs and choosing how these needs will be met (Carpenter, 2002). In many practice contexts, the growing influence of the citizen rights discourses can enable social workers to advocate for client decisions that run counter to dominant discourses within mainstream health and welfare settings. Partly as a result of citizen rights initiatives in law and policy making, many mainstream health and welfare institutions are required to involve service users in decision-making. These initiatives have also led to a broader public awareness of citizen-directed alternatives in many areas of service provision. Social workers can use these changing policy practices and levels of public awareness to support citizen self-determination.

In myriad ways, the citizen rights discourse has returned some power to the hands of the people oppressed within modern health and welfare systems, and helped to break down the isolation, self-blame and stigma experienced by many service users, especially those with chronic illnesses or disabilities. The legal protections of the rights of citizens using health and welfare systems have also improved. For example, in many countries over the past three decades, people living with intellectual disabilities have gained increased legal protection against enforced sterilization; a practice that previously occurred with little legal regulation (Stansfield et al., 2007). According to the testimonials of members of citizen rights movements (see Campbell and Oliver, 1996; Crossley and Crossley, 2001; Carpenter, 2002), the processes of support, critical awareness raising, skill development and collective action have energized many members and enabled them to achieve substantial improvements in their quality of life on their own terms. By challenging service providers to recognize the broad range of service users' needs, other than the 'cure' of a condition, the citizen rights discourse has facilitated the creation of services that expand the opportunities for service users to live a quality of life of their choosing. These initiatives move beyond a focus on addressing 'health' or 'welfare' needs to promote the social, cultural and economic wellbeing of service users (Crowther, 2007).

The citizen rights discourse has contributed to the substantial expansion of citizen-led services in many fields of health and welfare provision, especially among people with disabilities (Campbell and Oliver, 1996; Crowther, 2007). These services break down the professional domination of service delivery processes in health and welfare and diversify the range and form of services available to oppressed service user groups. Citizen-led services usually move beyond direct service provision to health and welfare minorities to supporting the capacity of service users to participate in organizational governance and broader social change activities (Campbell and Oliver, 1996, p. 169). Again, the citizen rights discourse moves beyond a narrow construction of client need to incorporate a recognition of needs and interests with the aim of promoting social inclusion and celebrating social diversity.

Despite the many strengths of the citizen rights discourse, there is currently much debate, within and outside citizen rights movements, about the limits of this discourse for promoting service users' interests and wellbeing (see Corker and Shakespeare, 2002; Shakespeare, 2006). One area of contention is the reliance on fixed identities forged around social categories of gender, race, class, wellness, ability and so on. These identity categories can be extremely useful and politically necessary (Thornton, 2000, p. 19). However, a reliance on fixed identities, for example the definition of oneself as 'a person with a disability' or 'a breast cancer survivor', disregards the 'temporal and fluid character' of identity (Thornton, 2000, p. 21). In other words, a focus on fixed identities overlooks the extent to which one's identifications may vary over time as, for example, one's condition may alter, and the meaning of each identification often changes through time, circumstance and context. For example, a person with a mental illness may find that their mental health status is not always the most salient aspect of their identity, especially during periods of wellness.

In constructing identity around specified characteristics – 'a differently abled person' or 'a mental health survivor' – the citizen rights discourse can rely on the suppression of differences and conflicts among members of specific communities. While this may be politically necessary at times, a reliance on a fixed collective identity can become oppressive when it involves the suppression of differences, such as variations in political perspectives, interests and identifications (Humphrey, 1999, p. 182). For example, women with disabilities and women of colour have raised concerns about the extent to which the concerns of white, middle-class, able-bodied women have dominated feminist debates about sexuality and reproductive rights (McCarthy, 2009). Similarly, some members of HIV/AIDS citizen movements have challenged the dominance of health initiatives around the needs of gay men on the grounds that the interests of other groups, such as HIV-positive women and lesbians, are marginalized (Humphrey, 1999, pp. 177–8).

Furthermore, when specific identities and interests dominate an identity group, members of that collective will face pressure to conform to group norms. Humphrey (1999, p. 183) warns that:

> all communities engender their own norms which will consolidate over time; and a community grounded upon a particular identity is likely to essentialize that identity and to enforce homogeneity, to a greater or lesser extent.

Hence, individuals who choose not to conform to claims made on behalf of the collective face the threat of sanction and, possibly, exclusion (for a discussion, see Campbell and Oliver, 1996, pp. 78–80). Social workers seeking to promote the value of self-determination may, at times, need to support individuals to express identifications and views that run counter to a collective identity, such as mental health service survivor.

Another set of concerns relates to the conflict perspective on which some forms of citizen rights discourse are based. Over the past decade, debate has emerged regarding the limits of the social model of disability, on which much disability activism rests, to acknowledge the role of impairment in shaping the life experiences of people with disabilities and the options for creating social inclusion and social justice. In critiquing the social model of disability, Shakespeare (2006, p. 56) states: 'whereas they [social modelists] say ... that "people are disabled by society, not by their bodies", I would argue that "people are disabled by society and by their bodies"'. Shakespeare (2006, p. 65) questions the aligning of disability rights activism with civil rights movements, given that the 'complex reality of impairment' contributes to unique challenges to achieving equality.

The alignment of health and service user activism with civil rights discourses can also render invisible the complexities of power relations at the levels of interpersonal and institutional practice. Certainly, drawing on a citizen rights discourse, advocates have exposed areas of human rights abuses such as the sterilization of young children (see Brady, 1998; Stansfield et al., 2007). Yet, when a citizen rights discourse is invoked as the primary framework for decision-making, it can fail to honour the difficult interpersonal dimensions of decisions that bear significantly on the care workload of 'stakeholders', such as family members. For example, in the above practice example, it is unhelpful to reduce parents' desire to prevent their adolescent daughter becoming pregnant as a 'denial of the reproductive rights' (McCarthy, 2009, p. 206).

A related concern is the potential for oppositional identity politics to alienate potential sources of support within the general community and among powerful groups within health and welfare institutions. For example, some activists have adopted oppositional tactics towards those individuals responsible for developing and implementing cochlear implant technology on the basis that it may deny deaf people the right to lead full and productive lives as deaf people. They have included picketing medical conventions concerned with the use of implants with placards describing surgeons as the new 'Butchers of Belsen' (Hyde and Power, 2000, p. 119; see also Sparrow, 2005). Oppositional tactics such as these, which fix individuals as allies or enemies on the basis of identity categorization, threaten to undermine potential coalitions for change. Writing from a disability rights perspective, Crowther (2007, p. 794) also warns of the risk of marginalization of the movement's concerns 'if productive partnerships are sacrificed on the altar of ideological purity and isolationism shapes action'. This is not to deny that powerful professional and economic interests may need to be confronted in the quest for change, rather it is to recognize that powerful allegiances may occur with individuals who might also be members of these groups.

A further problem is that an oppositional approach to power and identity can give rise to what Nietzsche, an eminent philosopher, has referred to as the politics of 'ressentiment' (Healy, 2000, p. 53; Thornton, 2000, p. 19). The term 'ressentiment' refers to a form of hostility exercised by members of an oppressed group towards individuals and groups who are seen to benefit from an unjust social order. In the politics of ressentiment, individuals who are perceived as privileged are held personally responsible for the existing social order that perpetuates their advantage. This attitude can arise from the process of consciousness raising when the citizen comes to understand themselves as a survivor who bears 'witness to the hidden injuries done to them by others – or by fate' (Rose, 1999, p. 268). On the one hand, the consciousness-raising process can be experienced as liberating as one comes to challenge negative stereotypes about the self as issues not of personal deficit but of structural oppression for which others are entirely responsible. On the other hand, this can limit one's capacity for power by placing responsibility for change in the hands of the other, more powerful person/group and by limiting one's identity as the stigmatized self. Rose (1999, p. 269) points out that, in the politics of ressentiment, one's identity

> is organized around the ideas of suffering, of demanding recompense, of making amends, of holding to account – a way of making sense of stigma by reversing it and attaching oneself to it as the very mark of one's virtue.

If the aim of the citizen rights discourse is to diversify citizens' opportunities for choice, constructing our identities in terms of citizen or group member can again close down these choices.

Finally, the citizen rights discourse can, perhaps inadvertently, reinforce some dimensions of the neoclassical economic discourse, particularly the drive to achieve greater economic efficiency in service delivery. Care must be taken lest the demand of citizen rights movements for increased control over service delivery and reduced professional involvement be used by governments and other funding bodies to justify a reduction in social services funding. Calls for increased citizen involvement must be coupled with demands for the necessary government investment so that all citizens are supported to realize their right to participate in the service system and in society (Crowther, 2007).

Religious and Spiritual Discourses

We move now to a consideration of how discourses associated with religion and spirituality construct service users' needs and service provision in health and welfare institutions generally and in social work practice in particular. Although most social workers view the profession as a secular one, we shall see that health and welfare contexts and the social work profession are strongly shaped by religious and spiritual beliefs and ideas. We begin by differentiating between spirituality and religion and outline key themes in these discourses. We then discuss how these discourses impact on social work contexts and service delivery, and consider the uses and issues concerning the operation of religious and spiritual discourses in social work practice contexts.

What are Religious and Spiritual Discourses?

In the secular world, the terms 'spirituality' and 'religion' are often used interchangeably. Yet, for many scholars, practitioners and service users, there are important differences between these two terms. Lindsay (2002, p. 48) defines religion as 'a systematic body of beliefs and practices related to a spiritual search'. The concept is connected to how individuals make meaning of their life (Zahl, 2003; Holloway and Moss, 2010). Spiritual beliefs and practices vary and can include meditation and prayer sessions through to radical social action. In addition, as Hutchison (1998, p. 58) asserts: 'religion also refers to a communal expression of some form of mutual aid and some communal compassionate concern for people and the environment in which they live'. In short, religious discourses usually produce forms of organized activity in addition to supporting individual spiritual search.

By contrast, spirituality refers to the search for meaning and purpose in life (Lindsay, 2002; Zahl, 2003). According to Hutchison (1998, p. 58), spirituality's 'primary focus is on the individual and the psychological processes by which he/she organizes some type of world view and consciously relates to that world'. Unlike religion, spirituality does not necessarily involve organized practices and institutions for the expression of faith. However, this does not mean that religion and spirituality are necessarily separated from one another; only that the search for spiritual meaning can occur in the absence of an organized and institutionalized base for that search. Furthermore, many groups not formally associated with religious faiths or institutions, such as some feminist and environmental groups, are strongly committed to spiritual activities as part of a broad change mission (Lindsay, 2002, p. 35).

Key Themes in Religious and Spiritual Discourses

Despite the considerable diversity of religious and spiritual discourses, we can detect at least four common themes. First, religious and spiritual discourses draw attention to a non-material world. This belief in, and focus on, a non-material world is in sharp contrast to the focus of Enlightenment thinking on the rational, observable world. The non-material world may include one's internal world, such as one's beliefs and values. Many religious discourses also focus on a non-material world beyond our earthly existence, such as the afterlife.

Second, religious and spiritual discourses focus on our relationship with a divine or mysterious power. Notions of the divine vary across religious and cultural groups, as does the individual's relationship with the divine. For example, Christian and Jewish religions imagine God as a higher being. By contrast, some forms of indigenous spirituality see spirituality as embedded in our natural environment (see Bennett et al., 2013). Furthermore, many non-Western religious traditions do not separate people from 'the divine'; for example, Hindus believe that the divine is within (Nigosian, cited in Crompton, 1998, p. 33).

Third, a primary purpose of religious and spiritually oriented activities is to promote spiritual wellbeing. In most religious and spiritual belief systems, good works in the world are a likely outcome of this quest for spiritual wellbeing, but they are not the primary purpose of these works. According to Swift (1956, p. 1), the central purpose of the church is

> through worship to build and to sustain the means whereby man [sic] and God may become more closely related. Concern for the humanity of man to man [sic] results inevitably from this communion with a God of love and justice, but is always secondary to it in so far as it is in any sense religious.

Yet, for other spiritual groups, one's spiritual wellbeing is entwined with action in the material world. For example, liberation theologists assert that one's personal relationship with the divine should be expressed through revolutionary action aimed at freeing the oppressed from social and structural oppression (Lindsay, 2002, p. 27).

Fourth, religious and spiritual discourses produce moral frameworks grounded in religious and spiritual belief systems (Hutchison, 1998, p. 59; see also Kissman and Maurer, 2002). Despite the diversity of different religious and spiritual belief systems, most promote value systems that can be broadly defined as promoting human wellbeing and care and compassion for others (see Hutchison, 1998). The moral frameworks emerging from diverse religious and spiritual belief systems offer profound challenges to the key ideas underpinning dominant discourses. For example, religious and spiritual discourses can challenge biomedical principles around the preservation of life, as, for example, an individual may refuse potentially life-saving intervention on the grounds that it contravenes their religious belief systems and thus compromises their relationship with God. Similarly, notions of compassion and care can also challenge the emphasis on rationality and economic efficiency found in neoclassical economic discourses.

Spiritual and Religious Discourses in Social Work Practices

While most postindustrial societies are increasingly secular societies (Levine, 1998, p. 118; Lyons, 2001, p. 58), religious and spiritual discourses profoundly shape social service delivery and social work practices in many service contexts, especially the nongovernmental sector. The influence of new public management means that in countries such as Australia, New Zealand, Canada and the UK, private charities, often with a religious base, have a renewed role in service provision. Furthermore, although social work is a secular profession, the International Federation of Social Workers and the International Association of Schools of Social Work recognize that social workers 'acknowledgement of spiritual issues should be an essential part of the knowledge base of social work' (Holloway and Moss, 2010, p. 19). Here, we consider key ways in which these discourse shape contemporary social work practices.

Professional social work was founded in religious organizations (for a discussion, see Lindsay, 2002; Holloway and Moss, 2010). In most postindustrial societies, including Australia and New Zealand, the Nordic countries and the UK, charities based in mainstream Catholic and Protestant religions were the forerunners of modern social work. In the USA, Christian and Jewish faiths provided the basis for American social work (Levine, 1998, p. 119). As a result of its origins in religious charities, professional social work shares a common value base with some mainstream religious faiths, particularly Christian and Jewish faiths. Recognizing this commonality, some social workers see the profession as a vocation that is consistent with their religious or spiritual commitment to the service of others. For example, in her study of 30 social workers committed to either Christian or Buddhist belief systems, Lindsay (2002, p. 77) found that all of them asserted that 'the common emphasis on social justice and empowering people to live full, authentic lives linked social work to their spiritual beliefs'.

Another way religious and spiritual discourses impact on social work practice is that, sometimes, social workers are called upon to respond to the religious or spiritual needs of service users. In some areas of social work, the spiritual issues facing clients are readily apparent, such as in palliative care, but service users may raise spiritual and religious issues in many other areas of practice too. According to Speck (cited in Lyall, 2001, p. 48), the kinds of situations in which spiritual and religious issues are likely to come to the fore include:

- loss of meaning, such as the breakdown of an important personal relationship or the loss of employment

- intense suffering, such as the suffering associated with a serious mental illness or a drug addiction

- a sense of guilt or shame, which may be raised for parents of children who are abused

- a concern about the ethical issues involved in various forms of professional intervention, such as the decision over whether or not to embark on in vitro fertilization treatment

- a lack of the sense of God or anger towards God, which could arise, for example, as a result of the death of a loved one.

Service users may turn to social workers to work on religious or spiritual issues precisely because they see the profession as a secular one. Service users may see the profession's lack of alignment with a specific religious or spiritual base as providing a safe environment in which to discuss spiritual concerns, such as anger at God or a loss of belief. Some commentators argue that understanding the religious and spiritual needs of service users is a key dimension of holistic care, inseparable from attending to material and emotional needs (Edwards, 2002, p. 83; Kissman and Maurer, 2002, p. 35). Arguably, then, practitioners should be mindful of the way individuals make sense of their experiences (Bland et al., 2009, p. 64) and comfortable talking about spirituality if issues of this nature are raised by service users (Holloway and Moss, 2010).

An understanding of spiritual and religious beliefs and practices is also important to culturally sensitive practice. First Nations people often express a spiritual connection to the land and to community that influences how they interact with health and welfare systems (Bennett et al., 2013). For example, spiritual beliefs may require individuals and families to engage in mourning for a specified period and may require absence from work and appointments, such as meetings with health and welfare professionals. By understanding the nature and significance of spiritual ceremonies for the diverse cultural groups with whom social workers practise, we can assist our clients to negotiate health and welfare systems. Holloway and Moss (2010, p. 2) also point out that as social workers seek to engage with ethnic minorities in culturally sensitive ways, the profession is being challenged to recognize the extent to which, for many people, 'a religious framework for their living is fundamental to their quality of life and approach to problems'.

A further way religious discourses shape social work is through the renewed influence of religious organizations in social service delivery. The profession of social work originally emerged in the religious charities of the late nineteenth century in the UK and the USA, but as the state assumed increased responsibility for provision of social services, the profession moved away from religious charities and into the public sector. Across the postindustrial world, the trend towards the privatization of social services, which has gathered pace since the 1980s, has led to an expanding role for religious organizations in the delivery of services (Harris et al., 2003). Privatization involves the transfer of responsibility for service delivery from governments to the nongovernmental sector (J. Healy, 1998, p. 10) and many of the medium to large established nongovernmental social services organizations in postindustrial societies have a religious base (see Industry Commission, 1995; Hutchison, 1998, p. 63). Moreover, many of these agencies are founded in the mainstream religious traditions of postindustrial countries, particularly Christianity and Judaism (see Hutchison, 1998, pp. 63–4; Harris et al., 2003). Consequently, social work graduates will increasingly work in religiously affiliated organizations. Similarly, clients will be increasingly served by organizations with dual religious and service missions.

Yet, religious organizations face constraints on the extent to which religious discourse is able to infuse the structure and provision of social services.

Tensions exist between the law, particularly human rights and equal opportunity laws, and religious discourses that seek to promote differential treatment based on specific beliefs or values. In 2012, in the UK, the Upper Tribunal dismissed the appeal of Catholic Care, a private adoption agency, which was seeking to exclude same-sex couples from using its adoption services (National Secular Society, 2012). In his ruling, the Hon. Mr Justice Sales took into account the requirements for equality under the law and 'the general social value of promotion of equality of treatment for heterosexuals and homosexuals' (Catholic Care and Charity Commission for England and Wales, 2012, p. 24, para. 66). But, in some contexts, religious charities continue to experience some freedom to discriminate on the basis of religious discourse. For example, in Australia, nongovernmental community service organizations can include a demonstrated commitment to a particular religion as a criteria for employment in senior positions in these charities, even where the charity is in receipt of substantial public monies to fund such posts.

Review Question

In what circumstances, if at all, should religiously affiliated organizations be allowed to require employees to demonstrate commitment to the religious belief system of the organization? In what circumstances, if at all, should such a requirement be outlawed?

Critical Analysis of Religious and Spiritual Discourses

Here, we consider how religious and spiritual discourses may support and extend or limit social work practices and social service delivery. First, many religious and spiritual discourses, including Buddhism, Christianity, Islam and Judaism, are aligned with, and offer support for, the humanitarian value base of social work (Canda, 1988; Lindsay, 2002). Thus, in some practice contexts, the religious mission of the organization and the social work service mission are compatible. For example, Hutchison (1998, p. 57) argues that:

> In the Judaic-Christian tradition … church-related agencies are well situated to play a major role in providing compassionate care for vulnerable and poor populations and in advocating on their behalf for policies that make services more affordable and accessible.

One benefit of a religious discourse is that services constituted through this discourse may offer more holistic responses to service users than is typically available through many secular welfare services. In particular, service providers in religiously affiliated services are likely to see spiritual needs as part of a range of service users' needs and, in some contexts, this may be important to service users. Also, religiously affiliated organizations tend to construct response to need as not only the preserve of service professions but the responsibility of the whole faith community. From this perspective, these agencies are able to draw on members of their faith community to provide support and care outside the official service contract between the funding body and religious organization (Harris et al., 2003). For example, a religiously affiliated employment service may be able to involve businesspeople within their community to provide employment opportunities for service users, or a religiously affiliated mental health service may be able to involve community members in general social support of people living with mental illness. In this way, services based in religious communities may, in some instances, offer more comprehensive and cost-efficient services than secular organizations (Harris et al., 2003, p. 95).

Despite these benefits, many social work commentators raise concerns about the religious and spiritual discourse in social service provision. These concerns include that religious institutions have, historically, played a role in the oppression and dispossession of some service user groups. For example, in countries such as Australia and Canada, mainstream churches are charged with historical involvement in the colonization of Indigenous people through missionary activities that failed to recognize their spiritual belief systems and sought instead to impose Christian belief systems on them. Also, as historical and recent investigations have shown, religiously based child welfare institutions were the site of great care, but also of horrific abuse for the children in their care and protection. Thus, some groups of service users, such as the adult survivors of child welfare institutions, may be reluctant to accept services from religious organizations. Alongside this, we also need to consider that religious or spiritual discourses can sometimes be malevolent. As Holloway and Moss (2010, p. 37) observe:

> we need to acknowledge that not all religions and spiritual expressions are benign in their human intent. Satanism and the Nazi exultation of the music of Wagner are two examples which we would put in this category.

A further criticism is that religious discourses are incompatible with the human science discourses through which professional social work is constituted. Some hold the view that religious and spiritual ideas are incompatible with the image of a modern profession as founded in rational and objective knowledge (Edwards, 2002).

Another area of conflict is that religious and secular community services may construct their primary purpose in different and quite conflicting ways. Members of religious communities, as well as secular commentators, question whether religious organizations should be involved in non-religious service provision. Some members of faith-based services are concerned that government funding will dilute the religious mission and value base of their services (Levine, 1998, p. 123). The autonomy of religious organizations is severely constrained by dependence on government funding as, for example, programmes are shaped by funding criteria and the require-ments of the service contract. This can constrain the activities of religiously affiliated service providers. For example, religiously based services may have a core mission to advocate for the poor and the oppressed, yet their service contract may also require them to refrain from public critique of govern-ment policy.

Some commentators raise concerns about the potential inaccessibility and inappropriateness of faith-based services to non-religious service users and service providers. As Levine (1998, p. 133) points out: 'Clearly, sectarian agencies were established to serve the needs of distinctive clienteles or promulgate specific goals.' These goals may conflict with social service provision. For example, youth and family support agencies often provide services, such as referral to family planning services or information on safe sex practices, that may conflict with the belief systems of some religiously affiliated organizations. Similarly, some service providers may be reluctant to access services with links to specific religious groups, even if these links are primarily historical associations. For instance, a Muslim family may feel reluctant to use the services of an organization with a Christian title.

Further concerns are raised about the potential for religious discrimina-tion against service providers and other personnel involved in the adminis-tration and delivery of social services. Most religious organizations have a core mission to spread the word and the love of God and see it as essential that organizational members, including service providers, share this mission. In many countries, faith-based organizations in receipt of govern-ment funds must comply with equal opportunities legislation associated with freedom of religion (see Levine, 1998, p. 128; National Secular Society, 2012). Yet, discrimination against people of other faiths, or of no faith, may occur in quite subtle ways. For example, Hutchison (1998, p. 68) concedes that religious organizations

> enunciate a spiritual interpretation of reality that views persons as members of communities that provide the type of support and interaction that leads to health growth and development. They try to recruit board and staff who share similar values.

This emphasis on similarity of values can also lead to the marginalization of groups that do not identify with these mainstream Christian or religious traditions, such as people of indigenous faiths, Buddhists, Hindus, Sikhs or

Muslims. Other forms of religious differentiation are less subtle. For instance, faith-based community service organizations often require employers to declare acceptance of the religious mission of the organization; this can take the form of workers' statement of willingness to work in sympathy with the value stance through to much more constrictive practices such as requiring employees to sign a statement of faith or show evidence of church attendance as a condition of employment (Levine, 1998, p. 128).

Practice Exercise **Recognizing spiritual needs**

Imagine you are a social worker at a haematology oncology (blood cancers) unit of a paediatric hospital. The children who are inpatients in this unit often face extremely painful treatments and a substantial minority of them die from their cancers. Many families attending the unit have complained to you that, while they are happy with the standard of medical and nursing interventions, they do not believe that their spiritual needs are being adequately acknowledged at this time of great spiritual need for them.

Concerns have been raised by families from a range of religious dominations, although those of non-Christian faiths appear to have experienced least recognition of their spiritual practices. In particular, families of non-Christian faiths have stated that hospital staff members have usually ignored their requests for recognition of their spiritual practices, such as blessing their child's room prior to the child's initial entry to it, or opportunities for prayer time with the child prior to major medical interventions.

- How would you, as a social worker, go about promoting greater recognition of religious and spiritual need and diversity in this practice context?

Environmental Social Work

Over the past two decades, as public debate and concern have grown about the impact of climate change, environmental discourses have become important considerations in many areas of public policy. In the past five years, an environmental social work literature has emerged, seeking to articulate how environmental discourses can reshape the foundations of our profession (Besthorn, 2012; Dominelli, 2012; Gray et al., 2013). The emerging discourse, referred to here as 'environmental social work' challenges the profession's privilege of the human environment and emphasis on rational problem solving; features that contribute to the neglect of the non-human environment and holistic responses to human need. Besthorn (2001, p. 38), a leading proponent of the environmental social work discourse, argues that deep ecology perspectives require social workers to 'seek holistic and spiritually sensitive ways of thinking and practising ... and a new way of being with oneself, others, and the world around us'.

The features of the environmental social work discourse are still being debated; however, several themes can be discerned. First, recognition of the physical environment is a necessary extension of the 'person-in-environment' perspective that has long shaped the profession. Drawing on deep ecology, Besthorn (2012, p. 255) argues that 'Deep justice ... recognizes all things in the cosmos as nested in a complex web of interconnections between the human and non-human. All are seen to have intrinsic worth and moral considerability.'

Second, environmental social workers argue that the value of social justice compels the profession to become involved in movements for environmental sustainability. As McKinnon (2013, p. 156) states: 'it is becoming more and more obvious that negative environmental consequences are experienced disproportionately by the most vulnerable members of society'. According to the environmental social work discourse, social workers have an ethical duty to address environmental issues in part because environmental degradation disproportionately affects disadvantaged populations (Dominelli, 2012; McKinnon, 2013).

Proponents of the environmental social work discourse urge social workers to engage in the critical interrogation surrounding the distribution of environmental resources and in building the reliance and sustainability of local communities. For example, Dominelli (2012, p. 62) suggests that social workers should ensure that 'locally relevant and culturally appropriate strategies are put in place that respect people, living things that share their habitats and the physical environment in their communities'. Although some argue that the environmental social work discourse should shape all realms of social work (McKinnon, 2013), the articulation of environmental practice implications has, to date, aligned the discourse with macro-practice methods, particularly policy advocacy and community development. The implications for reshaping practice contexts in health and welfare institutions where the practice focus is primarily with individuals and families is unclear.

Despite the growing interest in environmental social work, there are good reasons for social workers to adopt a critical and cautious attitude towards this discourse. The first issue concerns whether environmental social work offers new insights or opportunities for social workers. Since its inception, the profession of social work has been characterized by a person-in-environment focus. The concept of social sustainability may be less about the reorientation of practice, and more a reminder of the profession's responsibility for achieving changes in the social environment.

Conversely, social workers need to question the extent to which activities to achieve environmental sustainability are within the scope of social work practice. While there can be little doubt that service users are more likely than others to be disproportionately affected by environmental degradation, social workers are not typically engaged in the kinds of activities that create environmental harm, nor does the profession have substantial capacity to influence those industries from which the majority of such harm arises. The capacity and scope for social workers to influence industries such as mining, global transportation or chemical manufacturers are limited. Furthermore, by seeking to incorporate environmental sustainability activities in our practice, we risk displacing or ignoring those aspects of our work, such as mental health and family support or child protection work, for which social workers' expertise is well established.

Third, there is a concern that the uncritical embrace of the concept of social sustainability may lead social workers to absolve government and private industry of their need to change. Smith (2010, p. 51) asserts that the concept of social sustainability often referred to within the discourse of environmental social work can support a neoliberal agenda:

> The rhetoric is to devolve power to citizens, who with the help of the TS [third sector] (alongside the local state) will act as 'neoliberal subjects' and address the tensions of neoliberalism by promoting social capacity, social cohesion and communitarianism.

The concern here is that, far from promoting social justice, social sustainability can be used by government to absolve itself of responsibility for the harms arising from unjust social and environmental policies.

Conclusion

In this chapter we have considered the ways in which alternative discourses construct client needs and service missions. We have considered how discourses associated with citizen rights, religion and spirituality, and environmental social work can extend our capacities to achieve our practice purposes and, in particular, how these ideas challenge the dominant discourses shaping many contemporary practice contexts. Yet, these discourses, like all discourses, carry within them truth claims that can silence other ways of knowing and responding to the needs of service users and realizing our purpose and values in practice.

Summary Questions

1 Thinking about your area of social work practice, or an area you intend to work in, identify what you see as the strengths and limits of the citizen rights discourse for achieving social justice with and for service users.

2 How do religious discourses shape social work practices today?

3 Some social workers and service users argue that social workers should respond to the client's spiritual needs as an essential dimension of holistic practice. What is your view?

4 What are the themes within an environmental social work discourse?

Recommended Reading

Citizen Rights

● Shakespeare, T. (2006) *Disability Rights and Wrongs*. (Hoboken, NJ: Taylor & Francis).
Critically examines the key principles of a social model of disability and the disability rights movement. Critiques the social model for failing to adequately acknowledge the role of impairment in terms of the lived experience of disability and options for creating greater justice and social inclusion for people living with disabilities. Fascinating account of different philosophical conceptions of disability as they play out in medical, social care and activist approaches to practice.

Religion and Spirituality

● Bennett, B., Green, S., Gilbert, S. and Bessarab, D. (2013) *Our Voices: Aboriginal and Torres Strait Islander Social Work*. (South Yarra: Palgrave Macmillan).
Written by Aboriginal and Torres Strait Islander social workers in Australia, it incorporates discussion of the nature and significance of spiritual ceremonies and how social workers can demonstrate respect for the spiritual dimensions of social work practice with Aboriginal and Torres Strait Islander people.

● Holloway, M. and Moss, B. (2010) *Spirituality and Social Work*. (Basingstoke: Palgrave Macmillan).
Comprehensive introduction to contemporary debates about religion and spirituality in social work practice, with a clear analysis of social workers' responsibility and role in recognizing religious and spiritual aspects of social work practice.

● Lindsay, R. (2002) *Recognising Spirituality: The Interface between Faith and Social Work*. (Crawley, WA: University of Western Australia Press).
Examines the history of religious organizations in the development of professional social work. Reports on a study of social workers' and service users' experiences of religious and

spiritual themes in social work practices. Useful for all interested in this topic but especially recommended for Australian readers.

Environmental Social Work

- Dominelli, L. (2012) *Green Social Work: From Environmental Crises to Environmental Justice.* (Cambridge, Polity Press).
  Considers environmental issues from a social work perspective. Argues for the inclusion of the physical and natural environment in which we live as part of the scope of social work practice. Analyses and seeks to extend the role of social workers in the continuum of practice from the prevention of environmental degradation to the creation of more environmentally just societies.

- Gray, M., Coates, J. and Hetherington, T. (eds) (2013) *Environmental Social Work.* (New York: Routledge).
  Includes works by some of the leading authors in the emerging field of environmental social work. Seeks to draw attention to the limitations of an almost exclusive focus on social systems in social work and encourage the incorporation of the natural environment and recognition of environmental issues within social work practice.

- Mary, N.L. (2008) *Social Work in a Sustainable World.* (Chicago: Lyceum).
  Outlines the case for a shift in social work discourse to the embrace of environmental concepts. Drawing on the historical development of the profession, argues that social workers must engage with concepts of environmental sustainability and change if the profession is to make a meaningful difference to the significant environmental challenges facing the world and affecting disadvantaged populations most.

Recommended Website

- **www.un.org/disabilities**
  The United Nations Enable website is dedicated to disability issues. Provides information on the Declaration of the Human Rights of People with Disabilities and other information about UN support for the social and economic participation of people with disabilities.

PART 3

SOCIAL WORK THEORIES FOR PRACTICE

We turn now to theories for practice. Consistent with other social work theorists (Howe, 1987, p. 16; Payne, 2005), the term 'theories for professional practice', also known as social work theories, is used here to refer to formal theories intended to guide and explain social work practices. They have been developed for social workers in relation to specific domains of social work practice. As outlined in the dynamic model of social work practice (Figure 2.1), formal theories are integral to the professional base of social work. These theories substantially shape our purpose in social work practice, as they define who or what should be the subject of social work intervention and the practical approaches social work should use to achieve their purposes as presented in these theories.

Chapters 6–10 consider five sets of social work theories (see Figure P3), each with distinct ways on constructing our professional purpose, practice principles and applications.

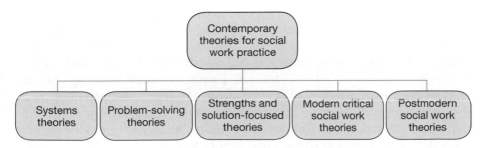

Figure P3 Contemporary theories for social work practice

In this introduction to the five groups of theories for practice, we critically consider the historical, geographical and institutional contexts in which each approach was developed and for which it was originally intended. In each chapter, we consider at least one (and sometimes more) specific theories for practice that have emerged within each group. We consider the assumptions, principles and techniques for application of the theories in practice. This critical review of the context in which the theory emerged and the assumptions and principles underpinning it is intended to assist you, the reader, to evaluate the potential and limits of each theory for your context of social work practice.

These five approaches have been selected on a number of criteria, all centred on the relevance of theories to social work practice. The first criterion is relevance to the contemporary institutional contexts of health and welfare services. Social work is usually performed by social workers in health and welfare agencies, rather than by individual service providers; this is especially the case for novice social workers (Donnellan and Jack, 2010). In these contexts, social workers often face significant time and other resource constraints, which make resource-intensive approaches, such as psychodynamic approaches, unfeasible. Indeed, although we have outlined the continuing influence of psychodynamic ideas on mainstream practice, the complete psychodynamic framework is rarely used as a guiding theory for practice in mainstream service agencies. For this reason, and because of the extensive criticism of psychodynamic approaches by social workers (see Chapter 4), they are not included here. These same constraints make more structured and time-limited approaches to practice, such as task-centred practice (see Chapter 7), relevant to many practice contexts.

The second criterion is relevance to the purpose of social work as it is constructed through our value base and within contemporary practice contexts. All the social work theories discussed emphasize, and promote, partnership between service providers and service users. Partnership approaches are consistent with the core social work values of promoting client self-determination and equity (Trotter, 2013). In addition, the notion of partnership has become enshrined in policy and legislation in a range of health and welfare fields from disability to child protection services (for a discussion, see Campbell and Oliver, 1996; K. Healy, 1998; Connolly and Morris, 2012). The new emphasis on partnership contributed to the convergence of influences from the political Right (as seen in the increasing influence of neoclassical economic discourse), which has tended to emphasize service user self-responsibility, and the political Left (as reflected in the new social movements associated with citizen rights discourses), which has supported a rights-based approach to service provision. In various ways, these divergent political forces and discourses have led to a growing concern about professional expertise and welfare state paternalism. This, in turn, has contributed to increased policy support for partnership-based approaches to practice.

The third criterion is the relevance of the theories to the formal knowledge base of social work. All the theories we consider are substantially developed within social work practice and by researchers and practitioners associated with the social work field. Reference to theories for practice developed from other disciplines have been incorporated, such as motivational interviewing, but only where they can assist in the development or implementation of theories for social work practice. Some theories for social work practice might also be described as interdisciplinary, such as solution-focused theories and narrative approaches. Importantly, while acknowledging their interdisciplinary base, we demonstrate that social workers were substantially involved in leading the development of these theories and articulating their relevance to social work practices (see White and Epston, 1990; Berg, 2000; Berg and Kelly, 2000; White, 2003).

A fourth criterion is that of extending the boundaries of the social work theory base. In recent decades, 'post' theories, such as postmodernism and poststructuralism, have influenced social sciences and social work theory development. The reputation and popularity of narrative therapy, which is derived from postmodern theories, have also contributed to growing practitioner interest in these theories. Chapter 10 provides an accessible introduction to 'post' theories and shows that social workers often use postmodern concepts in practice, as they recognize context and individual differences in constructing their understanding of client needs and their practice purposes.

In each case, we consider the original contexts and purposes for which these theories were developed and applied, as well as principles and techniques for the application of these theories in practice. The intention is not to direct you to choose a particular approach, but to assist you to actively engage in constructing your purpose and to make informed choices about the possibilities offered by contemporary social work theories for your practice.

6

THREE WAVES OF SYSTEMS THEORIES

Systems perspectives underpin knowledge development in the social work profession. Some social work theorists argue that recognition of the systemic character of human problems and the need for intervention to improve the interaction between the client and their broader environment distinguishes social work from other human service professions (see Meyer, 1976). Systemic analyses focus on interactions within and across multiple 'social' systems, which can include the interpersonal system of family and friendship ties, neighbourhood systems, organizational systems, social policy systems, and social structural systems. Systems theory emphasizes the role of these systems in contributing to individual and community wellbeing and for providing multiple points for social work intervention to improve the fit between the individual and their social environment.

The enduring popularity of systems theories in social work texts and in practice can be attributed to their concordance with social work's long-standing mission to understand and respond to people in their environment (Gordon, 1969, p. 6; Bartlett, 1970, p. 89). Systems theories provide ways of understanding problems and issues; however, it is widely agreed that systems frameworks do not provide intervention methods (see Leighninger, 1978; Wakefield, 1996a, 1996b; Mattaini and Meyer, 2002). The development of complex systems theories over the past three decades has contributed to renewed attention to the development of systems perspectives in social work (see Warren et al., 1998; Hudson, 2000; Stevens and Cox, 2008; Wolf-Branigin, 2009).

In this chapter, we consider the origins of systems perspectives in social work. We discuss the assumptions and practice applications of three waves of systems perspectives – general systems theory, ecosystems perspectives, and complex and chaos theories. We conclude with a discussion of the strengths and limitations of systems perspectives in practice.

Systems Theories in Context

Systems theories, like all the theories for practice we consider, draw on discourses originating outside the social work field. So, while systems theories have helped to guide and explain our work, the core concepts within these theories are not developed in, or intended for, social work practice. In Figure 6.1, systems theories are placed first to reflect their historical position as the first set of theories that social workers adapted specifically for use in social work practice. First, we consider the origins and application of systems theories in social work.

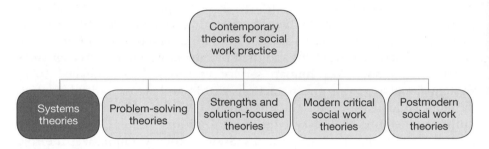

Figure 6.1 Systems theories in context

The Origins of Systems Theory in Social Work

According to Woods and Hollis (1990), Frank Hankins, a US sociologist at the Smith College School of Social Work, first introduced the term 'systems theory' to social work in 1930. Yet, even before the term was proposed, social workers in the emerging profession adopted a 'person-in-environment' perspective (Kemp et al., 1997, p. 23; see Richmond, 1917). Richmond (1917, p. 365) argued that social workers must balance personal and social change orientations, as she asserted that 'social reform and social case work must of necessity progress together'.

During the middle part of the century, a psychological focus dominated social work practice knowledge, particularly in the USA (Kemp et al., 1997, p. 21). It was not until the 1960s that a dual focus on the person and their environment returned to prominence in social work theory. In 1964, Florence Hollis, a leading social work theorist, urged social workers to adopt a 'psychosocial' perspective, that is, to recognize the 'social and psychological' aspects of assessment intervention (Woods and Hollis, 1990, p. 14). At this time, psychodynamic theory had lost its power as a unifying influence in social work and the profession was fragmenting as a result of tensions between social workers adopting psychological approaches and those seeking to address the societal contexts of practice. During the 1960s and 70s, some commentators argued that systems theory could provide a unifying framework for the profession, as it recognized the diverse systems, individual and social, in which social workers intervene (see Bartlett, 1970).

The First Wave: General Systems Theory

While systems theories have been referred to by the social work profession since the 1930s, it was not until the 1960s that social workers articulated a distinctive systemic approach to practice. During this period, Gordon Hearn and his colleagues in the National Association of Social Workers in the USA pioneered the application of this theory to social work (Hudson, 2000, p. 216; see also Hearn, 1969). The initial proponents of systems theory emphasized its potential to provide scientific credibility to the profession and develop an integrated theoretical foundation that would 'capture the central elements of social work practice in all its varied forms' (Gordon, 1969, p. 5). General systems theory (GST) challenged the individualistic focus evident in much of the professional social work literature during the middle part of the last century and encouraged social workers to give 'substantially more attention to environmental change' (Hearn, 1969, p. 65).

General systems theory was derived from Ludwig von Bertalanffy and sociological attempts to apply biological systems theories to the social world (Leighninger, 1978, p. 448). From his earliest writings, dating back to the 1920s onwards, von Bertalanffy (1968, pp. 11–12), a biologist, argued that systems approaches were more appropriate than 'causal' models for dealing with complex interactions in all types of systems – biological, mechanical and social. Von Bertalanffy (1968) argued that systems ideas were relevant to human services professions, such as psychology and psychiatry. He challenged behaviourist views that presented humans as 'reactive automatons' and instead argued for recognition of 'active personality systems' (von Bertalanffy, 1968, p. 207). By drawing attention to the *transactions* between the individual and their social environment, von Bertalanffy (1968, p. 219) proposed that an individual's mental health can only be understood in relation to whether the individual has 'an integrated framework consistent within the given cultural framework'; in other words, from a general systems perspective, mental health challenges are considered to be produced through the exchange between the individual and their cultural environment rather than arising primarily from the individual psyche. Von Bertalanffy (1968, p. 219) challenged psychotherapists to redirect their attention from 'digging up the past' to a focus on insight into current conflicts, attempts at social and psychological reintegration, and orientation towards future goals. This proposal was a radical departure from the psychoanalytic frameworks that dominated social work, psychiatry and psychology during the middle part of the last century. Today, systems perspectives can be used to challenge the individualistic focus of the dominant discourses shaping health and welfare services, as discussed in Chapter 3.

General Systems Concepts

The original proponents of GST used biological terminology when applying this perspective to social work. Although this terminology was intended to enhance the scientific credibility of social work, many social workers were alienated by it. Here, we consider some of the core concepts in GST – transaction, homeostasis, entropy, equifinality and feedback. We will use the case study of Stella to consider how we can apply GST concepts.

Case Study **Stella**

Stella is a 10-year-old girl with mild autism. Autism is a developmental disability that affects an individual's perception of, and capacity to interact with, their social environment. Autism is more commonly diagnosed among males than females, so Stella's situation is a little unusual. Stella was diagnosed with autism as a young child and she also has a mild intellectual disability. She has not attended any specific programmes or therapy for her autism. Her parents are committed to ensuring Stella's participation in mainstream society, and she has always attended mainstream nurseries and schools.

Stella and her parents have come to see you in your role as a social worker in a children's mental health service. Stella and her parents are worried about the problems Stella has experienced in developing a friendship network. Stella has encountered bullying at school, none of the children want to play with her and they push her and call her names. Stella has some large bruises on her arms and legs as a result of the physical bullying, but, from Stella's perspective, her biggest problem is her lack of friends. Stella's parents are distressed not only by her isolation but also by the aggression to which she has been subjected. They have previously tried changing schools but the problems re-emerged at this new school she now attends. They would like to keep Stella at the school as they feel she has some supportive teachers who could be enlisted to help her.

Transaction

First, the concept of 'transaction' between person and environment is central to GST (Gordon, 1969, p. 7). From a general systems perspective, the role of the social worker is to understand the transactions between the individual and their environment and to promote change in the transactions 'for the purpose of producing growth-inducing and environmental-ameliorating transactions' (Gordon, 1969, p. 10). Focusing on transactions, social workers seek to analyse the 'inputs' from individual or environment and then 'throughputs' from the 'organism to the environment and from environment to organism' (Gordon, 1969, p. 7). In Stella's case, a transactional analysis would focus, in part, on identifying her input into the situation she is encountering. For example, we would explore Stella's communication skills and behaviours to understand, with Stella and her parents, how her behaviour might contribute to the hostility she is encountering. A transactional analysis would also attend to how aspects of the environment provoke and sustain the problems Stella is encountering. For example, we might explore what resources are missing, such as disability support services in the school, that might facilitate Stella's participation in her school environment.

Homeostasis

The concept of 'homeostasis' refers to 'the tendency of a biological organism to seek and keep some kind of operating balance in its internal processes, or, at least, to keep processes within certain limits' (Leighninger, 1978, p. 448). Social workers took this concept to mean that the maintenance of a steady state is 'essential for growth of the human organism' (Bartlett, 1970, p. 103; see also Gordon, 1969). Working with Stella, we could use the concept of homeostasis in at least two ways. First, it would enable us to recognize resistance to change in Stella and in the many systems in which she is operating. For instance, the school community may resist change because they perceive a threat to current resource allocation; in other words, they may fear that if resources are directed to resolving Stella's issues, then other school issues may be neglected. One way of resolving this is to work with the school to secure improved resource allocation for children with disabilities. A second way we can use homeostasis is to seek improved environmental conditions that are vital for human growth. Stella's parents don't wish to change her school arrangements, so we could explore other non-school options for Stella to develop a peer network. Here, we might focus on Stella's talents and capacities, in arts or sports for example, that could be used to link her to a non-school network.

Entropy

The concept of 'entropy' refers to the 'the tendency in the universe to move towards disorder' (Hearn, 1969, p.65). Bringing together the notion that homeostasis was essential and entropy should be controlled, Hearn (1969, p. 66) argued that the role of the social worker was to increase the order of the individual and environmental systems with which they work. Returning to Stella, from a general systems perspective, we can understand Stella's social environment to be in a state of entropy, insofar as there are dysfunctional interactions between Stella and her peers and the school environment. The role of the social worker here is to improve the transactions between the environments and, in so doing, reduce the entropy within and between systems.

Equifinality

Equifinality is the assumption that there are always multiple solutions to a problem (Leighninger, 1978, p. 452). The practical implication of this concept, according to Mattaini and Meyer (2002, p. 6) is: 'One might enter a case through multiple avenues, more than one of which will lead to comparable results.' Applying this concept to Stella's situation, we can see that there are multiple systems in which we might intervene to address her problems. Rather than seeking a single correct solution, we can consider a broad range of intervention approaches that could include:

● family counselling to enable Stella and her parents to deal with the stress they are encountering

● social skills training with Stella, including developing her capacity to assert her rights to emotional and physical safety

● intervention at the school, including meeting teaching staff to develop strategies for reducing bullying and seeking funding for a disability support worker in the school

● policy interventions aimed at increasing recognition of, and resource allocation to, children with disabilities.

The principle of equifinality suggests that all these interventions could contribute to change in the issues confronting Stella.

Feedback

The concept of 'negative feedback' refers to the processes of monitoring and correction through which systems regulate themselves (Leighninger, 1978, p. 460). An example of this is learning and changing our behaviour on the basis of past experiences (Bartlett, 1970, p. 103). In Stella's situation, we could identify past situations where Stella has successfully managed problems like those she now faces and how we might incorporate these strategies into her current environment.

The concept of 'positive feedback' is a process by which the characteristics of a system are amplified and become entrenched. For instance, in social systems, we often see that certain differences, such as those attributed to class, gender and ethnicity, are reinforced and ingrained within myriad social relationships. In GST, then, the term 'positive feedback' does not refer to qualities that are necessarily positive, but rather that this form of feedback 'feeds on itself and breaks out of old bounds, creating either precipitous breakdown or seemingly sudden leaps to higher levels of creativity and functioning' (Hudson, 2000, p. 218). In Stella's situation, this concept could be used to analyse how the bullying behaviour towards her has become entrenched and to explore what sorts of intervention might 'short-circuit' this behaviour.

General systems theory contributed to the development of a number of practice models, most prominent being the unitary models presented by Pincus and Minahan (1973) and Goldstein (1973). They had significant international influence in the development of social work theories for practice (see Specht and Vickery, 1977; Boas and Crawley, 1975). Ultimately, however, many social workers have judged GST to be fundamentally flawed (see Mune, 1979; Payne, 1994, p. 9). Critics argue that its reliance on abstract concepts and the 'mechanistic, nonhuman nature of much of its language' alienated most practising social workers (Kemp et al., 1997, p. 4; see also Mune, 1979). In addition, GST maintained a relatively narrow focus on the interaction between the individual and their immediate environment and, as such, did not address the issue of broader systems and structures on service users' lives. A further criticism is that the concept of 'system equilibrium' led to an over-emphasis on system maintenance functions and negative feedback loops in sustaining problems (Hudson, 2000, p. 217). For example, the violent behaviour of a family member could be seen as a symptom of the system and thus something for which all family members were responsible. Proponents of the second wave of systems theories attempted to overcome these problems.

The Second Wave: Ecosystems Perspectives

During the 1970s, the ecosystems approach to practice superseded GST. Germain and Gitterman's life model of social work practice and the ecosystems work of Carol Meyer are widely identified as the leading formulations of ecosystems perspectives in social work (Wakefield, 1996a, 1996b; Payne, 1997, p. 143; see also Kemp et. al., 1997, p. 41). Here, we focus on the work of these social work leaders.

The ecosystems perspective brings together GST with an ecological view to expand the focus and relevance of systems perspectives to direct social work practice. The ecosystems perspective retains the GST notion of environmental wholeness, that is, recognition that the parts of the system can never be entirely separated from each other (Mattaini and Meyer, 2002, p. 6). Some of the biological terminology used in GST is also retained in ecosystems models (Mattaini and Meyer, 2002, pp. 11–13).

Ecosystems thinkers use ecology as a metaphor for encouraging social workers to focus on transactions within and across systems and to seek sustainable, not only short-term, change (Kemp et al., 1997, p. 44; Mattaini and Meyer, 2002, p. 8). On the basis of this metaphor, systems theorists argue that social work assessment and intervention should focus on 'person:environment' transactions (Mattaini and Meyer, 2002, p. 6; see also Meyer, 1976, p. 129). Proponents of the ecosystems approach use the distinctive term 'person:environment' to 'repair the conceptually fractured relationship' between person and environment (Germain and Gitterman, 1996, p. 1). Drawing on the ecological metaphor, person:environment transactions are understood to be complex and nonlinear. In recognizing complexity, Germain and Gitterman (1996, p. 7) discourage social workers from searching for 'original causes', whether they be psychological or socio-logical in nature, and instead focus on understanding and intervention to improve person:environment exchanges.

Second, the ecosystems perspective encourages social workers to recognize that problems arise because of 'a poor fit between a person's environment and his or her needs, capacities, rights, and aspirations' (Germain and Gitterman, 1996, p. 8). Lack of fit between the person and their environment can occur for many reasons, including anticipated life transitions like retire-ment, as well as chronic environmental stressors, such as poverty. Addressing earlier criticisms that the ecosystems perspective failed to address structural injustices, later formulations incorporated a recognition of power, 'habitat' or social location, and diversity of lifestyles (see Germain and Gitterman, 1996).

Third, the purpose of intervention is to improve these transactions by promoting adaptation between the person and their environment. According to Germain and Gitterman (1996, p. 5), 'the ecological metaphor helps the profession enact its social purpose of helping people and promoting respon-sive environments that support human growth, health, and satisfaction in human functioning'. Proponents of the ecosystems approach frequently contend that it is the focus on enhancing systemic transactions, rather than improving the functioning of isolated systems, that distinguishes social work from other human service professions such as psychiatry and psychology.

Like the general systems approach, an ecosystems perspective guides assessment and offers general directions for intervention, but it does not propose specific intervention methods (Germain and Gitterman, 1996, p. 45; Mattaini and Meyers, 2002, p. 18). The ecosystems perspective is intended to enable social workers to recognize complexity and avoid reduc-tionism in assessment and intervention.

The Life Model of Social Work Practice

Here, we discuss the application of ecosystems perspectives using 'the life model of social work practice' formulated by Carel Germain and Alex Gitterman (1996). The life model is characterized by three stages – initial, ongoing and ending. We discuss each of these phases by reference to the following case study.

Case Study **Tracy**

Imagine you are a social worker practising in a family support service. The social worker from the juvenile detention centre has referred Tracy to you to provide supportive case-work focused on the impending birth of her first child. Tracy is 17 years old and is seven months pregnant. Since she was 14, Tracy has spent extended periods in youth detention for a series of stealing offences, and has recently been released from a youth detention centre.

Tracy is of Anglo origin and her ex-partner, the father of the unborn child, is originally from India. Tracy does not plan for him to have any role in the parenting of the child. His family does not know about Tracy's pregnancy. Tracy has a difficult relationship with her parents; she was placed in foster care as a young child due to her parents' alcoholism. Tracy has no relationship with her foster family; she states that she was sexually abused by her foster father and wants nothing to do with that family. Apart from the periods in detention, Tracy has been homeless since she was 14.

Tracy's sister Leanne has now offered Tracy a place to stay for as long as she needs. Leanne is 24 years old and has two children (6 and 3). Tracy is happy to accept Leanne's offer and she tells you she has always had a good relationship with Leanne. In the referral file from the government authority, you learn that Tracy would like to return to school. While in detention, she made good progress with her formal education and would like to complete school. You also learn that the government authority plans to monitor Tracy's parenting as there are concerns about her capacity to care for the child, given her family background and her own harmful use of drugs and alcohol. Tracy has received rehabilitation treatment for heavy use of alcohol, dating back to when she was 14, and she also acknowledges that she has occasionally used heroin. However, Tracy insists that while she has been pregnant, she has not used drugs and has limited her alcohol consumption.

Initial phase: getting started

The primary purpose of the initial phase is for the social worker and service user to establish an active partnership based on 'mutuality and reciprocity' (Germain and Gitterman, 1996, p. 94). This partnership recognizes social workers' and service users' different knowledge and skills: 'Social workers bring professional knowledge and skill to the therapeutic encounter. Those served bring experiential knowledge of their life issues and their life stories' (Germain and Gitterman, 1996, p. 94). This purpose is achieved, first, by the demonstration of empathy. Thus, we would aim to clarify how Tracy sees her situation and, particularly, what she would like to achieve through her work with you. We should also clarify our role, including any obligations and constraints imposed by the agency or other statutory authority.

Second, in this first phase, the worker and service user work together to identify and, where necessary, prioritize 'life stressors'. Germain and Gitterman (1996, p. 60) describe a life stressor as an event or transition that contributes to maladaptation in the 'person:environment' fit. Together with Tracy, we would identify her strengths and capacities as well as the stressors in her life.

Ongoing phase: working towards goals

Our primary purpose in this phase is to promote adaptation in the 'person:environment' relationship so as to maximize Tracy's wellbeing and that of her child (Germain and Gitterman, 1996, p. 8). An ecological assessment forms the foundation of practice in this phase. The central skills involved are goal clarification, facilitation, coordination, and individual and systemic advocacy (Germain and Gitterman, 1996). In an ecological assessment, the service provider and service user work together to gather data about, and analyse the impact of, multiple systems on the service user's situation.

Many ecosystems theorists use an ecomap to assist the assessment process (see Meyer, 1993; Mattaini and Meyer, 2002). The ecomap is a 'graphic system for viewing the relevant connected case-elements together, within a boundary that clarifies for the practitioner the case system as the focus of work' (Mattaini and Meyer, 2002, p. 4). This pictorial representation enhances our capacity to see the complexities in the service user's situation much more powerfully than words alone (Meyer, 1993, Ch. 6). In addition, the use of an ecomap can also enhance client opportunities to participate in the assessment.

There are many ways of representing an ecomap (see Meyer, 1993). Many social work commentators use Brofenbrenner's (1979) approach, in which a series of concentric rings represent different system levels (Figure 6.2). In this model, microsystem refers to informal systems, such as home, the family and the local community, mesosystem refers to formal systems that have a direct impact on service users' lives, such as schools and social services, and macrosystem refers to society as a whole and the large social institutions of government and business.

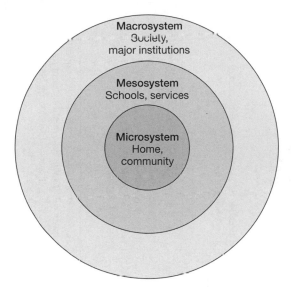

Figure 6.2 An ecomap framework

Using an ecomap, we would assess the impact of different systems on Tracy's situation and, on this basis, develop a plan for action directed at each of these systems, as shown in Table 6.1.

Within the overaching goal of enhancing person:environment fit, one of our primary purposes in this phase is to enhance and strengthen service users' 'adaptive capacities and problem-solving abilities' and promote environmental adaptedness (Germain and Gitterman, 1996, p. 50). The social worker's role, then, is to promote change at the micro-, messo- and macro-levels. Germain and Gitterman (1996, p. 50) suggest that the social worker enhances service user capacities through 'the methods of enabling, exploring, mobilizing, guiding, and facilitating'. One way we could enhance Tracy's capacity is by recognizing the strengths she already possesses. For instance, we acknowledge the capacities Tracy has demonstrated by surviving her abuse experiences and life on the streets. In the role of 'guide', we could help Tracy identify strategies for meeting identified needs such as antenatal care.

From an ecosystems perspective, we would promote a supportive community for Tracy. Community support would ensure that she has some independence from her personal supports, such as her sister, and the health and welfare systems that have had such a dominant influence on her life. At a micro-level, we may seek to link Tracy to peers, such as young mothers, or young people returning to secondary education. If these community networks are absent, we may take an active role in creating these networks with Tracy.

Table 6.1 Ecosystem intervention plan for working with Tracy

System level	Strengths and concerns	Action	Methods
Microsystem – home and family	Has good relationship with older sister Leanne	Strengthen tie with sister	Casework, family support skills, knowledge of support agencies
	Is estranged from her parents; however, acknowledges that she would like them to be a part of her child's life	Address estrangement with family of origin	Consider a family group meeting with parents to work to improve family relationships
	Tracy also states she experienced sexual abuse by a foster father from age 10–12	Discuss with Tracy the impact of the abuse for her and consider options including legal redress and assistance with managing personal trauma	Consider referral for sexual assault and trauma counselling
Microsystem – community and neighbourhood	Tracy is recently released from a lengthy period in juvenile detention. She is also separated from her partner and has no support other than her sister. She is about to give birth and could benefit from links to other young parents	Address peer isolation	Link to peer network, work on social skills
		Address local community isolation	Link to community support services, particularly those that could assist in the transition to parenting e.g. birthing services and parenting support services
Mesosystem – institutions	Tracy has experienced significant educational disadvantage. When given the opportunity, has demonstrated interest in and potential for learning	Promote educational pathways for Tracy	Access information on educational opportunities; challenge barriers that might prevent return to school, e.g. absence of childcare facilities
Macrosystem – policy change	Government policy provides limited support for young parents to gain access to educational and employment opportunities and support them in their transition to parenting	Address lack of support services, educational and childcare options for young parents and homeless women	Use research and policy development on support services, educational, childcare and alternative care systems to promote policy change
		Address injustices faced by young people abused in foster care	Link Tracy to peer support and advocacy networks where she may work collectively with others to address the injustices confronting her

At an institutional level, we could support Tracy in her wish to return to school by identifying and facilitating her access to educational institutions. If we are unable to locate supportive institutions, we may need to advocate at local institutional and broader policy levels for increased access to education for Tracy and other young people in similar situations.

It is important that social workers are aware of, and responsive to, the need for policy change. According to Germain and Gitterman (1996, p. 53):

> social workers and clients seek to influence organizational practices and legislation and regulations at local, state, and national levels in the cause of social justice. The influencing method includes such skills as coalition-building; positioning; lobbying; and testifying.

Tracy's situation points to a number of public policy issues. Apart from the issue of support for young people to access educational opportunities, there are issues about the plight of young people abused in alternate care systems and the importance of early intervention and support systems for young parents.

Phase three: the ending phase

A well-planned termination of the intervention is integral to the overall structure of the systems approach (Germain and Gitterman, 1996, p. 56). Some practical ways we could prepare Tracy for the termination phase of our work together include discussing the duration of the intervention at the outset and regularly referring to it throughout the intervention process. Germain and Gitterman (1996, p. 59) stress that the social worker and the service user should discuss the practical implications of, as well as their emotional responses to, the termination of the service relationship. Consistent with the emphasis in ecosystems perspectives on comprehensive service delivery, we should engage Tracy in an evaluation of our work together and ensure that adequate plans are in place for her to access support once our intervention is complete.

The Third Wave: Complex Systems Theories

Since the late 1980s, a third wave of systems theories has gained growing recognition in the social work field. Known as 'complex systems' or 'complexity theories', they emerged originally in the disciplines of maths, physics and engineering (Bolland and Atherton, 1999; see also Capra, 1996). Chaos theory is a related theory (see Doll and Trueit, 2010). Drawing on the work of Byrne (1998), Stevens and Cox (2008, p. 1322) note that the term 'complexity theories' refers to complex adaptive systems, that is, the domain between 'linearly determined order and indeterminate chaos'. Proponents of complexity theories argue that open systems are dynamic and characterized by nonlinear change processes (Doll and Trueit, 2010).

Over the past three decades, these theories have had a growing impact on a range of fields including information technology, business, management, health sciences, social sciences and the humanities (Doll and Trueit, 2010). Colin Peile, Australian social work theorist, was among the earliest proponents of complex systems ideas in social work, as exemplified in his work on the creative paradigm (see Peile, 1988, 1993, 1994). During the late 1990s and early 2000s, several social work authors advocated for further consideration of complex systems theories in social work (see Warren et al., 1998; Bolland and Atherton, 1999; Hudson, 2000).

While this third wave of systems theory has not yet reached the status of a new paradigm for social work, as predicted by Hudson (2000), work on the applications of complex systems theories in social work is continuing (see Wolf-Branigin et al., 2007; Stevens and Cox, 2008; Wolf-Branigin, 2009; Green and McDermott, 2010; Jones, 2010; Doll and Trueit, 2010). Theorists argue that complexity theories provide a way of articulating the intuitive knowledge possessed by most social work practitioners about the nonlinearity and unpredictability of change processes (see Warren et al., 1998; Bolland and Atherton, 1999). These theorists argue that complex systems ideas enrich existing ideas about systems theories in social work (see Hudson, 2000; Stevens and Cox, 2008).

A complex system is one in which the behaviour of the whole system is greater than the sum of its parts. Darley (1994, p. 1) states that:

> The defining characteristic of a complex system is that some of its global behaviours, which are the result of interactions between a large number of relatively simple parts, cannot be predicted simply from the rules of those underlying interactions.

Complex systems researchers use inductive approaches to consider how local phenomena, including apparently simple interactions, contribute to evolution to larger complex systems. There are several features to complex systems.

First, complex systems are characterized by nonlinearity. A linear relationship features a constant relationship between two variables; for example, if the rate of unemployment in an area increases, there is a proportionate increase in the rate of crime. By contrast, in nonlinear relationships, a change in one variable, or set of variables, will be associated with disproportionate changes in another variable, or set of variables. For example, as the rate of unemployment in an area rises, there is a sudden and disproportionate increase in the rate of crime. The saying 'the straw that broke the camel's back' captures the idea of the disproportionate relationship between an event and an outcome where the outcome arises from a preceding accumulation of events rather than the final event itself (Hudson, 2000, p. 220).

Second, whereas general systems theorists suggest that, typically, social systems are stable, complexity theorists argue that change is a usual feature of complex social systems (Warren et al., 1998, pp. 364–5). Feedback mechanisms contribute to the growing complexity of these systems over time (Capra, 1996, p. 123). In particular, the complexity of relationships within systems is amplified by 'repeatedly self-reinforcing feedback' (Capra, 1996, p. 123) – similar to the concept of positive feedback in general systems theory. Within nonlinear systems, certain events, or experiences, can have a snowballing effect, that is, there is a repetition (or iteration) of the effect of the event or experience so that it has a disproportionate effect on the life of the individual, group, family or community. For example, some institutional care settings can exacerbate, rather than alleviate, a person's distress and illness by repeatedly reinforcing the 'sick role' to the point where the person becomes the role (see Goffman, 1991). Again, common expressions such as 'downhill slide' or, conversely, the idea of 'going from strength to strength' capture something of the concept of 'self-reinforcing feedback'.

Third, complex systems are characterized by extreme sensitivity to initial conditions. This means that small changes at initial phases in the system's development can lead to substantial and complex changes in the behaviour of the system (Capra, 1996, p. 132). Complexity theorists refer to this extreme sensitivity to small and initial changes in the system as the 'butterfly effect' – this metaphor is used because of the 'half-joking assertion that a butterfly stirring in Beijing today can cause a storm in New York next month' (Capra, 1996, p. 132). The butterfly effect is relevant to a globalized world, where changes in one part of the world can have immediate and substantial impact on other parts. Similarly, in social work practice, sometimes a short-term, well-timed intervention can have a disproportionately positive impact on the capacity of service users to achieve their goals. Indeed, recognition of the potential for a high impact in short-term interventions underpins practice models such as problem-solving and solution-focused therapy.

Fourth, complex systems are characterized by complex, rather than random, behaviour. Warren et al. (1998, p. 363) describe this as 'deterministic chaos'. Importantly, complexity and chaos theories do not imply that the 'real world' comprises random unpredictable events, rather that the behaviour of complex systems shows 'a deeper level of patterned order' (Capra, 1996, p. 122) than is suggested by the 'linear cause and effect models familiar to social scientists' (Warren et al., 1998, p. 358). For example, discussions on the disadvantages of location suggest that the choices parents make (or are constrained to make) about where they live can have a substantial impact on their children's educational outcomes, but these effects can be complex; with some studies showing that children from mixed income areas fare better than children in either uniformly high or low income areas (Carpiano et al., 2009). Complex systems theory recognizes that any 'outcome', such as children's wellbeing, is determined by the interaction of multiple factors, across interpersonal, community and structural contexts (Mainzer, 1996, pp. 279–80). Overall, complexity theorists do not see people as victims of their social context, nor do they see them as entirely free agents, rather there is a complex interaction between the person and their environment (Wolf-Branigin, 2009; Doll and Trueit, 2010).

Finally, the notion of 'phase change' used by complex systems theories is particularly relevant to social workers in community development contexts. 'Phase change' refers to the moment at which the system switches from one pattern of complexity to another (see Mainzer, 1996, p. 10). Warren et al. (1998, p. 364) observe that human systems can rapidly shift from one form of organization to another. For example, critical periods of phase change occur in communities undergoing processes of urban deterioration or gentrification. These are periods when the community quality of life indicators, such as rates of crime and levels of volunteering, indicate a qualitatively different place, either for better or worse. Understanding the processes of phase change could help us to advocate for policies that can promote or sustain positive changes in communities. For instance, if we can show that a certain level of social mix, such as number of homeowners in a geographical area, affects other outcomes such as child protection risk, we may use this information to argue for strategies to improve homeownership options in some communities (see Mainzer, 1996 p. 277).

Complex systems theories require us to question linear cause-and-effect notions and focus instead on understanding relationships, while recognizing that our understanding will, at best, only ever be partial. Doll and Trueit (2010, p. 846) assert that:

> To think complexly means to think in terms of relations, more to be-in-relation (with ourselves, our colleagues, the situation in which we find ourselves); to accept the relationality inherent in a situation; to realize that our interpretations of the complexity inherent in a situation are at best partial, and indeed may be different from another's interpretation, and to be humble in our own assessment of both the situation and our own interpretation.

Complex systems theories encourage social workers to allow for ambiguity and recognize that all knowledge, such as that gained through expert assessment or lived experience, is limited. These theories also emphasize the interconnections between actors and thus encourage us to reject linear causality in favour of understanding how phenomenon are organized and produced through interactions at local levels of practice (Wolf-Branigin, 2009). Practitioners are also required to identify how these interconnections are part of the system they are seeking to understand and change (Stevens and Cox, 2008).

Social work researchers have a developing interest in the application of complex systems ideas to the discipline. Warren et al. (1998, p. 366) assert that 'nonlinear dynamics offers the possibility of a far deeper and more nuanced understanding of the ways in which human systems arise and change than is now available'. Bolland and Atherton (1999) contend that these theories affirm the understanding already held by most practising social workers of the nonlinearity of human systems. For example, the recognition of the complex interactions between individual systems and social structures is consistent with social workers longstanding focus on 'person-in-environment' approaches. Stevens and Cox (2008) also add that complex systems theories draw attention to the ever-changing nature of open systems and to recognition that systems can change abruptly, rather than only in a linear or predictable fashion. For example, we know that people's lives can be transformed by a sudden crisis associated with illness or accident and, similarly, communities can be radically altered by the introduction or removal of a resource, such as a site of employment or a community service.

Despite the intuitive appeal of complex systems theories, we can also identify a number of limitations to the application of these theories to social work. A major difficulty with complex systems theories for social workers is their reliance on specialist mathematics, including advanced statistical techniques. For example, Wolf-Branigin (2009, pp. 120–1) argues that in order to study complex systems, social work researchers should incorporate methods such as spatial analysis, hierarchical linear modelling and social network analysis. Hudson (2000) and Bolland and Atherton (1999) also point out that chaos theorists have incorporated specialist mathematics, such as fractal geometry, in the development of this set of theories. Just as social workers were somewhat alienated by the first wave of systems theories' reliance on biological terminology, we might also question how realistic it is to expect social workers to engage with, let alone develop expertise in, specialist statistical methods and complex mathematics, given the breadth of terrain already covered by our discipline. Moreover, we must be wary that social work researchers' capacity to translate research findings grounded in complex systems to social work practice may be limited by the reliance of these perspectives on mathematical disciplinary knowledge.

A second and related concern is whether research techniques used by complexity researchers to simulate complex weather systems or even economic systems should be applied to the study of social processes. Puddifoot (2000, p. 84) points out that 'there remains a considerable gap between idealized theoretical models and anything resembling real social behaviour'

(see also Mainzer, 1996, p. 280; Hudson, 2000, p. 228). At best, the application of complex systems theories to social work research is in its early
exploratory phases and certainly does not warrant a paradigm shift. However,
advances have been made in social science techniques in the past decade,
particularly in the field of spatial analysis, which have some potential for
knowledge development in social work practice (Wolf-Branigin, 2009).

Complex systems ideas have the potential to affirm the complexities of
social work practice and policy processes. Yet, as criticisms of these ideas
show, we must be wary of the simplistic application of these models to
social work. Two questions are pertinent here: What aspects of social work
can complex systems theories illuminate that escape current practice models
(Puddifoot, 2000, p. 92)? For example, complex systems theories renew our
appreciation of the important role of local social interactions in creating,
not only reflecting, broader social processes (see Mainzer, 1996, pp. 276–9).
How might we use these models in ways that bridge, rather than widen, the
gap between social work research and practices? Some researchers suggest
that qualitative research methods, which incorporate inductive and
nonlinear knowledge development processes, can help to illuminate
complex social processes (see Vallacher and Nowak, 1997). It seems important that complex systems theories are incorporated in ways that build a
bridge between quantitative and qualitative methods (Wolf-Branigin, 2009).

Strengths and Limitations of Systems Theories in Social Work

This chapter has considered arguments for and against each wave of systems
theory. Here, we summarize the overall strengths and weaknesses of systems
theories for achieving our purposes in social work practice.

Strengths

A key strength of systems perspectives is that they provide a framework for
understanding and responding to people in their environments. Systems
approaches discourage the pathologization of either the individual or their
environment, instead encouraging the social worker to analyse the interactions within and across systems. According to Mattaini and Meyer (2002, p. 4):

> The ecosystems perspective is a way of seeing case phenomena (the person and
> the environment) in their interconnected and multilayered reality, to order and
> comprehend complexity, and avoid oversimplification and reductionism.

Second, systems theories can provide a unifying conceptual foundation for social work as a profession focused on understanding and responding to people in their environment. As neoclassical economic discourses increasingly dominate social work practice contexts, we will face more pressure to identify our contributions to social service delivery. The systems perspective offers the profession an option for defining this contribution. For example, as systems 'specialists', professional social workers can provide forms of assessment at individual, group, community and organizational levels that promote systemic understanding and sustainable systemic change.

Third, systems approaches encourage social workers to respect the contributions that different methods make to practice and to develop basic competences across the range of intervention approaches. As Germain and Gitterman (1996, p. 474) state:

> An ecological view helps us appreciate that no theory, concept, model or approach can take everything into account. The complexity of the human condition requires that we develop both a broad perspective as well as specific accommodations and competencies.

This framework can provide an antidote to competition between practice methods; the message of systems theories is that we need a range of perspectives and intervention methods.

Weaknesses

Despite the influence of systems perspectives on the knowledge base of social work, we should also recognize their limitations. First, social work commentators criticize the lack of clarity about core systems concepts. What constitutes a system? What are the boundaries of a system? What are the attributes of a system (see Mune, 1979, p. 65)? This lack of clarity contributes to an absence of theoretical and empirical justification of systems' viewpoints in practice (Wakefield, 1996b, p. 206). Instead, practitioners are invited to accept central claims derived from systems theories – such as all parts of a system are complexly intertwined and that changes in one part of the system will inevitably lead to changes in other parts – without any external justification of these claims. In short, systems theories offer appealing metaphors for practice, yet the application of these theories to practice has not been developed through empirical research. If social workers are able to develop and incorporate qualitative and quantitative methods for analysing systems, there may be hope for the development of a substantial empirical base for systems perspectives in social work (see Wolf-Branigin, 2009).

Second, some commentators point to inconsistencies between social work values and systems theories (see Wakefield, 1996a, 1996b). A focus on function and exchange within systems can leave out questions of structural injustice and abuse of power (Wakefield, 1996b, p. 201). For example, feminist theorists have shown that family system functioning often depends on the exploitation of women's labour. Moreover, as Wakefield (1996b, p. 201) also points out, the systemic focus on interactions and networks can cause social workers to lose focus on the uniqueness of the person. In practice, we may also encounter concerns that a focus on individual and environment interactions downplays the individual's capacity and responsibility for change.

Third, commentators are concerned that systems perspectives draw on disciplines that are distinct from social work. The first wave of systems theory draws heavily on biological disciplines, while the third wave draws on maths and physics disciplines. Some commentators question whether concepts from these disciplines can be applied directly to social processes, such as social service delivery (Mune, 1979; Wakefield, 1996b; Puddifoot, 2000). Also, the specific language used to describe key concepts, whether the language of biological sciences, physical sciences, or complex mathematics, is likely to alienate practitioners who already cover considerable conceptual terrain in their work. This importation of systems ideas from other disciplines will further entrench the division between formal knowledge and practice knowledge in social work.

Fourth, systemic perspectives provide little guidance on how to move from a holistic analysis to systemic intervention. All three waves of systems perspectives urge us to recognize the person in their environment, but to act, we may need to break down this gestalt into smaller pieces. One problem here is that a systems perspective recognizes all the information available to us but does not help us to prioritize information. For example, returning to the case study of Stella, we know that her family, peer and school system are all important, but a systems perspective does not help to clarify which system is most vital to Stella's wellbeing and thus most deserving of our attention.

A systemic analysis does not necessarily enable us to use the enormous bank of information gathered in the development of a systemic analysis to form systemic action strategies; indeed, the sheer amount of information may prevent such action. As Leighninger (1978, p. 454) asks: will social workers 'while recognizing the social nature of many problems, find them so complex that they despair of solving them and go back to individual therapy as the only profitable use of their talents?' Proponents of systemic approaches, particularly ecosystems perspectives, have argued that social workers should have a generic skill set in order to practise holistically. This seems an incredible demand, given the growing diversity of social work practices. As Wakefield (1996b, p. 196) points out, in most complex endeavours 'specialization rather than a comprehensive approach by each individual increases efficiency and effectiveness'.

Conclusion

In this chapter we have explored three waves of systems theories and their influence on social workers' knowledge bases. We can see that systems perspectives remain a contested view in social work. At the very least, systems perspectives provide a way of articulating the complexity of interactions between individuals and their environments. For many social workers, this is an intuitively appealing framework. Even so, we can see substantial concerns about the adoption of these viewpoints in practice. Notwithstanding these limitations, systems theories remain key conceptual frameworks for contemporary social work practice.

Summary Questions

1 What are the criticisms of the first wave of systems theory, also known as general systems theory?

2 What are the similarities and differences between ecosystems theory and complex systems theory?

3 What do you see as the uses and limits of complex systems theory for social work practice?

Recommended Reading

Ecosystems Theory

- Germain, C. and Gitterman, A. (1996) *The Life Model of Social Work Practice: Advances in Theory and Practice*, 2nd edn. (New York: Columbia University Press).
  One of the leading formulations of the ecosystems perspective as a practice model. Thorough overview of the theory and practice of ecosystems perspectives in practice.

- Meyer, C.H. (1993) *Assessment in Social Work Practice*. (New York: Columbia University Press).
  Widely cited text by a leader in ecosystems perspectives in social work, provides an accessible introduction to the use of ecosystems perspectives in social work assessment and an excellent explanation of the use of ecomaps.

- Wakefield, J. (1996a) Does social work need the eco-systems perspective? Part 1: Is the perspective clinically useful? *Social Service Review*, 70(1), 1–32.

- Wakefield, J. (1996b) Does social work need the eco-systems perspective? Part 2: Does the perspective save social work from incoherence? *Social Service Review*, 70(2), 183–213.
  Companion articles making a powerful case against ecosystems perspectives in social work, but argument has relevance for the application of other waves of systems theories. Argues that social work is unified by a common purpose of promoting minimal distributive justice, and that an ecosystems perspective is unnecessary and may be unhelpful for achieving this aim. Both articles provide an excellent critical analysis of the development and deployment of systems perspectives in social work.

Complex Systems and Chaos Theories

To date, there are few books in the discipline dedicated to complex systems or chaos theory; however, there are many interesting journal articles explaining the third wave of systems ideas and their application to social work. This list provides informative, introductory reading on the nature and use of complex systems and chaos theories for social work.

- Hudson, C.G. (2000) The edge of chaos: a new paradigm for social work? *Journal of Social Work Education*, 36(2), 215–30.
  Excellent overview of the application of complex systems theories and chaos theories to social work.

- Stevens, I. and Cox, P. (2008) Complexity theory: developing new understandings of child protection in field settings and in residential child care. *British Journal of Social Work*, 38(7), 1320–36.
  Outlines how complex systems concepts can advance child protection practice. Highlights the value of these perspectives for recognizing dynamic features of the systems within which social workers practise. Valuable because of its grounding of complexity concepts within a core field of social work practice.

- Wolf-Branigin, M. (2009) Applying complexity and emergence in social work education. *Social Work Education: The International Journal*, 28(2), 115–27.
  Accessible introduction to complex systems theories in social work, with a particular focus on research methods for advancing social workers' use of complex systems theories in knowledge building for practice.

Recommended Website

- **www.complexssociety.eu**
  Complex Systems Society is dedicated to the advancement of interdisciplinary research developing and applying complex systems theory. Includes discussion blogs and information about forthcoming conferences and events.

7

PROBLEM-SOLVING APPROACHES
Focusing on Task-centred Practice

Problem-solving approaches are characterized by collaborative, highly structured, time-limited, goal-focused approaches to practice. Of all the approaches considered in this book, problem-solving theories yield the most comprehensive models for direct practice. These practice models derived from problem-solving theory define social work purpose and practice strategies at each phase of assessment and intervention. As such, problem-solving frameworks are among the most readily usable by inexperienced social workers, although there is also scope to develop advanced practice within these approaches (Reid, 1977, p. 11). Most commentators, including the critics of problem-solving approaches, acknowledge that these models enable workers to meet the growing demand from funding agencies for cost-effective, accountable services (Kanter, 1983; Epstein and Brown, 2002). However, they remain the subject of debate, despite their use in many fields of social service delivery.

In this chapter, we discuss the origins of the problem-solving approach. We then consider the features and application of the task-centred model and briefly compare it with crisis intervention. We discuss motivational interviewing and consider how the principles of this approach can enhance problem-solving approaches. Lastly, we explore the strengths and weaknesses of problem-solving approaches.

Problem-solving Practice in Context

Figure 7.1 highlights the problem-solving approach. Its positioning on the left-hand side but after systems theory recognizes that it is a well-established theory for practice, but its historical lineage is shorter than that of systems theory. It is worth nothing, however, that while systems theories have a longer presence in the formal base of social work compared to problem-solving practice, systems perspectives fell out of favour during the psychodynamic phase of professional social work, and only re-emerged as a major influence in the 1960s and 70s, by which time problem solving had become a significant force in the formal base.

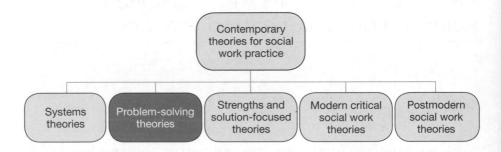

Figure 7.1 Problem-solving social work in context

The Origins of Problem-solving Practice

In 1957, Helen Harris Perlman (1906–2004), a leading social work scholar from the University of Chicago, published *Social Casework: A Problem-solving Process*. This seminal text positioned problem solving as the central task of social work practice (Epstein and Brown, 2002, p. 46). The idea was controversial, given the powerful influence of psychodynamic theory on social work practice at that time (see Chapter 4). Perlman (1957, p. xi) remained committed to psychodynamic ideas and saw the problem-solving process as reforming, rather than replacing, psychodynamically oriented casework. Indeed, the crisis intervention approach to problem-solving practice incorporates psychoanalytic ideas about the psychological usefulness of trauma.

The ideas of John Dewey (1859–1952), pragmatist philosopher, also influenced Perlman and later advocates of problem-solving practice. Dewey paved the way for collaborative, goal-focused problem solving with his view that 'human activity is an instrument for problem-solving and that truth is evolutionary and based on experience that can be tested and shared by all those who investigate' (Epstein and Brown, 2002, p. 70). This perspective offered profound challenges to psychodynamic ideas that had emphasized the hidden and unconsciousness nature of service users' problems.

Perlman proposed a highly structured and focused approach to social work intervention, an approach that she believed, paradoxically, unleashed the creative potential of social work. In a precursor to the modern slogan 'think global, act local', Perlman urged social workers to adopt different levels of analysis for understanding and responding to problems. Perlman (1957, p. 29) asserted that:

It is quite possible to understand the nature of a problem in the whole, but it is rarely possible to work on the whole. In casework, as in any other problem-solving activity, the overt action must be partial, focused, and sequential even though the mental comprehension may be total.

Perlman's separation of the process of analysis from response has resonance for social workers today, as many of us find our work constrained by resource and time limits. In its emphasis on partial and focused activity, Perlman's problem-solving model suggests that meaningful work is possible despite these constraints.

Perlman (1957, p. 87) stressed that problem solving should be a joint effort between social workers and service users and should aim to develop service users' capacity to solve problems independently of the worker. These principles of collaborative action and developing clients' capacities remain central to contemporary problem-solving approaches. The ideal of partnership enshrined in Perlman's approach was not intended to imply that both parties' contribution was the same. Indeed, Perlman (1957, p. 166) insisted that in the early stages of assessment, the social worker should develop a 'diagnosis' that incorporated the worker's and the client's view of the situation, which outlined the resources both would bring to bear on the problem-solving effort. Consistent with the principle of mutual clarity that characterizes contemporary problem-solving practices, Perlman (1957, p. 166) insisted that diagnosis is 'simply an argument for making conscious and systematic that which already is operating in us half consciously and loosely'.

The Rise and Rise of Problem Solving

While Perlman's model of problem-solving practice offered challenges to the social work profession, it also found fertile ground within it; in part because of changes in social service organizations when it first appeared. During the 1960s in particular, social workers experienced growth in employment opportunities in an expanding public sector, which was accompanied by changing tasks and expectations for social workers (Dominelli, 1996, p. 155). The psychodynamic framework that had dominated social work during the middle of the twentieth of century was unsuited to practice in these new environments, which focused on a far broader range of concerns than service users' psychological health. The problem-solving model found receptive terrain within the profession, as a series of landmark studies began to call into question the long-term, relatively unstructured interventions that had become accepted practice in clinical work (Trinder, 2000; Kirk and Reid, 2002). In addition, in these new organizational contexts, social workers faced increased demands for accountability to their employing body, and task-centred approaches' focus on transparency and evaluation of practice are consistent with these demands.

Task-centred Practice: A Brief History

Task-centred practice provides the basis for a broad range of contemporary practice methods. It is recognized as the foundation for generalist social work practice, which incorporates micro-, meso- and macro-practice methods (Garvin, 2003) and is consistent with case management approaches. When applied in interpersonal practice settings, task-centred practice is consistent with other goal-focused interpersonal change approaches such as CBT and motivation interviewing. Task-centred practice recognizes the social worker as an active partner in the change process.

While Perlman's problem-solving model set a new direction for social work practice, it was soon superseded by other problem-solving models. One of the most prominent and perennial of these is the task-centred approach. As Gambrill (1994, p. 578) defines it: 'The task-centred model is a short-term problem-solving approach in which the focus is on tasks that clients and practitioners carry out to resolve problems that clients have agreed to work on.' It was originally espoused by Reid and Epstein (1972), two North American social work scholars, and was intended for therapeutic practice with individuals and families who had voluntarily committed to social work intervention (Reid, 1977, p. 2). Social workers have now adapted this approach to practice in a broad range of settings, including statutory probation and child protection and various community service fields (Epstein and Brown, 2002, p. 99; see also Marsh and Doel, 2005; Trotter, 2006).

The task-centred approach grew out of Reid and Shyne's (1969) comparison of brief and extended therapy and Studt's work on structured interventions (Reid, 1977, p. 1). These projects suggested that clients made comparable and sometimes better progress in short-term interventions (limited to about eight sessions) than clients in longer term interventions. Moreover, researchers found no statistically significant differences in the durability of changes made in short- and long-term interventions (Reid and Shyne, 1969, p. 151). Reid and Shyne (1969, Ch. 7) proposed that time-limited, structured, focused interventions led to greater concentration on and effectiveness of the problem-solving effort. The positive findings on short-term structured interventions were controversial from the start, partly because of their challenge to the psychodynamic paradigm, but also because social workers questioned the generalizability of the model (see Kanter, 1983). We discuss these concerns later on.

In 1970, in response to the findings on the relative effectiveness of short-term therapy focused on behavioural change, Reid and Epstein established the task-centred project at the University of Chicago, with the objective of developing scientifically valid social work approaches 'that could be learned efficiently, increase the effectiveness of direct services, and increase the ability to conduct research on treatment practices' (Epstein and Brown, 2002, p. 92). The model was aimed at 'problems in living', which Reid and Epstein (1972, p. 20; see also Reid, 1977, pp. 2–3) described as:

- interpersonal conflict

- dissatisfaction with social relations, such as social isolation

- problems with formal organizations

- difficulty in role performance

- problems with social transitions, such as entering or leaving an institution

- reactive emotional distress, such as anxiety provoked by a traumatic experience

- inadequate resources, such as a lack of money or housing.

Some problems, such as practice with people suffering from chronic psychiatric illness, were excluded from this list. More recently, however, task-centred practitioners have added a category of 'other: any problem not classifiable' to the list of issues this model can address (see Epstein and Brown, 2002, p. 135). Some proponents of task-centred practice now suggest that this model offers a unifying approach for social work (see Doel, 1998; Garvin, 2003), although others, as we shall see, have significant reservations about the theory (see Gambrill, 1994).

One way of thinking about the task-centred framework is that it provides a 'shell' in which other theoretical perspectives can be incorporated so long as they do not disrupt the requirements that the intervention is structured, focused and time-limited. Indeed, Reid and Epstein encouraged social workers to draw thoughtfully on a broad range of theoretical perspectives in developing practice interventions (Epstein and Brown, 2002, p. 103; see also Reid, 1992). Mark Doel (1998, p. 197), British social work theorist, contends that the task-centred approach has moved 'into more radical territory, embracing notions of partnership, empowerment and anti-oppressive practice, and signalling practical ways of realizing these ideas'. In short, this model appears to offer practitioners and service users a great deal of discretion about the approaches they use to achieve target goals. Later in this chapter, we consider how the principles of motivational interviewing can support problem-solving approaches, such as task-centred practice.

Key Principles of Task-centred Practice

Here we outline the eight practice principles of task-centred practice, before going on to outline the model in practice.

1: Seek Mutual Clarity with Service Users

Task-centred practitioners seek to maximize clarity between social workers and service users about the purpose and process of the intervention (Ford and Postle, 2000, p. 53). Clarity is important for promoting a constructive working relationship based on realistic expectations of the intervention process. Clarity is achieved by the worker and service user jointly determining the focus and processes of the intervention, the establishment of written or oral contracts, and a regular collaborative review of progress towards target goals.

2: Aim for Small Achievements rather than Large Changes

Task-centred practice focuses on enabling service users to make small and meaningful changes in their lives. Doel and Marsh (1992, 106) assert that this is 'a departure from the grand reformism of social work in bygone days. The desire for radical change, at either a personal or societal level, is understandable, but leads to disappointment.' This focus on small, local, achievable change activity is based on the assumptions that it is beyond the scope of social work practice to produce large-scale change and it is not necessary to address all the identified problems at once. This is because successful problem-solving experiences will have knock-on effects for other problems in people's lives, which may enable them to live with these problems or deal with them without social work intervention (Epstein and Brown, 2002, p. 144).

3: Focus on the Here and Now

The task-centred approach is structured around a limited number of problems, no more than three, which are the targets of intervention. Drawing boundaries about the problem to be worked on increases the effectiveness and efficiency of the practice process and limits the potential for 'loose, diffuse, and rambling work' (Epstein and Brown, 2002, p. 143). In contrast to the psychodynamic models that preceded them, task-centred practitioners have little interest in people's personal history, other than understanding historical factors that may directly impact on the current problem-solving effort. Indeed, Epstein and Brown (2002, pp. 102–3) assert that 'accumulating substantial past history is inefficient and may mislead the client about the intentions of the practitioner'.

4: Promote Collaboration between Worker and Service Users

Like Perlman's problem-solving model, task-centred practice is based on the active participation of worker and service user as partners in the problem-solving effort. Each is expected to take an active, although different, role in the problem-solving process. According to Epstein and Brown (2002, p. 73), task-centred practitioners 'tend to be active, and direct, to teach, advise, and instruct'. Through their mutual contract, the service user is also held accountable for developing, implementing and monitoring change strategies.

5: Build Client Capacities for Action

Task-centred practitioners focus on responding to client problems in localized and practical terms. According to Epstein and Brown (2002, p. 99), most troubles have two components: the client lacks either the resources or the skills required to alleviate a problem. While acknowledging that problems may have their origins in other 'causes', such as 'deeper' psychological problems or unjust structural conditions, task-centred practitioners aim to build client capacities to deal with the identified target problems. While not necessarily ignoring the personal or structural origins of client problems, task-centred practitioners see dealing with these original causes as beyond the scope of the problem-solving effort and unnecessary for addressing the target problems of the service user (Reid, 1977, p. 12).

6: Planned Brevity

Reid and Epstein used the term 'planned brevity' to refer to intervention processes that are limited to no more than 15 sessions over a short period of up to three months (Reid, 1977, p. 7). In many practice contexts today, this would not be considered brief intervention, but when task-centred casework was introduced, long-term therapeutic interventions were common. Proponents of task-centred practice argue that the planned brevity of intervention has benefits for service users and service provider organizations. Service users benefit because, as practice research shows, deadlines motivate change and the problem-solving efforts of workers and clients are concentrated (Reid and Epstein, 1972). Service provider organizations benefit as brief interventions allow for the cost-effective deployment of staff resources in increasingly stretched welfare agencies.

7: Promote Systematic and Structured Approaches to Intervention

The task-centred model offers a standardized approach to social work intervention that is also sufficiently flexible to apply in a broad range of practice contexts. The standardization of the model helps to ensure mutual clarity between service provider and service user and external accountability as the practice proceeds sequentially through a predetermined and scientifically tested intervention framework. Epstein and Brown (2002, p. 96) assert: 'Being systematic can protect clients and practitioners from extremes of bewilderment, frustration, and irrelevancy. Systematic practice minimizes waste of time, effort, and money and encourages effective practice.' Yet, within this overall model, practitioners and service users have considerable discretion in determining the actual content of intervention (Reid, 1977, p. 11).

8: Adopt a Scientific Approach to Practice Evaluation

The task-centred model emerged during a period of growing scepticism within the profession about the validity of established practice methods, and external demands for accountability. These pressures continued to intensify in the intervening years. In response to these concerns, Reid and Epstein (1972) were committed to developing a model of practice that was based on scientific findings, developed through scientific methods, and amenable to scientific research. Most proponents of task-centred practice argue that social workers should systematically review and monitor the casework process using scientific methods and scientific research, rather than relying on intuition or anecdotal evidence of progress (Epstein and Brown, 2002, pp. 217–18; Trotter, 2006).

Task-centred Practice: Putting the Model into Practice

In the task-centred model, workers and service users work intensively on a mutually agreed set of target problems. 'Tasks' are the vehicle through which target problems are addressed and service users' skills are developed. Reid (1992, p. 38) asserts that: 'An ultimate goal in the use of tasks is empowerment of the client – to enable the client to design and carry out their own problem-solving actions.' The following description of the model draws primarily on the original model devised by Reid and Epstein (1972) as well as Epstein and Brown's (2002) further development of the approach and Trotter's (2006) application of these ideas to work with involuntary clients. The task-centred approach has five phases, which should flow sequentially in order to maximize client outcomes (Epstein and Brown, 2002, p. 93). Occasionally, it may be necessary for us to revisit earlier stages of the process with service users, and, in such cases, we should aim to return to the stage we were at prior to the interruption of the sequence. Assuming that our problem-solving intervention will occur over eight sessions, we indicate the approximate point in the intervention process where each step should occur. We will use a case study to help us demonstrate the phases of the approach and practise some of the skills associated with it.

Case Study **Task-centred practice**

Imagine you are a social worker in a large teaching hospital, and one of your responsibilities is discharge planning for older people where there are complex personal or family situations.

You receive a referral for George, who is in his late seventies. He was admitted two days ago for urgent investigation of chest pains. He cares for his wife Flo, who is also in her late seventies and has Alzheimer's disease. In the notes, you read that George needs to do everything for her, including dressing, bathing and helping her go to the toilet. You also read that when George was admitted, the Carer Respite Centre arranged for a live-in care worker to look after Flo, as it became apparent that George would only need to be in hospital for about four days.

After the first day, the care worker tells her supervisor that while she was helping Flo to shower and dress she noticed that Flo looks very underweight and may be malnourished. The care worker also found that the cupboards and fridge had little food in them. The centre then contacts you. When you first meet George, he is anxious to get home to look after Flo, and he insists he doesn't need any help, and no one but him can understand Flo and care for her. The case notes indicate that they have one son who lives overseas and visits about once a year. On retirement 15 years ago, George and Flo had moved to the seaside some distance from the community in which they had worked and raised their son. Case notes from a previous hospital admission for Flo note that George and Flo have a supportive relationship and have been married for over 50 years.

Pre-intervention Phase

The purpose of the pre-intervention phase is to understand and establish the context of intervention, prior to and during session one. This involves understanding the reasons for referral (if referral has occurred) and clarifying with the service user any limits or boundaries to the practice relationship.

The task-centred model was originally designed for clinical practice with voluntary service users. In this context, it was understood that the target problems would be identified by service users as something they 'recognize, understand, acknowledge, and want to attend to' (Epstein and Brown, 2002, p. 93). Yet, as social workers moved increasingly into public welfare agencies, advocates of the task-centred model have recognized that tasks other than those identified by the service user themselves may have a bearing on the problem-solving effort (see Trotter, 2006). If a referral is involved, we should clarify the referral source's goals and:

● Whether any compulsion, legal or otherwise, underpins these goals. Is their contact with you compelled by a third party such as the courts or another service agency?

● What reporting requirements do you or the service user have to the original referral source? If so, who is responsible for feedback to the referral source?

In the process of understanding the source of the referral, you may also need to negotiate expectations with the referral source, bearing in mind the respective agency's policies about confidentiality and so on. The practice principle of mutual clarity means that you should communicate any obligations you have to the referral source, or anyone else, to the service user. Moreover, understanding the referral agency's view does not mean it is necessarily accepted as the focus of work. As we work with the service user on defining the target problem, it may be necessary to defer or even reject the referring source's view of the most pressing problem.

The principle of mutual clarity requires us to clarify the role of the agency and service providers with service users, whether voluntary or involuntary, in this pre-intervention phase. Trotter (2006) suggests that the themes that should be addressed in the initial phase of engagement include:

● *the role of the worker:* emphasizing the helping aspects of the work and any legal or other obligations that may impact on the social work process. For example, you should inform the client of your reporting requirements, if any

● *confidentiality and its limits:* the service user should be aware of under what conditions information disclosed in the casework process might be shared with others and how the client would be informed about this

- *service users' expectations of the casework process*
- *what is negotiable and what is not:* some things that might be negotiable include places and times of meetings, while non-negotiable things might include processes for dealing with allegations of abuse or violence.

Step 1: Defining Target Problems

The purpose of this step (first session) is for the worker and service user to arrive at a shared understanding of the issues of concern and to begin to narrow down the focus of intervention. Task-centred practitioners seek to explore and, as far as possible, prioritize the service user's view of the problem, although, in many instances, the worker's perspectives and those associated with external mandates, such as the courts, must be taken into account. The achievement of a mutually agreed definition of the target problem is no easy task, given the differences between service providers and service users. These differences may include different worldviews, obligations, values and identifications – such as age, gender, class. They are likely to be especially pronounced in practice with involuntary clients who may hold ambivalent, and even hostile, feelings about the intervention process (see Trotter, 1999, Ch. 5). The strategies of problem survey and problem ranking are intended to ensure that the service user's view, and those of relevant stakeholders, is understood prior to reaching a shared definition of the target problem(s).

The focus on understanding the service user's view of the problem is consistent with the social work credo of 'starting where the service user is at' and is vital for building a working relationship with the service user. Beyond this, task-centred practitioners also recognize that service users' involvement in defining the problem is critical to concentrating their efforts on the change process (Epstein and Brown, 2002, p. 136). For example, George is more likely to be motivated to work on target problems that are consistent with his definition of the problem and his goals, rather than those he regards as imposed from an external source, such as the care worker or the hospital.

The problem survey

In this first step, task-centred practitioners use a problem survey, or problem search, to develop a comprehensive understanding, for both themselves and service users, of the issues at hand. In this process, the service user and worker list the issues, as they see them, in as concrete and practical way as possible and in the service user's own words (Trotter, 2006, pp. 110–12); this ensures that workers and service users are both clear about the problem and what needs to be done. For example, in undertaking a problem survey with George, he may suggest the following issues:

- I want help to return home as soon as possible

- I am finding it difficult to cope with basic jobs around the house like preparing meals.

As our purpose is to develop an understanding of the target problem, the worker should encourage discussion of a brief history and context of each problem. For example: How long has this been a problem? How severe is the problem? What is its impact on your life? What strategies have you used to manage it so far?

While the views of the client are central to the problem clarification process, it is usual for the worker to take an active role in identifying the issues to be resolved. In this role, workers may challenge definitions of the problem that are unrealistic or undesirable. For example, in working with George, we may acknowledge his strengths in caring for his wife, Flo, while also challenging his view that he doesn't require further support. Here, 'undesirable' definitions of the problem are those that conflict with our legal mandates or professional value base. For example, if the hospital team were to define the problem as 'George cannot manage Flo's care and thus Flo should be referred to a nursing home', we might challenge this definition as inconsistent with our professional value of promoting client self-determination.

How we manage competing definitions of the problem depends on our practice context. Where the service user is a voluntary client and there is no overriding threat to others, the service user's definitions of the problems should prevail (Epstein and Brown, 2002, p. 162). However, there are at least two contexts in which the worker is duty-bound to insist on specific problems being considered in this phase. The first is when the worker is legally mandated to address specific problems, such as child protection or self-harm concerns (see Trotter, 2006). The second is where the worker has formed a judgement of a potential risk the service user might pose to themselves or others. In terms of our professional accountability to the service user, our employing agency and our professional value base, it is vital that we raise these issues in this initial phase. Returning to the case study, we should raise our concerns about Flo's possible state of malnourishment as a problem for further investigation, if George has not already raised this concern.

Problem ranking

Once a list of problems is established, the worker and service user analyse priority areas of intervention. Task-centred practitioners insist that only a limited number of problems can be addressed within any task-centred intervention cycle. Epstein and Brown (2002, p. 155) suggest a 'rule of three', that is, to limit intervention to no more than three issues. In the problem-ranking process, problems the client is most anxious to resolve are usually given highest priority (Reid and Epstein, 1972, p. 21), although, again, legally mandated problems should be prioritized as well. Some of the questions we might ask at this stage include:

- What is the most urgent problem and why?

- What problem is the service user most motivated to work on?

- What, if any, problems are the worker and service user required by external mandate to work on? For example, the health team you work with may insist that concerns about Flo's care are addressed with George.

Step 2: Contracting

The aim of this step (second session) is for the worker and service user to reach an explicit agreement about the target of their intervention and how the target problem(s) is to be addressed. This agreement will form the basis of a contract between service workers and service users (Epstein and Brown, 2002, p. 189). The main purpose of the contract is to ensure mutual clarity and accountability between worker and service user. In contexts where clients are involuntary or reluctant participants in the intervention process, contracts are more likely to be written (Epstein and Brown, 2002, p. 167). A contract should include practical information about the working relationship between service providers and service users, such as the duration, frequency and location of meetings, as well as detailed information about the goals of intervention.

Goals of intervention

Drawing on the work completed in step one, the worker and service user should identify up to three target problems that will be focus of their work together. The service user should be primarily responsible for determining the order of problems to be addressed. The goals should be stated in the service user's own words and on their own terms. If the service provider has other goals on behalf on the agency, such as those related to legal compliance, these need to be indicated as the service provider's goal in the contract. So, in working with George, possible goals for intervention include:

- Flo's health status to be investigated by a medical team and a plan of action to address her apparent health problems

- George and Flo to get more home help to enable George to remain in the primary care role for as long as possible

- George's health problems to be thoroughly assessed and monitored.

A statement of the tasks

In task-centred practice, tasks have a dual purpose – to directly address the target problem(s) and to develop the service user's problem-solving skills. With this purpose, and our target goals in mind, we work with the service user in determining practice tasks. Once tasks are decided, they should be spelled out in detailed and concrete ways. For example:

- George will contact the home help service to arrange an assessment for home care support by 3 February

- Karen (social worker) will arrange for the community health team to investigate Flo's health status by 3 February.

The responsibilities of worker and service user

In the process of completing our detailed task list, we must also clarify who is responsible for task achievement. In assigning responsibilities, we should bear in mind that a key intention of task-centred practice is to develop the client's problem-solving abilities; hence, we must resist any temptation to do 'for', rather than do 'with', the service user. In developing our contract, we should also be mindful of time limits and ensure that tasks are achievable within our time frame (Epstein and Brown, 2002, p. 183).

Task-centred practitioners argue that contracts help to maximize clarity between workers and service users and can provide a vehicle for collaboration in defining practice goals and processes. The establishment of a contract can also provide concrete evidence of a commitment to the intervention process (Epstein and Brown, 2002, p. 169). On the other hand, social work commentators have raised numerous concerns about contracting. Dominelli (1996) questions the mutuality of the contracting process, arguing that clients may have little option but to enter into contractual arrangements. For example, a client seeking only material assistance may feel forced to enter into a contract for other assistance as a condition of receiving the aid they seek. Questions are raised about service user and worker accountability to practice contracts. In each practice context, we need to be clear about the legal and other practical ramifications of the contract, who may have access to the contract, and the consequence of failing to meet contractual obligations.

Step 3: Problem-solving Implementation

Most of the change work occurs in this step of the model (3–7 sessions). In this phase, we refine the problem and the tasks, support task performance, and review task performance. Let's consider each aspect of this step.

Refining the problem and tasks

In earlier stages, we defined the target problem. As we begin to act on the problem, it may be necessary to review our definitions of it. For example, the medical team may discover that Flo's low weight is due to a disease, not malnutrition, and thus we may need to review our plan of action with George altogether. In order to ensure mutual clarity and that our tasks fit the target problem, it is important that we continually review our definition of the problem and tasks throughout this phase.

Supporting task performance

Consistent with the aim of building service users' problem-solving capacities, the worker facilitates their performance of agreed tasks. The worker may foster skill development by, for example, encouraging the service user to rehearse task activities. For instance, if George has never previously contacted a service agency, we may role play with him the task of contacting the home help agency. The worker may encourage the service user to anticipate obstacles to successful task completion and discuss problem-solving strategies for overcoming these problems. For example, as we assign tasks, we might query what George will find easy and difficult about each task and consider how we can help him to address the identified problems. In order to support task performance, we might also discuss incentive and reward strategies for task achievement. For instance, if George enjoys a game of bowls and lunch at the bowling club, we might encourage him to schedule in an extra visit to the club as a reward for completing tasks associated with his target problem.

Reviewing task performance

Remembering the importance task-centred practitioners place on systematic intervention and evaluation as opposed to anecdotal evidence or intuitions about performance, this requires us, at the very least, to systematically gather information about the service user's task performance and the status of the target problem. By regularly reviewing task performance, we can acknowledge the gains made by them and also address task non-performance. Review of non-performance of tasks provides an ideal opportunity to address issues with the service user and revise our contract. For instance, we may find George has not contacted the local home help service. As we probe the reasons for this, George reveals to us that he is worried about losing his independence. We might use this revelation to explore ways George can access support for Flo in ways that maintain his sense of dignity and self-control.

Step 4: Termination

The well-planned termination of an intervention (last session) is integral to the overall structure of the task-centred approach. You will recall that task-centred practitioners believe that a clear and looming deadline is vital for concentrating worker and service user efforts on change (Reid and Epstein, 1972). For this reason, task-centred practitioners are cautious about the extension of an intervention beyond the agreed contract between service user and worker; any such extensions should be time-limited and focused. As Epstein and Brown (2002, p. 230) warn: 'The practitioner should be vigilant about the tendency to drift into open-ended treatment (driven perhaps by desires to attain elusive goals) without a clear contract.'

From the outset, the worker should have communicated the time limits to the intervention and this should be reinforced throughout the process. For example, if we have contracted with the client to meet them for eight sessions, we might remind them of the place of the current session in relation to the overall sequence: 'This is our fourth meeting, we have four more meetings to go; how are we doing so far?'

The key purpose of the termination meeting is to review overall progress towards addressing the target problem and to point to the future (Epstein and Brown, 2002, p. 230). In line with the principle of systematic intervention and review, the review of what was, and wasn't, accomplished should incorporate a range of information sources, such as client's and worker's perceptions of the process, any 'evidence' parties have gathered about accomplishments, such as data collected over the course of the intervention, and reflections on key learnings and expectations for the future. Epstein and Brown (2002, pp. 233–4) also suggest that we should initiate a discussion of how the service user might maintain any progress made during the intervention. For example, we might probe how George will get the support he needs to continue in his role as carer for Flo.

Comparing Task-centred and Crisis Intervention

We should not leave this discussion of problem-solving without reference to 'crisis intervention', another popular model of practice. A comparison of the two methods is useful for highlighting the different ways the principles of problem-solving practice can be applied. This comparison will also illuminate the practical applications of these two models.

While social workers sometimes use the term 'crisis intervention' to refer to practice in the context of disasters or high-risk situations, it also refers to a distinctive approach to problem solving. Crisis intervention first emerged in the 1940s through the work of two American psychiatrists, Gerard Caplan and Eric Lindemann (Kanel, 2003, p. 14). Crisis intervention was introduced to social work in the 1960s in the field of mental health, particularly through the work of Howard Parad (1965; see also Parad and Parad, 1968) and later Naomi Golan (1978).

Caplan defines a crisis as 'occurring when a person faces an obstacle to important life goals that is, for a time, insurmountable by the customary means of problem-solving' (cited in Golan, 1986, p. 302). Within the crisis intervention approach, crises are both an inevitable part of the life course, often associated with life changes such as the transition from childhood to adolescence, and arise through hazardous events, for example the loss of a job or serious illness. The approach centres on the idea that crises present both threats and opportunities and that, if handled well, crises can contribute to personal growth. Caplan argued that not only are crises inevitable but they are actually essential for personal growth (Kanel, 2003, p. 3). Like the task-centred model, crisis intervention offers a time-limited, structured approach and is characterized by distinct phases of intervention, each with a clear purpose and specific tasks.

Both models are oriented towards the long-term empowerment of clients by developing their capacities for independent problem resolution, and, in their contemporary forms, draw on cognitive and behavioural ideas (see Kanel, 2003, p. 39). However, these models differ markedly in some key theoretical assumptions and the rationale behind their shared practice principles. While models are eclectic, the crisis intervention model is more strongly aligned with psychodynamic ideas focusing on the internal world of the client. For example, crisis intervention is intended to use a crisis as an opportunity to promote psychological growth, whereas task-centred practitioners aim to resolve 'problems in living'.

In addition, both models promote brief intervention but for different reasons. Whereas task-centred practitioners limit the duration of intervention, in part because they believe that people are motivated by limited time frames and achievable goals, crisis intervention practitioners insist on time limits because they believe that the period of crisis, and thus the window of opportunity for change, is brief (see Golan, 1986, p. 298; Kanel, 2003, p. 3).

Proponents of crisis intervention also view their role as involving the resolution of an immediate crisis. Cournoyer (2012, p. 259) states that 'the main focus is on addressing immediate problems and pursuing short-term goals', including reducing distress and mobilizing resources. By contrast, task-centred practice is not specifically focused on points of crisis but rather on the development of problem-solving skills to build the client's capacities for independent problem solving. In short, crisis intervention sees a crisis as an opportunity for change, while task-centred practitioners see intervention as an opportunity for knowledge and skill development.

A further difference is that the crisis intervention model gives far greater emphasis to the exploration and expression of client feelings. This is because crisis intervention theorists view the expression of feelings as a precursor to meaningful change. Finally, differences also exist in the role of the worker in the two models. Both assume that the worker should adopt an active role in the problem-solving activity, although in the crisis intervention model, the worker becomes less directive over time, as the client becomes 'ready to "take charge of himself" [sic] once more' (Golan, 1986, p. 324).

Review Question

What are the advantages and disadvantages of a crisis intervention approach, compared to a task-centred approach, for working with George and Flo?

Links to Motivational Interviewing

We turn now to consider how motivational interviewing (MI) could support problem-solving approaches, such as task-centred practice. Over the past two decades, MI has become an increasingly well-recognized approach to interpersonal helping. Social workers, especially those working with individuals, have expressed growing interest in the relevance of MI to practice. Hohman (2012) contends that MI is consistent with the core values of social work practice, particularly notions of partnership and service user empowerment, and can be readily integrated into diverse contexts of interpersonal work. Because MI is primarily a psychological theory, developed by and initially for clinical psychologists working the field of behavioural psychotherapy, we did not include it as a theory for social work practice (Miller and Rollnick, 2002). However, we do briefly outline MI principles, given their relevance to, and increasing use in, problem-solving work in social work. MI is consistent with problem-solving approaches developed by social workers because of the common focus on working collaboratively with people in a goal-directed way to achieve behavioural change (Hohman, 2012).

Miller and Rollnick (2002, p. 25) define motivational interviewing as '*a client centered, directive method for enhancing intrinsic motivation to change by exploring and resolving ambivalence*'. MI is underpinned by four principles. These are, first, that of expressing empathy, what Miller and Rollnick refer to as 'acceptance' of the individual's perspectives and feelings about their situation. As widely recognized by social workers, the expression of empathy can be a powerful basis for change as it contributes to trust in the worker and reduced defensiveness to problem exploration (see Trotter, 2006). In working with George, we could demonstrate empathy by inviting him to discuss his home life, his long partnership with Flo and his hopes for Flo and their life together.

The second MI principle is to 'develop discrepancy', which means that the worker facilitates awareness of 'a discrepancy between present behaviour and important personal goals and values' (Miller and Rollnick, 2002, p. 39). For example, in working with George, we might explore with him the kind of quality of life he would like for Flo into the future and then examine the extent to which he is currently achieving this; this can lay the groundwork for exploring what needs to change for him to achieve his hopes for the future.

The third principle is that of 'rolling with resistance' (Miller and Rollnick, 2002, p. 40). The worker acknowledges the person's ambivalence towards change and assists them to explore this. Returning to George, we could explore with him what he likes and doesn't like about his home life and the care he is able, or not able, to offer Flo and how alternatives, such as the introduction of home care services, might create positive or negative effects in relation to his goals for Flo and him.

The fourth principle is self-efficacy. The worker should seek to enhance 'a person's belief in his or her ability to carry out and succeed with a specific task' or goal (Miller and Rollnick, 2002, p. 40). Consistent with the problem-solving perspective, the role of the worker is to support task performance and goal achievement, rather than doing *for* the client. In line with the optimistic outlook of the strengths perspective (Chapter 8), MI also recognizes the powerful role of hope and optimism in achieving change. One way a worker can demonstrate an optimistic approach is by listening for, and reflecting back to the person, situations where the client has previously succeeded with similar challenges. This technique is sometimes referred to as 'utilization' and involves utilizing past successes from the client's life to demonstrate their capacity to achieve their current ambitions. For example, in working with George, we might be able to identify other points in his life where he has successfully adapted to change, such as the transition to retirement.

We have outlined the core MI principles and how they might be applied to enhance a problem-solving approach to work with the case study of George. Currently, there is a great deal of interest in MI and research into its effectiveness in social work practice. At the end of the chapter, there are some references for those who wish to explore this approach further.

Strengths, Weaknesses and Issues in Problem-solving Approaches

The following discussion focuses mainly on the task-centred approach, although many of these points also have relevance for crisis intervention.

Strengths

Problem-solving processes are consistent with case management – or care management – models that are now common approaches to social service provision (Dominelli, 1996). Task-centred practice, in particular, allows social workers to offer time-limited, highly structured, problem-focused services that are relatively easy to administer and evaluate by social service agencies. Task-centred practice can contribute to the revaluing of social work practice by service agencies and can lessen the conflict social workers sometimes feel between their institutional contexts and their professional practice frameworks. Apart from this point of consistency between practice context and intervention methods, proponents of task-centred practice identify a number of key strengths to this approach.

A major strength of task-centred practice is that it promotes clarity of thinking and action between service providers and service users (Goldberg et al., 1977, p. 6). This limits the potential for confusion and frustration between service providers and service users. Also, the principle of mutual clarity encourages service providers and service users to carefully think through what can be achieved in their time together, thus enhancing accountability to the problem-solving process and reducing the scope for unrealistic expectations and disappointments.

In addition, by involving service users in determining. practice goals, processes and outcomes, the approach is consistent with the core social work values of respect and self-determination. Doel and Marsh (1992, p. 97) go even further to argue that task-centred practice promotes an openness to the client's worldview and, as such, is consistent with anti-oppressive practices. Consistent with the value of respect, it challenges us all to recognize and support service users' capacities to address their problems (Doel and Marsh, 1992, p. 97).

Also, the model aims to empower service users to address the problems they face in daily living without ongoing support from social service agencies. Given the well-known problems of long-term involvement with social services, such as scope for surveillance by the state, the quest to promote independence from social services should, wherever possible, be appreciated by service users and service providers.

A further strength is its commitment to accountability. Research suggests that social workers' evaluation of their own practice tends to be subjective, irregular and difficult to assess by others (see Munro, 1998; Healy and Meagher, 2001). By placing the issue of continuous practice evaluation at the centre of direct practice, task-centred practitioners challenge us to look squarely at our effectiveness and how we develop strategies for communicating this to other stakeholders, particularly those using and funding services.

Weaknesses and Issues

Despite their popularity in some practice and academic contexts, problem-solving models are also the subject of extensive critique. Some commentators question the generalizability of the model, arguing that it is only suitable for relatively superficial problems with people who are atypical of social service users. Gambrill (1994) argues that task-centred practice relies on a selective use of behavioural approaches, leading to an oversimplification of the strategies and the complex character of problems, such as depression, to which Reid and Epstein apply this approach. Kanter (1983, p. 229) criticizes Reid and Shyne's study of brief intervention, on which the task-centred model is founded, on the grounds that 'the study's participants tended to be young, middle income, motivated, and free of gross pathology'. Thus, according to Kanter (1983), the task-centred model is simply irrelevant to the vast bulk of service users who have to face entrenched and complex issues. Thus, there is considerable risk that problems encountered in the application of the model will be attributed to the service user, who may be placed in the 'too hard' basket, rather than lead to further questioning of the model.

A related concern is that the structured, time-limited, goal achievement framework is inappropriate for practice with some kinds of issues, especially those with significant emotional content. Or, to put it differently, there are some areas of social work practice in which goal achievement is less important than simply 'being with' the client. Consider, for example, a young mother dying of breast cancer. A task-centred approach may help us to assist her in practical preparations for her death, but could lead us to be grossly insensitive to the significant emotional issues arising in this situation. To some extent, the crisis intervention model may provide an alternative approach for emotionally charged situations, but its underpinning assumption – that crises are resolved in four to six weeks – is problematic in enabling the worker to provide longer term support, as may be required in this example.

The model can also be criticized for failing to take account of the structural factors contributing to the apparently personal problems facing service users. Gambrill (1994, p. 593) remarks that task-centred practice 'encourages an approach that leaves untouched the conditions that contribute to many problems clients confront'. This insight points to concerns about the potential incompatibility of the task-centred approach with our profession's central value of social justice. By failing to recognize the structural contexts of clients' problems, we might question whether this model may lead our profession to ignore the structural conditions of clients' lives and neglect our responsibility to pursue the goals of achieving greater social and economic equality.

From a citizen rights perspective, we might also question the scope for partnership and participation within the model. Dominelli (1996) criticizes this model on the grounds that its claims to partnership are illusory in the context of inequalities within the practice context and in society more generally. We know that power inequities are an ever-present reality in social work practice – between service users, services providers and service agencies – but, for Dominelli (1996, p. 157), the problem is that the task-centred model does not adequately acknowledge these differences nor does it 'encourage challenges to a system that causes a client's distress'.

Partnership is also problematic in contexts where service providers and service users have vastly different, and possibly irreconcilable, views of a problem. The value given to partnership in this model reflects its therapeutic origins and its intended use for practice with voluntary clients. But what of situations in which the client is not entirely voluntary or where your concerns, as the worker, are in conflict with the client's views? For example, returning to our case study, we can see that working with George would become more problematic if there was a concern about domestic violence between the couple. In that situation, it may be difficult to reach an agreement with George about the focus of our intervention, because we would be duty-bound by our professional ethics, and in some contexts by law, to prioritize our concerns about possible abuse of Flo above all else. Indeed, we need to thoroughly investigate our concerns before we can be sure that helping George with his target goal – to return home – will not worsen matters for Flo. Similarly, in statutory social work contexts, the social worker is mandated by the courts to work on specific problems. If the client is unable to agree to contract to work on these problems – even as part of a more extensive contract – then task-centred practice is not appropriate.

The emphasis on a structured, time-limited intervention can be problematic with clients from some cultural groups. While Anglo-Saxon cultures tend to value ideals such as time effectiveness and structured, linear interventions that are consistent with problem-solving approaches, other groups, such as Aboriginal people, often hold a different view. Members of cultural groups with a more circular view of time and an emphasis on things such as relationship building and the sharing of stories are likely to be alienated by this approach.

The emphasis on strict time limits to each practice step poses a problem even in mainstream health and welfare institutions for which it was originally intended. In many of these contexts, practitioners and service users have little choice about the duration of their work together. The eight-session time frame, on which task-centred practice is based, may be too lengthy in some contemporary contexts of social work practice, such as acute hospital wards where the practice relationship may be limited to one or two sessions. Alternatively, in other contexts where protracted involvement is inevitable, such as some community support programmes, the time-limited model is also not feasible. In these contexts, Doel and Marsh (1992, p. 85) suggested that longer term involvements can be broken down into 'manageable chunks of work'. However, this does appear to be a contravention of the principle of planned brevity so central to problem-solving models.

Conclusion

For the beginning practitioner, problem-solving models offer comprehensive, structured frameworks that are readily applicable to practice; while for the advanced practitioner, they provide an overall direction for practice within which increasingly sophisticated and creative approaches can be developed. Yet, we have also seen that many social work commentators express reservations about these models. Notwithstanding these debates, problem-solving approaches have enjoyed enduring popularity in many fields of practice and this seems unlikely to subside in the near future. It is important, then, that we have a thorough critical understanding of these models and recognize their uses as well as their limits within our specific contexts of practice.

Summary Questions

1 Briefly describe the steps of task-centred practice outlined in this chapter.

2 Briefly describe how the principles of task-centred intervention would apply to social work practice with a specific client group of interest to you, such as young people or survivors of mental health conditions.

3 How does task-centred practice differ from crisis intervention?

4 What is motivational interviewing and how can it support problem-solving approaches to practice?

Recommended Reading

- Epstein, L. and Brown, L. (2002) *Brief Treatment and a New Look at the Task-centered Approach*, 4th edn. (Boston: Allyn & Bacon).
  Comprehensive framework for task-centred practice; addresses some of the issues in using this framework within contemporary practice contexts.

- Gambrill, E. (1994) What's in a name? Task-centered, empirical and behavioral practice. *Social Service Review*, 68(4), 578–99.
  Extensive critique of the claims of task-centred practice. Draws attention to the commonalities between task-centred practice and behavioural therapies and criticizes the task-centred approach for its neglect of structural contributors to clients' problems.

- Hohman, M. (2012) *Motivational Interviewing in Social Work Practice*. (New York: Guilford Press).
  Comprehensive introduction to MI principles; outlines the relevance of this approach to social work values and practice contexts. Incorporates the voices of social work practitioners using MI in a range of practice contexts.

- Marsh, P. and Doel, M. (2005) *The Task-centred Book*. (London: Routledge).
  Thorough introduction to task-centred practice, focusing on practitioner and client perspectives about the relevance of this approach to social work practice.

- Miller, W.R. and Rollnick, S. (2002) *Motivational Interviewing: Preparing People for Change*, 2nd edn. (New York: Guilford Press).
  Highly accessible book outlining the core principles and evidence base for MI. Well worth reading for those seeking a comprehensive understanding of the origins of this approach. The applications provided pertain to counselling contexts and social workers working in other contexts might also consider reading Hohman's work.

- Reid, W.J. and Epstein, L. (1972) *Task-centered Casework*. (New York: Columbia University Press).
  Seminal text on task-centred practice; outlines the rationale for, and the processes of, this practice approach.

- Trotter, C. (2006) *Working with Involuntary Clients: A Guide to Practice*, 2nd edn. (London: Sage).
  Excellent introduction to the evidence for problem solving in practice with mandated clients and a step-by-step guide to the implementation of this approach. Includes tips for managing difficult issues around confidentiality and authority; helpful guide for those working with mandated clients.

8

STRENGTHS AND SOLUTION-FOCUSED THEORIES
Future-oriented Approaches

During the 1980s, a dramatic reorientation of practice, particularly interpersonal work, began to emerge in social work and cognate disciplines such as counselling and family therapy. Proponents of these new approaches reject the problem focus, which, they contend, underpins social work and other human service professions (Berg and Kelly, 2000; Saleebey, 2012), and are oriented instead to finding solutions that draw on clients' strengths, and their hopes and dreams for the future. These future-oriented approaches include the strengths perspective, solution-focused brief therapy and narrative approaches. This chapter focuses on strengths and solution-focused brief therapy. Narrative approaches will be discussed in Chapter 9 because of the clear linkages between narrative practice and postmodern concepts.

In this chapter, we discuss the features of the strengths perspective and solution-focused brief therapy (SFBT). We outline the origins and theoretical foundations of these approaches and discuss their common features before considering how they differ. Common strategies and practice techniques used in these approaches will be discussed as well as their strengths and limitations.

Strengths and Solution-focused Approaches as Social Work Practices

Social workers have had significant involvement in the development of the strengths perspective and SFBT. The strengths perspective hails from North America, primarily the work of Dennis Saleebey, Charles Rapp and Anne Weick from the School of Social Welfare at the University of Kansas. In recent years, it has gained popularity in many other countries and practice contexts (see Chapin, 1995; Parton and O'Byrne, 2001; Pichot and Dolan, 2003; O'Connell, 2005; Sharry, 2007). Originally developed in mental health practice contexts, this perspective is now adapted for a broad range of practice contexts and practice methods, including child protection (see Turnell and Edwards, 1999), addictions (van Wormer and Davis, 2003), developmental disabilities (Quinn, 1998), social policy (Chapin, 1995) and criminal justice (van Wormer, 2001).

The growing popularity of the strengths perspective since its founding in the late 1980s can be partly attributed to its embodiment of social work values, particularly its emphasis on respect and service user self-determination. It emphasizes optimism, hope and creativity and, in so doing, offers an alternative to increasingly defensive and risk-averse practices that have become commonplace as result of the growing influence of the dominant discourses discussed in Chapter 3.

SFBT dates back to the 1950s and the work of Milton Erikson, and became popular during the 1970s. It draws on a range of disciplinary traditions, including psychology, philosophy and anthropology. Despite the eclectic disciplinary base of SFBT, professional social workers have made significant contributions to developing the foundations of this approach since the 1980s, particularly through the work of husband and wife team Insoo Kim Berg and Steve de Shazer (Berg, 1992; see also de Shazer et al., 1986; de Shazer and Berg, 1992). More recently, social workers have demonstrated the relevance of this approach to a range of contexts and methods of social work with individuals, groups and families (see Pichot and Dolan, 2003; O'Connell, 2005; Sharry, 2007).

Figure 8.1 highlights the strengths perspective and SFBT. They are positioned after systems and problem-solving perspectives to reflect their more recent influence on the formal base of social work practice. They are beside critical and postmodern approaches which, like the strengths perspective and SFBT, have become established in the formal base of social work over the past three decades. SFBT is often referred to simply as 'solution-focused therapy' or 'brief therapy'.

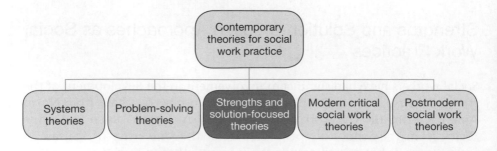

Figure 8.1 Strengths perspective and solution-focused practice in context

Like all theories for practice considered in this book, the strengths and SFBT approaches draw their intellectual foundations from behavioural and social science discourses as well as practice within specific service fields. Strengths and solution-focused approaches were originally founded in mental health services, and 'psy' perspectives, especially ideas of psychological resilience, inform these theories. The founders of SFBT drew on the research work of psychiatrist Milton Erikson (1954) and the Mental Research Institute, established in Palo Alto in 1958 (see de Shazer et al., 1986).

The sociological discourse, especially research on the social processes that produce stigma, also contributes to strengths perspectives (Saleebey, 2012), while solution-focused brief therapists draw on anthropology, particularly the work of noted anthropologist, Gregory Bateson (Weakland et al., 1974).

Both the strengths perspective and SFBT draw on the alternative discourses, discussed in Chapter 5. In particular, many of their aspects are consistent with consumer rights discourses, which challenge professional expertise by highlighting clients' knowledge of their concerns. The strengths perspective also highlights the importance of supportive communities for recognizing and fostering service users' capacities. Consistent with discourses associated with religion and spirituality, the strengths perspective recognizes that responses to the spiritual needs of the service user are a dimension of holistic service provision.

A strong interchange of ideas and practice techniques exists between the strengths perspective and SFBT (see Turner and Edwards, 1999; see also O'Connell, 2005). The approaches discussed in this chapter are based on a rejection of a central concern with problems and pathology found in many social work approaches and across human service professions. Proponents of the strengths perspective and SFBT see a problem focus as aligned to the medical model approach, which, they argue, leads to a concentration on pathology and deficit rather than capacity (de Shazer, 1988; Saleebey, 2012, p. 3). In the view of these practitioners, such a focus is antithetical to change. In both approaches, it is argued that 'if clients do create change in their lives or solve problems they do so *out of their strengths not out of their weaknesses*' (Sharry, 2007, p. 27).

The strengths perspective and SFBT are also critical of linear approaches to problem solving. Proponents of these approaches argue that effective responses to life challenges do not require a detailed understanding of, and plan to respond to, problems. Rather, the worker needs to gain a detailed understanding of service users' strengths, the triumphs they are already having over their problems, and the hopes and dreams they have for their future (see Saleebey, 2012) or the solutions they envisage to their problems (de Shazer, 1988; de Shazer et al., 1986).

Drawing on features of SFBT (see O'Connell, 2005), we can identify similarities between the strengths perspective and SFBT, including that both approaches:

● Recognize and focus on the strengths and capacities of service users to respond to their problems

● View service provision as a mutual learning process for service provider and service user

● Seek to depersonalize service users' problems, that is, the person is not the problem, rather, the problem is the problem

● Explore future possibilities rather than examine the past.

Despite the commonalities between these approaches, there are some differences. Saleebey (2012b, p. 302) states that unlike the strengths perspective, SFBT has not 'concentrated on the resources and solutions in the environment'. Solution-focused approaches generally focus on helping individuals to construct solutions to their problems and not to change their environment. At the same time, they are founded on the notion that problems are sustained by the environment in which they occur and that a change to the way an individual interacts with that environment can assist in resolving challenges (Weakland et al., 1974; de Shazer et al., 1986). Proponents of SFBT propose that any change in the way the client interacts with their environment is likely to disrupt the problem system, thus helping to create solutions (see Weakland et al., 1974; de Shazer, 1988). Notably, while the strengths perspective has been developed for use in macro-methods including community development (Kretzmann and McKnight, 1993) and policy work (Chapin, 1995), SFBT is almost exclusively linked to practice with individuals, families or groups.

A second difference is the extent to which proponents of these traditions describe their approach as a theory for practice. Proponents of the strengths perspective debate whether it is a theory, a distinct way of seeing the world, or a value position. Weick et al., (1989, p. 354) suggest that:

> If anything, a strengths perspective is a strategy for seeing; a way to learn to recognize and use what is already available to them [the service user]. The professional person thus becomes a translator who helps people see that they already possess much of what they need to proceed on their chosen path.

In this book, we refer to the strengths perspective as a theory of social work practice. This is because, like other practice theories, it offers guidelines for analysing and developing practice responses. In this sense, it fits the definition of social work theory as theory developed by social workers to explain and guide social work practices outlined in Chapter 1.

By contrast, proponents of SFBT clearly identify their approach as a theory of practice and as having a base in practice-based research. De Shazer (1988, p. xiii) emphasizes that his work on the development of SFBT is based on his continued involvement in the 'study of solution development'. He further states that the link 'between what we do (practice) and how we talk about or describe what we do (theory) is very strong' (de Shazer, 1988, p. xiv).

We turn now to outline the origins and features of the strengths perspective, including its extension to community development work in the asset-based community development tradition. We then discuss SFBT approaches.

Origins of the Strengths Perspective

The approach first emerged among social workers in North America practising in mental health contexts, mainly with people diagnosed with severe and chronic psychiatric conditions (Saleebey, 2012a, 2012b; see also Rapp, 1998). Saleebey (1996, p. 296) stated that the strengths perspective was developed in opposition to 'U.S. culture and helping professions [that] are saturated with psychosocial approaches based on individual, family, and community pathology, deficits, problems, abnormality, victimization and disorder'.

As the strengths perspective gains increasing international attention, it is important for us to understand how the geographical and institutional settings in which this approach originated have shaped its development and application. The origin of the strengths perspective in the USA is significant because there social work is more strongly aligned with the professions of psychiatry and psychology than in other countries, such as Australia, New Zealand, the UK and Scandinavia. Its origin in mental health contexts is also important, as this provides the primary frame of reference for the development of this approach. The original advocates of the strengths perspective sought to challenge key concepts in the biomedical and psychiatric discourses, particularly the emphasis on individual pathology that, in their view, dominated conventional mental health agencies. While biomedical and psychiatric discourses shape social work practices in many practice domains, other discourses, such as law and neoclassical economics, are also influential in shaping social work practice and our understanding of client 'needs', 'strengths' and 'deficits'.

Despite these contextual differences, the strengths perspective insight that social work is based on a deficit model resonates with social workers across many countries. Weick et al. (1989) attribute this common focus on deficit to the historical foundation of social work in religious charities and the assumption that service users' problems could be attributed to moral failings. Also, the psychodynamic tradition of social work, influential in shaping the modern profession, focused on uncovering and treating psychopathology (Weick et al., 1989, p. 350). Today, proponents of the strengths perspective argue that despite the profession's stated commitment to the values of client self-determination and respect, dominant practice approaches remain mired in the language of pathology and deficit (Weick et al., 1989; Saleebey, 2012b).

Knowledge Foundations of the Strengths Perspective

Before turning to the practice principles of the strengths perspective, we consider the sources of intellectual and practice inspiration for this approach. The strengths perspective draws on a broad scope of theoretical knowledge and empirical research in the social sciences and social work and is strongly aligned with solution-focused and empowerment approaches.

Proponents of the strengths perspective acknowledge Bertha Capen Reynolds (1887–1978) as an influential figure in its development (Saleebey, 2012a, p. 21; see also Kaplan, 2002). Reynolds was a social work practitioner and educator, whose work with the Maritime Union during the 1940s shaped her outlook on professional work practice. Drawing on this practice experience, Reynolds (1951, p. 130) criticized the profession's growing attachment to professional status and its uncritical adoption of the psychoanalytic discourse. Reynolds challenged the fledgling profession of social work to reject notions of professionalism that emphasized detachment, diagnosis and individualized treatment, as being ultimately destructive to service users' wellbeing. In turning away from a psychological treatment orientation, Reynolds (1951, p. 175) advocated that the profession recognize its political responsibilities to enhance the social and political inclusion of service users. Reynolds also urged social workers to focus on clients' strengths and capacities rather than concentrating on personal pathology. In a statement consistent with the strengths perspective, Reynolds (1951, p. 34) asserted:

> Recognition of what a client has to work with, in himself [sic], is a better starting point than an attempt to make him accept his [sic] failure, and that building him [sic] up as a person makes him [sic] more ready, rather than less so, to go on to further growth and accomplishment.

The work of Erving Goffman, the eminent sociologist, has also had a profound influence on the strengths perspective. Goffman's (1991) research on social labelling, stigma and marginalization showed that many of the practices adopted by human service institutions and professions contributed to the problems they were intended to overcome. For example, the use of the label 'schizophrenic' imposes a stigma on a person that has negative repercussions on their self-understanding and the way others respond to them. In recognition of the power of language to 'elevate and inspire or demoralize and destroy' (Saleebey, 2012a, p. 11), advocates of the strengths perspective urge workers to be sensitive in their language use, particularly in their description of clients' perceived capacities and deficits.

The strengths perspective also draws on empirical research about psychological resilience. Saleebey (2012b) points to research demonstrating that adverse life events are not strong predictors of future capacities. Reviewing research on childhood trauma and adversity, he contends that the majority of people do not reproduce the problems to which they were exposed as children. Resilience research also suggests that people can actually benefit from difficult life events (see McMillen, 1999). This is particularly true for acute experiences of adversity experienced as an adult, such as surviving a life-threatening illness or a natural disaster (McMillen, 1999, p. 456). We discuss problems in strengths theorists' interpretation of resilience research later in the chapter.

Similarities exist between the strengths perspective and ego psychology concepts. Psychodynamic and psychosocial casework theorists argued that social workers should seek to identify and reinforce 'ego strengths'. Both the strengths perspective and ego psychology emphasize the links between psychological strengths, such as ego strengths, and personal resilience in the face of adversity (see Garrett, 1958, p. 44). Interestingly, proponents of the strengths perspective do not usually link their approach to ego psychology. This may be because ego psychology was part of, and reinforces, a pathological view of service users. For example, Hamilton (1951, p. 296), a proponent of ego psychology in casework, warned that:

> caseworkers must not only ally themselves with the healthy parts of the personality ... but also make a new appraisal, as it were, of how the ego is weakened and dependency needs exacerbated by illness.

Nonetheless, given that the strengths perspective first arose among social workers in the mental health field, where 'psy' discourses are ubiquitous, it is likely that these ideas have contributed to the development of this approach.

Some proponents of the strengths perspective link it with empowerment approaches (see van Wormer, 2001; Saleebey, 2012a). Many features of the empowerment approach (see Payne, 1997; Parsons et al., 1998) are consistent with the strengths perspective. Both aim to recognize and build service users' capacity to help themselves and their communities and promote a mutual learning partnership between workers and service users.

However, advocates of empowerment perspectives focus more strongly on the social and structural origins of service users' difficulties than proponents of the strengths perspective. In concert with anti-oppressive practice perspectives, empowerment theorists (Parsons et al., 1998, p. 5) contend that social workers should 'help individuals see the roots of their problems in society' and foster collective action among service users directed at 'internal and external' social structures. The empowerment perspective articulated by Parsons et al. (1998) can be seen as a bridge between strengths and anti-oppressive approaches in that it combines core elements of both practice perspectives.

Practice Assumptions and Principles

The strengths perspective involves much more than a mantra emphasizing client capacities. The perspective refers to a distinct set of assumptions from which flow core practice principles. Here, we turn to these assumptions and principles.

Drawing on the work of Saleebey (2012a, 2012b) and Weick et al. (1989), we can identify the following key assumptions of the strengths perspective:

- All people have strengths, capacities, and resources.

- People usually demonstrate resilience, rather than pathology, in the face of adverse life events. This is because 'all human organisms have an inclination for healing' (Saleebey, 2012a, p. 10).

- Service users have the capacity to determine what is best for them and do not need human service workers to define their best interests for them.

- Human service professionals, including social workers, tend to focus on perceptions of service users' problems and deficits, while ignoring their strengths and resources. A key goal of the strengths perspective is to focus on and work with service users' and communities' capacities.

- Collaborative partnerships between workers and service users reflect and build service users' capacities. But human service professionals, including social workers, are reluctant to collaborate with service users in a spirit of mutual learning and genuine partnership, preferring instead to protect their professional power.

Now we turn to the practice principles arising from these assumptions. In this discussion, we also consider practical strategies for applying these principles. Five practice principles are outlined.

1: Adopt a Hopeful, Optimistic Attitude

Social workers have a professional duty to assume a positive and optimistic attitude towards service users. Optimism is essential because our outlook determines whether we can see, let alone build on, service users' strengths and resourcefulness (Turnell and Edwards, 1999, p. 62). This positive attitude requires us to be sceptical about labels that construct service users as incompetent or incapable of achieving an improved quality of life; instead, we should seek to fully recognize their capacities, resources and hopes and dreams for the future.

In practice, we must challenge ourselves, and others, including those in formal and informal helping networks, to question pathological and deficit-oriented views of service users and instead seek out evidence of clients' strengths, capacities and resourcefulness. For example, in working with families who are identified by authorities as being at risk of abusing their child, we could explore the relationships they feel positive about and that could help them build a support network for themselves and their children, such as extended family relationships, friendships, professional helpers and community networks (Turnell and Edwards, 1999).

In addition, we must convey to service users our belief in their capacities to resolve the immediate problems facing them and to achieve quality of life on their own terms. Sensitivity to our use of language is also vital here. At a minimum, a strengths-based approach requires that we separate the person from the problem that brings them to the social service agency. So, instead of describing a person as 'schizophrenic', we might refer to them as 'a person with schizophrenia'. Better still, if we must refer to the issues facing service users, we should describe them in terms that convey our respect for service users' resilience; so the service user is described as 'a survivor of schizophrenia'.

2: Focus Primarily on Assets

While advocates of the strengths perspective do not deny the reality of problems such as mental illness and addiction, they assert that we should resist making them the focus of our assessment and intervention. Rather, we must primarily recognize service users' assets, because we can only build on strengths, not on deficits.

We should focus on eliciting the full range of people's assets, including their personal capacities and the resources embedded in their social networks. For example, Quinn (1998, p. 105) argues that:

> It is easy to assume for example, that any adult with Down syndrome will be a happy, placid person who is satisfied performing routine, repetitive tasks ...

Instead, the entire range of possible cognitive abilities, physical capacity, and personal interests must be evaluated. The assumption should be made that the young adult can accomplish any task, until this is proven wrong.

Strengths-based practitioners argue that we, as practitioners, must change the way we listen to the client's account of their situation. A strengths approach to listening requires us to be on the lookout for signs of capacity and resourcefulness, rather than problems and deficits in service users' lives. Van Wormer (2001, p. 32) describes a strengths approach to listening:

> Listening is the method; listening to the client's story, not passively, uncreatively, but with full attention to the rhythms and patterns, and then, when the time is right, observing, sharing, until through a mutual discovery, events can be seen in terms of some kind of whole. The challenge is to find themes of hope and courage and in so naming to reinforce them.

A strengths-based approach suggests that the process of identifying and reinforcing service user capacities, of itself, contributes to positive change as it reveals existing strengths that might otherwise be overlooked. For example, say we are working in a school context and a young person is referred to us because of their absenteeism. The referral from the school principal tells us that, on average, the young person misses two days of school per week. From a strengths perspective, we would not focus on the two days missed per week, but turn our attention to what keeps the young person at school three days per week. Moreover, using a strengths-based approach to listening, we would seek out strengths, not only within the individual, but also within their formal and informal networks. So, we could ask the young person: 'Tell me about someone who wouldn't be surprised to know that you had managed to get yourself to school three days a week despite everything that is going on for you.' The focus on strengths within the young person's network helps us, as workers, and the service user to gain a list of the resources available to address the problem at hand.

A few words of clarification would probably help here, lest a strengths-based approach to listening be dismissed, out of hand, as naive or even dangerous. First, proponents argue that a strengths-based approach to listening does not require us to ignore evidence of risk, only that such evidence is put within a comprehensive understanding of the service user's situation (Turnell and Edwards, 1999, p. 65). For example, say we are child protection workers working with a young mother, Sally, who is suspected of neglecting her two-year-old son Ben. We might assess not only the risks to the child but also times when Sally has found the resources within herself and her community to give Ben the care he needs. In some situations, this information can be used to promote change in the service user's life.

In addition, although strengths-based listening requires us to question the labels applied to service users, this does not mean that we should ignore these categories altogether. Indeed, in some situations, labels, such as diagnoses, can bring clarity and relief. For instance, some people may find relief in the diagnosis of a medical or psychiatric condition to explain their puzzling and distressing symptoms. According to van Wormer (2001, p. 75), 'the secret' lies in how this diagnosis is used. In the strengths perspective, the labels applied to service users become a point of discussion and investigation with them rather something to be used by professionals over them.

A final concern is that too great a focus on strengths may lead us to either naively or insensitively gloss over service users' negative feelings and perceived deficits and, in so doing, cause us to lose credibility with service users and other service providers. So, it is important that we find ways of acknowledging service users' and other service providers' interpretations, while also promoting the strengths-based view. For example, returning to the example of Sally, the young mother suspected of neglecting her son Ben, we might ask: 'From what you've told me, I can see that you've found being a young mother, alone, very difficult and you feel that Ben has suffered a great deal. What good might come out of the struggles you've had for your relationship with him?'

3: Collaborate with the Service User

Like all the practice approaches considered in this book, the strengths perspective emphasizes the importance of partnership between worker and service user, recognizing that a partnership approach is consistent with social work values and that, at a practical level, solutions developed collaboratively are likely to be more useful to service users than those imposed by others, such as experts. In addition, proponents of the strengths perspective argue that the formation of practice partnership increases the resources available to solve the problem at hand. Through alliance, service providers and service user are best able to harness the resources and capacities of service users, including their capacities for self-help. Second, partnership work is a necessary, although not sufficient, condition for service user empowerment. Advocates of the strengths perspective contend that people can only grow when others, particularly 'helpers', 'actively affirm and support their capacity to do so' (Weick et al., 1989, p. 354; see also Saleebey, 2012a). Finally, in contrast to problem-solving approaches, proponents of the strengths perspective argue that finding solutions is a creative process that must engage all the understandings, including emotional and spiritual perspectives, and capacities of the service worker and service user (see Weick et al., 1989). In solution-focused approaches, on which strengths practitioners often draw, there is a recognition that solutions to problems often lie in emotional and irrational knowledge, that is, this non-rational knowledge provides the 'keys' to unlock problems. De Shazer (1985, p. 7) asserts: 'All that is necessary is that the person involved in a troublesome situation does something different, even if that behavior is seemingly irrational, certainly irrelevant, obviously bizarre, or humorous.'

Collaboration between service workers and service users can be encouraged in many ways. These include:

- *promoting a collaborative physical environment:* For example, ensuring that the space where we work with the service user is free of interruptions and furniture is arranged in ways that promote collaboration, such that worker and service user are sitting at the same level, face to face, with nothing obstructing our view of each other, such as a desk.

- *promoting a collaborative interpersonal relationship:* Strategies for achieving collaborative interpersonal relations are context specific, so it is important that, in seeking to enhance mutuality, we do so in ways that are appropriate to the environment. Some general ways of achieving mutuality may include:
  - encouraging mutual use of first names
  - the use of appropriate self-disclosure, particularly to indicate resources and assets you may use in responding to the service user's concerns
  - paying attention to service users' perceptions of the situation, especially their interpretations of the key issues and how these might be resolved
  - encouraging service users to participate in setting the agenda for your work together and evaluating the effectiveness of that work
  - being alert to opportunities for demystifying professional intervention processes, for example by clarifying biomedical terminology that has been applied to the service user or their situation.

- *encouraging collaborative and creative solution seeking:* We can encourage collaborative solution seeking by, for example, working with service users to 'brainstorm' possible solutions to their identified concerns. Consistent with the principle of optimism, we should encourage service users to put forward all possible responses to identified concerns, no matter how outlandish and unrealistic they may seem to us.

4: Work Towards the Long-term Empowerment of Service Users

Saleebey (2012a) argues that social workers must support the empowerment of service users through dialogue and action in partnership with service users and communities. In part, this involves recognizing and affirming service users' resilience and capacities in the face of adversity. Thus, we recognize that people are not only unharmed by negative life events but may actually develop capacities from them. In addition, the strengths perspective is aimed at achieving practical outcomes that enhance service users' capacity to improve their quality of life. The social worker's role is to facilitate service users' capacity to use existing strengths and resources, as well as developing new ones, to achieve their hopes and dreams.

From a strengths perspective, empowerment is achieved, in part, by a focus on future possibilities rather than past problems. Thus, rather than seeking to excavate the causes of problems, our work is oriented towards uncovering service users' hopes and dreams for the future. It is vital that we affirm service users' resilience and capacities, including those developed via adversity, rather than view them as victims of their situation or social structures. In addition, strengths-based practitioners seek to enhance empowerment by achieving practical outcomes with service users that are consistent with their hopes and dreams.

5: Create Community

Advocates of the strengths perspective stress the importance of social support for achieving resilience and enhancing quality of life. According to Saleebey (2012a, p. 13), belonging to a community is vital because 'most people want to be citizens – responsible, recognized, and valued members of a community'. Just as social workers' recognition of service users' strengths can enhance their capacity to activate these strengths, so, too, community recognition of, and support for, service users' strengths can help them to mobilize their capacities in the achievement of their hopes and dreams. In addition, community support can build and draw on the capacities of service users to help themselves and others.

In working with service users' strengths, we should recognize the strengths and assets embedded in service users' social networks. These strengths could include people who the service user experiences as affirming and supportive, and the roles that service users perform in their 'community' that develop or reflect their capacity for self-help and/or helping others. Social workers can be alert to opportunities to link service users to community networks that could affirm and build their capacity for self-help and community service. If such networks are absent, social workers can contribute to the development of support networks.

Solution-focused Brief Therapy (SFBT)

We turn now to a discussion of the features of SFBT, which shares many common assumptions with the strengths perspective. A core principle of SFBT is that service users already possess the knowledge and skill they need to address the problems they face. As de Shazer et al. (1986, p. 207) state: 'this is the key to brief therapy: *utilizing what clients bring with them to help them meet their needs in such a way that they can make satisfactory lives for themselves'*. The role of the social worker is that of assisting the client to uncover these capacities.

Change is achieved in several ways. The first is by focusing on solutions not problems. SFBT seeks to orient the worker and service users' attention to the question of how they will know when the complaint is solved (de Shazer et al., 1986). In contrast to problem-focused approaches, SFBT seeks to concentrate worker and service users' efforts on solutions. In the view of SFBT proponents, this involves a radical reorientation of social work practice away from problem-saturated approaches.

The second way change is achieved is by creating an expectation of, and increased sensitivity to the presence of, change. This involves exploring with the service user several positive aspects of their situation, including what they want to continue in their current situation, what triumphs they are already having over the challenges they are facing, and their hopes and dreams for the future. As de Shazer et al. (1986, p. 208) state: 'we connect the present to the future (ignoring the past, except for past successes), then we point out to the clients what we think they are already doing that is useful and/or good for them'.

Proponents of SFBT have developed the use of a range of questioning strategies that assist to create an expectation of change. Many of these strategies have been adopted by other future-oriented approaches, particularly the strengths perspective and narrative therapy.

The first type of question concerns encouraging the service user to identify what their life will be like once the problem is solved. This can occur in several ways, including asking them to describe how they will know that the problem they are facing is solved. SFBT also popularized the use of the 'miracle question' as a strategy for helping the service user to imagine their life without the problem. The miracle question involves asking them to consider, in detail, what their life would be like if a 'miracle' happened and the problem was no longer there. In so doing, the worker is seeking to gain a detailed understanding of the solution they are seeking and to build their belief that a solution is possible.

A second type of question, the 'scaling question', can also help to build service users' confidence in their capacity to achieve solutions. The scaling question involves asking the client to rate aspects of the problem or, more often, the solution. For example, a client experiencing anxiety is asked to rate, on a scale of 1–10, the extent to which they have felt calm and untroubled by anxiety over the past week, with 1 being a poor result and 10 being complete calm. If the client rates themselves at 5, the worker could then explore what helped to get them to 5, and what could they do over the next week to reach 7.

A third type of question involves developing the client's confidence in, and awareness of, their own capacity to address the challenges they are facing. The underpinning assumption is that clients are having successes with the troubles they are facing but that these successes often go unnoticed. 'Coping questions' focus on exploring how the client is coping with the challenges they are facing; they also demonstrate that the worker empathizes with the challenges confronting the individual. Examples of these questions include:

- 'With everything that has gone on for you over the past months, how come things are not worse?'

- 'Despite all the challenges that were thrown your way, you managed to remain calm. How did you do that?'

A fourth type of question is an 'exception seeking question'. This involves asking the client about times when they are not troubled by the particular complaints or concerns that have brought them into contact with social work or therapeutic services. For example: 'In the last week, can you tell me about times when you have felt untroubled by feelings of anxiety?' These questions seek to further illuminate service users' triumphs over their problems and provide the worker and the service user with clues about how sustainable solutions might be achieved. The worker explores with service users exceptions to the problem they are facing and makes these exceptions visible to them as evidence of change that is already occurring.

Finally, questions that explore clients' strengths and areas of life satisfaction are also important for creating a collaborative relationship with the service provider and preventing the working relationship from becoming problem saturated. For example, in a child protection interview, one might ask:

- 'What you are most proud of about your children?'

- 'What do you see as your greatest strengths as a parent?'

These questions help to balance out a focus on risks and problems and also assist the worker to build on strengths and solutions that already present in the service user's life. Furthermore, by exploring service users' strengths, the worker demonstrates that they respect the service user. SFBT emphasizes the importance of respect and collaboration between worker and service user, and urges workers to recognize that service users know more about their problems and the potential solutions to them than anyone else.

Another feature of SFBT is a focus on change through disrupting the vicious cycle that keeps the problem in place. In contrast to problem-solving approaches, which seek to develop a linear plan for problem resolution,

SFBT seeks to focus on small changes that undermine the problems. Indeed, proponents of SFBT argue that a focus on large goals is problematic, because 'the bigger the goal or the desired change, the harder it will be to establish a cooperative relationship, and the more likely that therapist and client will fail' (de Shazer et al., 1986, p. 209).

SFBT has had significant influence in a wide variety of fields of social work practice including and beyond counselling. Insoo Kim Berg, a social worker and co-founder with de Shazer in 1982 of the Brief Family Therapy Center in Milwaukee, applied SFBT to a wide range of practice contexts including child protection and drug and alcohol treatment services (Berg, 2000; Berg and Kelly, 2000). Nonetheless, unlike the strengths perspective, there has been little attempt to apply this approach to macro-methods, such as community work, and this is a significant limitation for social workers involved in generic or macro-practice. We turn now to consider how the strengths perspective has been applied to community work methods.

The Strengths Perspective in Community Development: An Assets Approach

While the strengths perspective emerged in a casework practice, its key themes are applicable to other practice methods, such as community development. Community development is a method used by social workers and others, such as town planners, which focuses on developing the resources of communities (Green and Haines, 2002, p. vii). The asset-based community development approach (often referred to as ABCD practice) shifts away from the needs-focused approach that, according to Kretzmann and McKnight (1993, p. 25), has characterized community development and instead focuses on the gifts, skills and assets within a community (Green and Haines, 2002, p. 9). According to Kretzmann and McKnight (1993, p. 13), 'strong communities are basically places where the capacities of local residents are identified, valued and used'.

The key features of the asset-based approach, as outlined by Kretzmann and McKnight (1993), are:

● *Change must begin from inside the community:* It is important that the community drives the change process, as the community will own and support changes and initiatives that it has developed. When the community 'owns' initiatives, the process of creating and sustaining change will build pride and independence within the community. Another reason is that, according to Kretzmann and McKnight (1993, p. 5), in the current climate of neoclassical economic reform, it is futile to depend on outside help and so 'the hard truth is that development must start from within the community'.

- *Change must build on the capacities and assets that already exist within communities:* There are at least four sites where assets can be uncovered – individuals; informal networks, such as neighbourhood ties; civic institutions, such as sporting organizations and self-help groups; and formal institutions, such as schools, charitable institutions, businesses, or government agencies.

- *Change is relationship driven:* Collaboration is fostered across different sectors, such as informal, community service, business and government agencies.

- *Change should be oriented towards sustainable community growth:* Advocates of the assets-based approach are critical of community development approaches that focus primarily on community maintenance, and on approaches that look outside the community for change initiatives (Green and Haines, 2002, pp. 9–11; Kretzmann and McKnight, 1993). Instead, they seek to achieve the long-term social and economic empowerment of disadvantaged communities by building assets within the community and using these as a basis for partnership with other communities and other sectors (see Green and Haines, 2002, p. 11). According to Kretzmann and McKnight (1993, p. 354):

> Clearly a community which has mobilized its internal assets is no longer content to be a recipient of charity. Rather, this mobilized community offer opportunities for real partnerships, for investors who are interested in effective action and in a return for their investment.

Review Question

Thinking about a context practice that interests you, and the social work role(s) within that context, identify the strengths and weaknesses of the strengths perspective for practice in that context.

Strengths of the Strengths Perspective and SFBT

Many practitioners, service provider organizations and social work commentators regard the strengths perspective and SFBT as a valuable addition to the professional base of social work. A key strength of these approaches is their recognition of the power of optimism and hope, on the part of both service worker and service user, for achieving significant improvements in the quality of service users' lives. It challenges us to constantly reflect on the subtle ways in which our attitudes and language as 'helping profes- sionals' can be used to enable or, conversely, disempower service users. At the very least, the strengths perspective and SFBT encourage us to critically examine assumptions that service users' destinies are constrained by the problems and issues they face.

In addition, the strengths perspective and SFBT can provide challenges to the dominant discourses shaping social work practice contexts. Whereas the biomedical and legal discourses promote professional detachment and privilege professional expertise, the strengths perspective and SFBT promote collaboration between workers and service users and encourage a sceptical stance towards expert knowledge. SFBT, in particular, offers a set of tech- niques, notably around the use of questions, that can help unlock service users' potential. These techniques have been applied across a range of social work practice contexts involving practice with individuals, families and groups.

The strengths perspective encourages us to focus on the social, as well as the individual context, of service user concerns. In contrast to the individ- ualistic orientation of the dominant discourses shaping social work practice, the strengths perspective draws our attention to how the resources within service users' informal and formal networks can be used, or developed, to assist them achieve their hopes and dreams (see Quinn, 1988). This focus on building sustainable community support networks for and with service users provides a useful framework for practice in situations where service users' concerns are not amenable to the types of short-term, structured interventions considered in Chapter 7. Indeed, this perspective is now widely utilized in community support work in a broad range of fields, including mental health, disability support, and child and family support agencies, although it is not limited to these contexts.

Weaknesses and Concerns about the Strengths Perspective and SFBT

Despite their considerable value as contemporary practice perspectives, we can also identify some common criticisms of the strengths perspective and SFBT. Both appear naive to the barriers, particularly structural obstacles, that service users experience in realizing small goals, let alone their hopes and dreams. The SFBT approach places a great deal of faith in the capacity of the individual to influence change in their environment through small changes in their own behaviour. Similarly, Cowger (1998, p. 33) argues that:

> The models and perspectives of strengths-based practice must become conceptually more holistic to include the political, structural, and organizational ramifications of the approach and to move beyond the narrow focus on promoting client strengths in direct practice perspectives to critical analysis and action at the institutional, organizational and policy levels.

At best, the strengths perspective adopts a liberal perspective, which focuses change aspirations at the individual and community levels, and SFBT rarely focuses on change outside the local spheres of individual or family interactions. For many social workers, working in anti-oppressive and empowerment traditions, this local change focus is too narrow. Moreover, from an anti-oppressive perspective, we would ask whether the concept of collaborative partnership, advocated by proponents of the strengths perspective and SFBT, is meaningful in the context of their failure to acknowledge the continuing inequalities between service providers and service users (see Dominelli, 1996).

SFBT and the strengths perspective can be criticized for their overemphasis on the capacity and responsibility of individuals and communities to achieve change particularly at the level of community and society. While SFBT proponents rarely aspire to broader social change, proponents of ABCD seem resigned to accepting that change efforts will necessarily be limited by the neoclassical economic policy context. Kretzmann and McKnight (1993, p. 5) argue that disadvantaged communities have 'no other choice' than to create change themselves (see also Weick et al., 1989, p. 354). Many social change advocates, such as anti-oppressive workers and members of consumer rights movements, would argue that there is another choice, that is, to transfer economic and social resources to disadvantage communities as a way of minimizing the impact of global economic and technological change on them (see Dominelli and Hoogvelt, 1996; see also Chapter 5).

While there have been some attempts to apply the strengths perspective and SFBT to statutory practice, further work is needed to ensure that the focus on solutions and capacities is appropriately balanced with workers' responsibility to identify and manage risk. For example, in contexts such as statutory child protection work, mental health risk assessment and criminal justice services, social workers have a statutory and ethical obligation to assess the risk service users present to themselves or others; thus, a primary focus on their strengths may not be viable and may exacerbate some service users' vulnerability to harm or to harm others. Social workers, particularly inexperienced workers, employed in these practice contexts need to take great care to communicate the theoretical foundations and principles of this approach as well as to understand its limitations within their practice context, otherwise there is a risk that practice based on the strengths perspective will be misinterpreted as merely naive, inexpert, or even dangerous, within the practice context.

The final criticism is that proponents of the strengths perspective have, thus far, failed to account for how certain attitudes and behaviours are counted as strengths. There are two problems. One is that, although strengths-based social workers claim a nonjudgemental stance, the concept of 'strength' is a culturally loaded term, as what counts as strength in one context may be seen as weakness in another. For example, in presenting evidence of resilience, Saleebey (2012b, p. 298) reports on a study that found that two out of three children identified as at 'significant risk' for adolescent problems 'had become caring and efficacious adults at age 32 and 40'. There is an implicit assumption here that certain dispositions, such as being 'caring' and 'efficacious', are strengths, yet the bases of these assumptions are not articulated. This failure to reflect on why certain attitudes and behaviours count as strengths leads to a second concern: What are the boundaries of dispositions and behaviours we will endorse as strengths? A strength in one context, such as asserting one's rights, might become dominance in another context. The lack of direction as to how a worker determines a strength is a weakness of this perspective.

The strengths perspective appears to be based on a questionable interpretation of the research on resilience. In his review of the resilience literature, McMillen (1999, p. 458) reports that people are more likely to become resilient in the face of adversity when they face acute events rather than chronic adversity. McMillen (1999, p. 462) also reports that 'children and people from lower socioeconomic classes might have the most difficulty benefiting from post adversity changes in life structure'. These two findings are significant, given that the adversity faced by many social service users is chronic rather than acute and they are disproportionately drawn from socioeconomically disadvantaged backgrounds. Similarly, returning to Saleebey's (2012b, p. 298) report on research findings that 'only one-third of children who had developed serious and emotional problems in adolescence had some continuing midlife problems', Saleebey does not address the fact that further interpretation of this research is that one-third of those identified at risk had experienced serious psychological problems into adulthood – a much higher rate than we would expect for the general population. In short, while the strengths perspective's emphasis on hope, optimism and human resilience is an important corrective to a pathologizing view of service users, we must also be careful of underestimating the elevated risks facing vulnerable populations. Understanding this risk is important for promoting preventive and protective measures for 'at-risk' populations.

Conclusion

The strengths perspective and SFBT are valuable additions to the social work practice base. They embody the humanitarian values on which the social work profession is founded, and provide a framework and practice techniques for promoting respect for service users' capacities and potential. But critical questions are raised about these approaches. Some rest on the limited recognition within both approaches of the structural barriers to service user empowerment. Chapter 9 considers the anti-oppressive approach, which, by contrast, focuses on understanding and responding to structural injustices.

Summary Questions

1   Proponents of the strengths perspective and SFBT aim to empower clients to realize a better quality of life on their own terms. What do you see as the strengths and limitations of both approaches for achieving this aim?

2   What is involved in the practice skill of strengths-based listening?

3   What types of questioning techniques do solution-focused brief therapists use to unlock client potential? How do these techniques work to unlock client potential?

4   What are the features of an asset-based approach to community development?

Recommended Reading

- Berg, I.K. and Kelly, S. (2000) *Building Solutions in Child Protection Services*. New York: WW Norton).
  Comprehensive, practical guide to SFBT and its application to working with families mandated to receive child protection services. A collaboration between Insoo Kim Berg, a leading figure in SFBT, and Susan Kelly, who has an extensive background in public child protection services in the USA.

- De Shazer, S., Berg, I.K., Lipchick, E. et al. (1986) Brief therapy: focused solution development. *Family Process*, 25, 207–21.
  Excellent overview of the SFBT approach developed by de Shazer, Berg and their colleagues at the Brief Family Therapy Center.

- Green, G. and Haines, A. (2002) *Asset Building and Community Development*. (London: Sage).
  Great introduction to the theory and practice of a strengths approach to community development.

- Kretzmann, J. and McKnight, J. (1993) *Building Communities from the Inside Out.* (Chicago: Center for Urban Affairs and Policy Research).
  Practical guide to the application of asset-based community development. Can be ordered from the Asset-Based Community Development Institute's website (see below).

- Saleebey, D. (ed.) (2012) *The Strengths Perspective in Social Work Practice*, 6th edn. (Boston: Pearson).
  Edited by one the leading figures in the strengths perspective; offers a comprehensive introduction to the theory of the strengths approach and its application to a broad range of practice fields, including mental health and addictions. If you only read one collection on the strengths perspective, this should be it.

- Turnell, A. and Edwards, S. (1999) *Signs of Safety: A Solution and Safety Oriented Approach to Child Protection Casework.* (New York: Norton).
  Demonstrates how the strengths perspective and solution-focused approaches can be practically applied to child protection work. The Signs of Safety approach is now internationally recognized and widely used in child welfare services.

Recommended Websites

- **www.abcdinstitute.org**
  Asset-Based Community Development Institute, where John Kretzmann and John McKnight, widely regarded as the founders of the ABCD approach, are located. Includes references to research papers, seminars, and practice projects on ABCD practice.

- **www.sfbta.org**
  Solution-Focused Brief Therapy Association posts information about workshops, conferences and research on SFBT. Readers can also purchase publications (books and DVDs).

- **www.signsofsafety.net**
  Signs of Safety is an innovative solution-focused and safety-organized approach to child protection casework. Provides information about DVDs, workbooks and training opportunities for this approach.

9

MODERN CRITICAL SOCIAL WORK
From Radical to Anti-oppressive Practice

In this chapter we consider modern critical social work. In its broadest sense, critical social work is concerned with the analysis and transformation of power relations at every level of social work practice. This chapter focuses on modern forms of critical social work and Chapter 10 considers post-modern influences on social work generally, including critical social work. The term 'modern critical social work' refers to forms of critical social work that are grounded primarily in modernist ideas about power and identity. 'Critical social work' refers to a broad range of practice perspectives, from radical to anti-oppressive practice. These draw on critical social science theories and focus on understanding and addressing the impact of broad social structures on the problems facing service users and the social work process itself. In this chapter, we discuss the historical foundations of modern critical social work and the radical approaches that preceded anti-oppressive practice. We outline and apply one contemporary form of critical social work, namely anti-oppressive practice, to a case study.

A range of modern critical social work forms exist, including radical, Marxist, feminist and structural social work. Anti-oppressive practice is also included in this chapter as a modern form of critical practice, although some proponents of anti-oppressive practice have incorporated post-modern ideas as this approach has evolved (Dalrymple and Burke, 2006). Modern critical social work approaches share a focus on the structural contexts of service users' problems and incorporate strategies of critical consciousness and collective action against injustice. Unlike other theories we've considered, these theories for practice are built on the rejection of some aspects of the psychological discourses that have made a significant contribution to modern social work (see Chapter 4). In particular, critical social work approaches reject a focus on psychological assessment and change promoted through 'psy' discourses. But, as we shall see, some core concepts from 'psy' discourses, especially the importance of self-reflection and the 'relationship' between worker and service user, have been incorporated into critical theories for practice.

Figure 9.1 locates critical social work after the strengths and SFBT approaches and before postmodern practices. Although critical social work perspectives emerged prior to the strengths and SFBT approaches, critical and postmodern perspectives involve a significant reorientation of social work practice regarding issues of power and identity and, as such, are separated conceptually from the approaches considered in Chapters 6–8. The critical focus on the operation of power and the social construction of identity within social structures (as is the case for critical social work) or within discourse (as is the case in postmodernism) represents a break with the liberal humanist notions of self and power on which many social work theories rely. Liberal humanism emphasizes and values the human capacity for individual agency and this ideal is reflected in the three theories for practice (systems, problem-solving, strengths and solution-focused) discussed in Chapters 6–8, as each valorizes the individual's capacity to achieve change. By contrast, despite some important differences, the theoretical foundations of critical and postmodern approaches to practice require social workers to question liberal humanist notions of rationality, individual agency and the operation of power (see Agger, 1991).

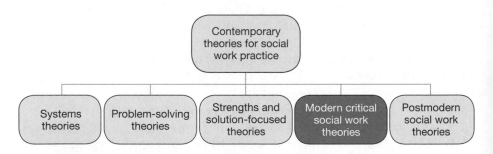

Figure 9.1 Modern critical social work in context

Modern critical social work is oriented towards understanding the structural conditions that impact on the genesis and maintenance of social problems and in which social work practitioners operate. Modern critical social workers emphasize that social workers should seek to address injustice at every level of their practice, from direct engagement with clients through to work aimed at challenging the inequitable distribution of resources. Critical social workers identify injustice as stemming from differences in power and access to material resources. While there is a wide variety of modern critical social work, as identified elsewhere (Healy, 2012, p. 192), all share the following characteristics:

1   A commitment to solidarity with oppressed and excluded individuals and communities (Leonard, 1994).

2   Identifying and, as far as possible, acknowledging the power differentials in all aspects of interpersonal relationships but especially between human service professionals and service users.

3   Recognition of the influential role of social, economic and political systems in shaping individual and community experiences and opportunities and the relationships between service providers and users (Leonard, 1995).

4   A commitment to the transformation of the processes and structures perpetuating domination and exploitation within the human service system and broader social structures.

The Foundations of Modern Critical Social Work

The term 'modern critical social work' refers to a broad range of practice approaches, including Marxist social work, radical social work, structural social work, feminist social work, anti-racist social work, anti-oppressive and anti-discriminatory social work. Despite their considerable diversity, the approaches share an intellectual debt to the critical social science paradigm (Healy, 2000, p. 18).

The key features of the critical social science paradigm that are especially relevant for modernist forms of critical social work include the claim that macro-social structures shape social relations at every level of social life (Healy, 2000, pp. 19–21). For example, some critical social science theories assert that capitalism shapes relations between middle-class and working-class people, patriarchy shapes relations between men and women, and imperialism constrains relations between European and non-European peoples. Drawing on these understandings, critical social workers seek to understand the original causes of oppression, within overarching social structures, and are committed to transforming these structures (see de Maria, cited in Reisch and Andrews, 2001, p. 5).

Critical social scientists also hold that the world is divided between the 'haves' and 'have nots' and that the interests of these groups are opposed and irreconcilable (Healy, 2000, p. 19; see also Mullaly, 1993, pp. 142–3). The 'haves' are members of privileged groups, such as the middle classes, males, Europeans, heterosexuals and able-bodied people, while the 'have nots' are located on the other side of the social divide, that is, the working classes, women, non-Europeans, gays and lesbians, and people with disabilities. In terms of these divisions, social workers are represented as powerful, because of their professional status and access to institutional power, while service users are represented as relatively powerless. As we shall see, modernist forms of critical practice require social workers to reflect on their access to power and to develop strategies for sharing power with service users who are assumed to be less powerful (see Dominelli, 1988, pp. 10–11; Dalrymple and Burke, 1995).

Another feature of the critical social science paradigm is the view that the oppressed are encouraged to accept their oppressed status via dominant ideologies that present the current social order as just (Fay, 1987, p. 70). For example, the dominant discourse of neoclassical economics focuses on individual choices and responsibilities but obscures the way in which these choices are constrained by patterns of advantage and disadvantage. Critical social workers argue that social workers should raise the consciousness of service users, that is, help them see that the causes of their problems lie not in themselves but in unjust social structures.

A final feature of the critical social science paradigm relevant to modern critical social work is the emphasis on empowering oppressed people to act, collectively, to achieve social change. In all forms of critical social science, the ideal goal of collective action is a society free of all forms of oppression and domination (Fay, 1987). In this paradigm, it is in service users' collective self-interest to agitate for social change. Drawing on these ideas, critical social workers aim to create opportunities for service users to participate in collective, rather than individual, responses to their concerns. So, for example, in responding to young mothers' experiences of violence, we would see individual support and counselling as a precursor to these young women's participation in the development of collective, and consumer-run, initiatives for challenging violence against young mothers (see Healy and Walsh, 1997; Healy, 2000).

The Early History of Critical Social Work

Although critical social work theories gained prominence during the 1960s and 70s, critical social workers have always existed within the social work profession. In the late nineteenth century, critical elements within the profession highlighted the impact of socioeconomic disadvantage on service users and encouraged social workers to forge links with social movements and the trade union movement (Reisch and Andrews, 2001, p. 35). Perhaps the best known 'first wave' critical social worker is Jane Addams (1860–1935), who worked in the settlement house movement in Chicago from the 1890s onwards and later won the Nobel Peace Prize in 1931 for her pacifist activities.

During the middle part of the twentieth century, a small number of leading social work commentators challenged the profession to move beyond its increasingly individualistic orientation. For example, in 1949, Norma Parker (see Parker, 1969), a leading Australian social work academic, advocated a human rights framework for analysing social issues and promoting service users' wellbeing. The historical evidence suggests that these social workers sometimes paid a high personal and professional price for their views, as they were often professionally isolated and vulnerable to persecution (see Reisch and Andrews, 2001). For example, in the USA, during the McCarthy era of the 1940s and 50s, Bertha Reynolds, a prominent early critical social worker, was forced to resign from her academic post and was effectively blacklisted from service organizations because of her association with the Communist Party (Reisch and Andrews, 2001, p. 115).

The Birth of Radical Social Work

During the 1960s and 70s, radical social work emerged as a distinctive practice approach and had a significant influence on social work education. The dramatic expansion of radical social work literature during this period can be attributed to a number of factors, including the growing influence of sociology, particularly critical sociology, on social work and social policy, critical social change movements, and the discovery of poverty as a public policy concern (Reisch and Andrews, 2001; see also Thompson, 2006). Across what we now know as the postindustrial world, a cadre of radical social work academics drew on Marxist philosophy to reorient social work towards its 'true' purpose – radical social change (Martin, 2003, pp. 23–4; see Bailey and Brake, 1975; Throssel, 1975; Corrigan and Leonard, 1978; Galper, 1980).

From a base in critical social science theories, particularly Marxism, radical social workers argued that social workers should recognize that the origins of service users' problems lay primarily in unjust social structures, rather than in their personal histories. They highlighted the inherent contradictions in the role of social workers, and questioned the potential for truly progressive practices in capitalist societies and urged social workers to constantly reflect on the social control dimensions of their ostensibly caring role (see Corrigan and Leonard, 1978, pp. 90–3). Radical social workers encouraged social workers to eschew the individualistic practices that characterized 'psy' approaches, in favour of working collectively with service users for social change. For example, Throssel (1975, p. 21) argued that:

> Any substantial change in the current oppression of whole groups of people requires not diagnosis and treatment of those groups but change in the others – the non-deviant, the 'normal' or 'healthy'. Thus, to overcome poverty (and its consequences), there needs to be a relinquishing of wealth by the rich.

Consistent with critical social science principles, radical social work theorists argued that service users would only act rationally in their own best interests once they understood that the true origins of their problems lay not in themselves but in oppressive social structures. Thus, critical consciousness raising was a key practice strategy employed by radical social workers and remains a cornerstone of modern critical social work practice.

Beyond Marxist theory, social workers can draw on other bodies of social theory. However, as we shall see, certain forms of social theory, particularly those associated with social movements such as feminist and anti-racist movements, feature more prominently in the modern critical social work literature than others, such as the neo-Marxist work of the Frankfurt School. Notwithstanding the significant influence of the Frankfurt School on critical social theory generally, its influence on critical social work has been limited. The small body of literature examining the potential of the Frankfurt School for social work practice has offered critical insights into existing contexts and methods of practice rather seeking to develop new approaches (see Gray and Lovatt, 2007, 2008; Houston, 2009). This limited engagement can perhaps be explained by the specialist philosophical discourse of the Frankfurt School, which may constrain its relevance to social workers without specialist philosophical training, and the pessimistic outlook that pervaded some of this literature regarding the potential for progressive social change under conditions of late modern capitalism (Healy, 2012). We turn now to an exploration of some of the different frames utilized by social workers in the context of increasingly diverse approaches to modern critical practice.

The Diversification of Critical Practice Models

Given their concern with a dramatic reorientation of social work, radical social workers had probably anticipated that their perspectives would contribute to tensions within the profession. Less expected perhaps was the growing discontent among radical social workers about the limited scope of a class-based analysis as a base for critical practice. From the 1970s onwards, a diverse band of critical social work projects 'emerged in connection with various intellectual movements, including feminism, race theory and Marxist criticism, that identified dimensions of economic and political domination in modern societies' (Gray and Webb, 2009, p. 77). The most prominent of these new critical practice models were feminist social work, anti-racist social work, and structural social work.

Feminist social workers critiqued the gender blindness of radical social work. They sought to broaden radical definitions of social oppression by placing women's experiences of gender oppression on the agenda of critical social work, alongside other forms of oppression, such as classism, racism and heterosexism (Dominelli and McLeod, 1989, p. 2). These feminist social workers argued that a gender analysis must be central to radical practice because the vast majority of social service workers and service users are female (Hanmer and Statham, 1999). In practice, they drew attention to women's specific experiences of oppression, such as their vulnerability to domestic and sexual violence, which had been largely unrecognized in the radical paradigm (Weeks, 1994; Hanmer and Statham, 1999). Like radical social workers, modern feminist social workers asserted that the true origins of women's oppression lay in the macro-structures, particularly those associated with patriarchy (Dominelli and McLeod, 1989, p. 33).

From feminist social movements, feminist practitioners incorporated practice principles that have influenced other forms of modern critical practice. One of these principles is that 'the personal is political'. By this, feminist practitioners meant that one's personal experiences have their origins in political structures and that our personal behaviour reflects and reinforces broader political processes (Dominelli and McLeod, 1989, p. 33; see also White, 2006). Thus, we should reflect in our personal and professional relationships the kinds of political changes we would like to effect. Another powerful idea in feminist social work is the notion of 'radical egalitarianism', meaning that service providers should seek to minimize the power differentials between service workers and service users (Dominelli, 2002a, p. 39).

Among radical social workers, there was also a concern that issues of racial injustice were inadequately addressed by class-focused analyses. From this, distinctive anti-racist approaches emerged during the 1980s, not as a threat to radical social work, but as a necessary extension of the apparently myopic focus on class-based oppression. Anti-racist social workers sought to show that racial oppression is a significant and distinct form of oppression, rather than merely an effect of class-based injustices (Dominelli, 1988; Hutchinson-Reis, 1989; Shah, 1989). Like radical social workers, anti-racist social workers adopted a critical stance towards modern professional social work, but extended the radical analysis to focus on the racial dimensions of oppression. For example, Dominelli (1988, p. 33) asserts that:

> As their attention is deflected onto resolving 'clients' personal problems', social workers expend considerable energy teaching clients to change their behaviour, making it conform more closely to 'acceptable' standards. For black clients, this has led white social workers to downplay the specific circumstances and avenues through which racism holds black people back and deprives them of resources, power, justice and dignity.

Anti-racist social workers sought to reform social work practice towards recognition of and collective responses to racial injustice (see Dominelli, 1988).

Structural social work represented another offshoot from radical social work. One of the earliest references to 'structural social work' was in 1974 when US social work scholars Middleman and Goldberg published a book on this topic. Since the late 1970s, Canadian scholars have been strongly associated with the development of this practice theory, initially in the work of Moreau (1979, 1990) and, more recently, in publications by Mullaly (1993, 2007), Carniol (1992) and Bishop (2002). In common with the other theories in this chapter, structural social work is based in the critical social science paradigm (Mullaly, 2007). As their name suggests, structural social workers are primarily concerned with analysing and confronting structural injustices, particularly 'how the rich and powerful within society constrain and define the less powerful' (Martin, 2003, p. 24; see also Mullaly, 2007). However, in contrast with radical social workers who focused on class-based oppression, structural social workers insist that 'all forms of oppression are, in reality, mutually reinforcing and overlapping' (Moreau, 1990, p. 64; see also Mullaly, 2007).

Structural social workers seek to alleviate the negative effects of 'an exploitative and alienating social order' and, ultimately, aim to transform the social order to one of greater material equality and respect for diversity (Mullaly, 2007, p. 245). Structural social workers' practice strategies draw on not only critical social science, but also ideas from critical social movements, particularly the women's movement, gay and lesbian rights movements, and the trade union movement (see Bishop, 2002; Mullaly, 2007). In addition, structural social workers draw on the insights of a range of critical social work theories, including radical, anti-racist and feminist social work (Mullaly, 2007). Again, like the critical practice models we have discussed so far, structural social workers promote consciousness raising on the grounds that 'the social order may seriously impair a client's capacities to accurately construe reality' (Moreau, 1990, p. 54). They also aim to facilitate collective rather than individualistic responses to structural injustices (Moreau, 1990, p. 53), and urge social workers to engage with progressive social change activities in order to address the structural injustices that lie at the heart of the issues facing most service users.

Critical Social Work Today

Within the social work literature, a diversity of critical social work practice writing continues to flourish. In the past decade, a significant body of work defending and reinvigorating the radical social work project has emerged (see Lavalette and Ferguson, 2007; Ferguson, 2008, 2011; Lavalette, 2011). This has coincided with, and been informed by, the emergence of social movements within the social work field, particularly the Social Work

Action Network in the UK. This contemporary body of radical social work writing sits alongside a large body of anti-oppressive, anti-racist, critical and feminist social work writings (Healy, 2000; Dominelli, 2002b; Fook, 2002; White, 2006).

Perhaps more than any other body of social work literature, modern critical social work writers draw attention to the oppressive circumstances and effects of social work practice. In their articulation of approaches to practice, this diverse group draws attention to the devastating impact of neoliberalism and new public management on the social work profession and on individuals and communities (see White, 2006; Mullaly, 2007; Ferguson, 2011). They are also critical of the role of social workers as agents of the state and urge social workers to challenge state practices and policies that disenfranchise vulnerable citizens.

Despite a unifying concern about changing societal and institutional conditions, there remains some dispute among modern critical social workers about both the utility of the term 'critical social work' and the diverse body of critical social work approaches. Ferguson (2008, p. 104) is critical of the extent to which contemporary critical social work theories depart from radical notions of 'the nature of social divisions and the possibility (and even desirability) of social change'. Ferguson (2008, 2011) critiques the extent to which a focus on 'identity', such as gender or ethnic identity, undermines recognition of the material base of oppression and the impact of the social structures of late capitalist society on the continuing marginalization of individuals and communities.

The radical social workers' case for recognition of the class base of oppression is compelling and a much needed reminder regarding the contribution of class inequality and material disadvantage to the lives of people with whom we practise. Yet the relationship between class and other forms of oppression as foci of social work analysis will, necessarily, be a matter for ongoing debate within the profession. Social workers working within the critical tradition make similarly compelling cases regarding the impact of identity-based oppressions that cannot be ignored nor subsumed within a class-based analysis of oppression. Indeed, the tension between the politics of redistribution and recognition is well recognized in sociological and philosophical debates about social justice (see Fraser, 1997; Olsen, 2008) and is unlikely to be resolved in favour of either side of the debate. For critical social workers, this means that we must recognize the multiple dimensions of oppression and acknowledge our dual responsibilities to address the economic and cultural bases of oppression. We turn now to outline anti-oppressive social work as one model of modern critical social work practice that seeks to recognize and address the multiple dimensions of oppression encountered in social work practice.

Anti-oppressive Practice

Over the past two decades, anti-oppressive social work has emerged and developed as a dominant theory of critical social work practice. Anti-oppressive practice first arose in the UK in the late 1980s (Martin, 2003, p. 29). During the 1990s, a series of landmark publications on anti-discriminatory and anti-oppressive practice, primarily by British authors (see Dalrymple and Burke, 1995; Dominelli, 1997; Thompson, 2006), led to international recognition of this approach. According to Dalrymple and Burke (2006, p. 7):

> Anti-oppressive practice is a critical social work approach that draws on critical social science theories and is informed by humanistic and social justice values, taking account of the experiences and views of oppressed people.

Anti-oppressive practice, like radical social work, is based on recognition of the structural origins of services users' problems and seeks to transform power relations in practice. Anti-oppressive theory also promotes social workers' role and responsibility in achieving social transformation (see Dominelli, 2002b). Yet anti-oppressive theory goes beyond the radical social work tradition in a number of ways, most particularly in its insistence that the personal and cultural bases of oppression must be integrated with the structural analysis of oppression and its recognition of interpersonal and statutory work as legitimate sites of anti-oppressive practice.

In this discussion, we refer to anti-discriminatory theory alongside anti-oppressive theory on the grounds that both theories share many core assumptions. However, we also alert the reader to debate among theorists about the commonalities and differences between the two schools. Dalrymple and Burke (2006, p. 4) claim that anti-oppressive practice places greater emphasis on changing social structural arrangements, while anti-discriminatory theorists rely more strongly on anti-discriminatory legislation as a vehicle for achieving change. However, anti-discriminatory theorists may contest this claim on the grounds that they too offer a comprehensive theory of practice aimed at challenging existing structural arrangements (Thompson, 2006).

Core Assumptions of Anti-oppressive Practice

A key assumption of anti-oppressive practice is that social workers must recognize multiple forms of oppression and that all forms of oppression should be acknowledged as harmful (Thompson, 2006). In anti-oppressive theory, oppression arises from unequal power across social divisions (Burke and Harrison, 2002, p. 229). For example, Mitchell (cited in Dalrymple and

Burke, 2006, p. 41) argues that women are oppressed by men, children and older people by adults, disabled people by able people and so on. Anti-oppressive theorists urge social workers to be constantly alert to the social divisions affecting service users' lives.

Anti-oppressive social workers argue that social divisions shape practice relationships and that we can reduce the disempowering effects of these differences by critical reflection on our position within social structures. According to Thompson (1992, pp. 169–70, cited in Thompson, 2006, p. 15): 'There is no middle ground; intervention either adds to oppression (or at least condones it) or goes some small way towards easing or breaking such oppression.' Anti-oppressive theorists emphasize that the social work role is an intensely political one, in which social workers occupy a privileged status, at least in contrast with service users. Hence, social workers must adopt an ongoing critical and reflective stance so as to avert, as far as possible, replicating oppressive social relations in practice (see Burke and Harrison, 2002).

Anti-oppressive theorists highlight the multiple levels of oppression including, but also going beyond, structural oppression. Thompson (2006, pp. 26–8) proposes a three-dimensional model of discrimination, the 'PCS' analysis, that describes the interaction across the personal or psychological, the cultural and the structural sources of oppression (see also Dalrymple and Burke, 2006; Mullaly, 2002). For Thompson (2006, p. 26), the personal level of practice refers to the personal feelings and attitudes of the service user, as well as the interpersonal relationship established between service providers and service users. The cultural level 'represents the interests and influence of society as reflected in the social values and cultural norms we internalize via the processes of socialization' (Thompson, 2006, p. 27). Anti-oppressive theorists require social workers to constantly reflect on the ways in which the social structures associated with capitalism, patriarchy and imperialism contribute to, and interact with, the personal and cultural levels of oppression (Thompson, 2006, p. 28).

Anti-oppressive theorists emphasize that various forms of oppression interact with other. For analytic purposes, they identify specific kinds of oppression, such as ageism and sexism, while also recognizing that, in practice, individuals may experience multiple forms of oppression (Mullaly, 2002, Ch. 7; Thompson, 2006). Recognition of this complexity has significant implications for collective action, insofar as anti-oppressive practitioners do not assume that a specific kind of oppression will necessarily provide the basis for commonality. For example, the experience of oppression encountered by a black single mother will, of necessity, differ from that of a black disabled man; thus, shared racial oppression cannot be assumed as a basis for commonality in all contexts. According to Mullaly (2002, p. 153), 'making links between oppressions, therefore, will require the recognition of both commonalities and specificities across different forms and experiences of oppression'. In addition, Mullaly (2002, p. 153) argues that we must recognize that complex interactions across oppressions can intensify the experience of oppression. So, for example, a person subject to two forms of oppression, such as class and race-based oppression, may suffer more than twice the level of oppression experienced by a person subject to only one of these forms of oppression (see Mullaly, 2002, pp. 153–6).

Anti-oppressive social workers recognize and seek to support a broad range of intervention strategies. A key strength of anti-oppressive theories is that they recognize interpersonal and statutory practice as legitimate sites of social work practice and, in so doing, seek to develop the potential for critical practice in these sites. For example, in contrast to radical social workers' wholesale rejection of statutory power (see Simpkin, 1979, Ch. 7), anti-oppressive social workers seek a more constructive engagement with constructive power, recognizing it as a necessary but often destructive form of authority (Dalrymple and Burke, 2006). In particular, anti-oppressive practice promotes a minimal intervention approach, which incorporates the idea that practitioners should intervene early and in ways that prevent the escalation of state involvement in clients' lives.

We turn now to a case study of the Hayden family.

Case Study **The Hayden family**

Imagine you are working as a social worker in a community-based child and family welfare service staffed by social workers, psychologists and a family worker who provide services to those with ongoing involvement from the statutory authority. Service providers can work for up to three years with a family requiring long-term support and therapeutic intervention. The service works closely with the statutory authority and other agencies, as many families referred have a broad network of services involved in their lives. You have received the following referral from the statutory child protection authority.

Family history of Hayden family re: child protection concerns

Julia – 35 years

Kathleen (subject child) – 12 months

Max (subject child) – 4 years

Cynthia – 14 years

Delia – 16 years

Jonathan – 18 years

Julia is a woman of Anglo-Saxon background whose own childhood was characterized by instability, loss and abuse. Julia's mum and dad split up when she was nine years old.

▶

Initially, Julia lived with her mum, but when her mother's new partner moved in, she was sent to live with her dad, who proceeded to sexually and physically abuse her. When Julia turned 14, she ran away to a refuge.

Julia experienced periods of homelessness and although a good student, she found it hard to maintain her schooling. She became pregnant at 16 to her then boyfriend, and gave birth to her first child at 17. Later, she married the father of her two daughters but the relationship was characterized by violence and drug abuse, and she has been struggling with a drug habit ever since. Her oldest three children were placed in care because of the violence and drug abuse affecting her parenting and she had irregular contact with them for several years. Three years ago, the children re-established contact with Julia and the two girls returned to her care six months later.

Julia has had a number of male partners but most of these relationships have been characterized by domestic violence and criminal activity. The family has been living in public housing ever since the birth of her four year old.

Despite her history of severe abuse, Julia has a clear picture of the sort of parent she would like to be and is able to articulate the steps she needs to take to get there. Concerns focus on her capacity to reach her goals. Julia has a supportive drug and alcohol worker who is an effective advocate; however, there have been concerns that this worker and the drug and alcohol service generally minimize the impact of the drug abuse on Julia's ability to parent. In this case, there has been a history of conflict and poor communication between the services involved with the family.

Reasons for referral to the child and family welfare service

Julia is experiencing difficulties in her ability to adequately parent her two youngest children. The statutory child protection officer tells you that there have been a number of reports on the two younger children related to neglect – in particular, emotional neglect – and whether or not Julia has the capacity to be a good enough parent. At one stage, she left her two young children with her mother and disappeared for two weeks on a 'drug binge'. After this incident, the youngest child was placed in the grandmother's care and has recently returned to Julia.

The concerns of the statutory child protection agency include:

- Julia's long history of drug use

- her criminal activity in relation to this

- her history of being involved in violent relationships

- her ability to understand the impact of drug use on her parenting capacity

- the impact of disrupted attachment on her youngest child.

She struggles to respond to her children's need and also has a tendency to rely on her older children to provide the parenting of the younger children. For example, her 16-year-old daughter, Delia, failed to attend college because she had to stay home to look after the youngest child.

We now discuss five key principles of anti-oppressive practice, and using practice exercises, you are asked to apply these principles to the Hayden family case study.

1: Critical Reflection on Self in Practice

Anti-oppressive social workers seek to maintain an open and critical stance towards their practice (Dalrymple and Burke, 2006; Thompson, 2006). This approach demands that we reflect on the ways in which our own biographies, especially how our membership of particular social divisions, shapes our practice relationships (Burke and Harrison, 2002, p. 231). We are also challenged to reflect on how the biographies of other professionals involved in intervention and assessment might affect their capacity to truly empathize with and understand clients' experiences. The assumption is that by reflecting on our membership of social categories, and where possible, replacing ourselves with workers of similar social backgrounds, we can begin to address power differentials in practice.

Practice Exercise **Critical reflection on self**

As the social worker at the child and family welfare service:

- Who do you see as the service user(s) in the Hayden family?

- Who would you see as the service user if you were working in a different service, such as the drug and alcohol service, or the local statutory authority?

- Using the anti-oppressive framework, what social divisions are you a member of, for example gender, class, race identities?

- How might your membership of these identity groups enhance or limit your capacity to work with the client(s)?

2: Critical Assessment of Service Users' Experiences of Oppression

Anti-oppressive practitioners assess how personal, cultural and structural processes shape the problems service users present to social service agencies. An anti-oppressive assessment requires us to consider how the service users' membership of specific social divisions and their historical and geographical context shape their experiences and the options for action available to them (Burke and Harrison, 2002, p. 232). In our analysis of service users' oppression, it is important that we consider the impact of major social divisions such as race, class and gender, as well as other divisions arising from inequality and discrimination, such as 'geographical location, mental distress and employment status' (Burke and Harrison, 2002, p. 232). In addition, the anti-oppressive assessment process turns workers' attention to a critical analysis of the prevailing ideologies shaping agency policies and resource allocation. For example, we might consider how the discourses of biomedicine, neoclassical economics and law might shape various professionals' assessment of the Hayden family and the services available to them.

The processes of critical reflection also extend to reflection on how the language one uses in assessment is shaped by dominant ideologies that convey and sustain oppressive power relations. Dalrymple and Burke (2006, p. 150) emphasize that in our practice:

> we have to be aware of the way in which language can reflect power relations and have an impact on the people with whom we are working ... It enables workers to label others and define what is acceptable and unacceptable behaviour. Terms such as disturbed, at risk and in need describe behaviour from a particular value perspective.

Anti-oppressive theorists contend that while they do not negate social workers' responsibilities towards the assessment of phenomena such as 'risk' and 'need', they insist that any assessment must also be 'theoretically informed, holistic, empowering and challenging' (Burke and Harrison, 2002, p. 234).

Practice Exercise **Undertaking critical assessment**

Using an anti-oppressive framework, discuss:

● What forms of oppression are these service users subject to? (Remember to consider major social divisions, for example class and sex, and other forms of discrimination, such as unemployment and isolation.)

● In your role as a child and family welfare worker, what dominant ideas or discourses will shape service provision to the Hayden family?

● How will these ideas shape service provision to this family?

3: Empowering Service Users

Anti-oppressive approaches to empowerment seek to overcome the cultural, institutional and structural, as well as personal, obstacles to clients taking greater control of their lives (Dalrymple and Burke, 2006, Ch. 5).

At the interpersonal level, anti-oppressive social workers promote service user empowerment by encouraging them to share their feelings of powerlessness (Dalrymple and Burke, 2006, p. 113). Again, like other forms of critical social work, anti-oppressive theorists support consciousness-raising processes that enable service users to understand how structural and cultural injustices shape their experiences of oppression, which highlight that service users are not alone in their experiences of powerlessness (Mullaly, 2002, p. 180).

Anti-oppressive theorists identify that a further barrier to empowerment may lie in service users' lack of capacities, or confidence in their capacities, to act. Thus, social workers working in the anti-oppressive paradigm work with service users to identify areas for skill development and to facilitate opportunities for service users to exercise and gain confidence in their capacities. Another way service providers can empower service users is by ensuring that their views are incorporated into the assessment process, especially where the service provider and service user disagree.

At an institutional level, anti-oppressive social workers promote changes to the organization and delivery of services in ways that enhance anti-oppressive practice and service user control (see Thompson, 2006). Anti-oppressive theorists insist that, because the processes of service delivery can serve to oppress or empower, it is crucial that service providers have opportunities to learn about, and maximize their potential for, anti-oppressive practice. According to Thompson (2006, p. 177), 'awareness training' for service providers can help to promote anti-discriminatory practice at every level of the service organization. Additionally, anti-oppressive theorists promote service user involvement in decision-making about the management of social service resources.

Empowerment at the structural level requires social workers to work towards fundamental reform of social, economic and political structures in ways that lead to the more just distribution of material resources and social power. Mullaly (2002, p. 194) suggests that the obstacles to structural empowerment can be addressed by the development of alternative services and organizations, engagement with progressive social movements, critical social policy practice, and revitalization of the political sector. Returning to the case study, we might use the knowledge we have gained by our work with the Hayden family to expose the inadequacies of current government policy and service provision to families affected by parental drug use.

Practice Exercise **A critical and multidimensional approach to empowerment**

- Identify at least one barrier to empowerment facing members of the Hayden family at each of the following levels: personal, institutional, cultural and structural.

- Identify and discuss two practical strategies you would use for addressing each of these barriers.

4: Working in Partnership

For the anti-oppressive social worker, the term 'working in partnership' means that 'service users must be included as far as possible as citizens in the decision-making processes which affect their lives' (Dalrymple and Burke, 2006, pp. 131–3). While all the practice theories we have discussed incorporate partnership as a practice principle, anti-oppressive theorists take the notion of partnership in a different direction. In contrast to task-centred practice or the strengths approach, which take partnership as some-thing that can be achieved relatively easily given the will of both parties, anti-oppressive theorists see partnership as a vexed issue. They contend that the potential for partnership is constrained by unequal power relations arising from:

- the stigma of service use

- vested power interests held by professionals and service provider agencies

- social control roles of service agencies

- agency accountabilities to third parties such as funding bodies rather than primarily to service users themselves (Dalrymple and Burke, 2006).

For anti-oppressive practitioners, partnership must begin with the genuine sharing of power and a commitment to collaboration at interper-sonal and institutional levels (Dalrymple and Burke, 2006, p. 133). Some ways of enhancing partnership at the personal level include open and clear communication about the nature and scope of the social worker's role. For example, it is vital that service users are made aware of your statutory responsibilities in relation to them and the organizational constraints, such as time limits, on your involvement with them. Partnership also demands that we value the individual by, for example, showing respect for their perspectives and their lived knowledge (Burke and Harrison, 2002; Mullaly, 2002).

At both personal and institutional levels, it is important to maximize service users' opportunities for participation in the decisions affecting them. Some ways of achieving this include establishing an agency charter in which service users' right to participate is endorsed and mechanisms are established for redressing a lack of opportunity to participate. At an agency level, this will also involve the allocation of resources, such as support staff, to ensure that service users can truly participate in decision-making.

Practice Exercise **Working in partnership**

- Identify one barrier to partnership that would face a social worker seeking to work in an anti-oppressive way with the Hayden family.

- Discuss two strategies you could use to overcome this barrier.

5: Minimal Intervention

Anti-oppressive social workers recognize that social services work is a contradictory activity in which social care dimensions are always intertwined with social control. However, anti-oppressive theorists concede that social workers may need to enact social control to prevent harm to the service user, as is the case in high-risk environments (see Dalrymple and Burke, 1995, p. 78). Anti-oppressive theorists adopt the principle of minimal intervention in order to reduce the oppressive and disempowering dimensions of social work intervention. Minimal intervention means that social workers should aim to intervene in the least intrusive and oppressive ways possible (Payne, 1997, p. 261; see also Dalrymple and Burke, 2006, p. 15). In practice, this usually means that social workers should focus on early intervention, with the primary aim of preventing the escalation of risk of harm to the service user.

Anti-oppressive social workers can achieve minimal intervention through a focus on early intervention and working towards increasing the availability and accessibility of services, particularly preventive services. For example, service workers might adopt an outreach model of practice that increases service users' knowledge and options to access support services that could help a person manage their struggles with mental health concerns.

Another way we might increase the service's accessibility and comprehensiveness is by linking existing services. For example, when working with a group of young parents, we might move beyond a focus on their parenting needs to increase their access to services such as literacy and educational services to address long-term barriers to social and economic participation.

Practice Exercise **Practising minimal intervention**

- How might you minimize the intrusiveness of your intervention with the Hayden family?

- Imagine that the manager at the child and family service has asked you for your ideas about how the organization might minimize the intrusiveness of its interventions with families like the Haydens. What practical strategies would you recommend for your organization?

Anti-oppressive Practice: Some Critical Reflections

Here, we consider the strengths, limits and concerns associated with this approach. The substantial body of recent publications on anti-oppressive practice attests to the contemporary popularity of this approach, at least among social work educators and authors. The key strengths of this practice model include its reconciliation of social work values and practice methods. Anti-oppressive practice places the value of social justice centre stage in all dimensions of social work practice. It does not blame individuals for their difficulties, but encourages us to adopt a multidimensional analysis, which recognizes the personal, cultural and structural dimensions of the oppression experienced by service users, such as the Hayden family. It ensures that, as practitioners, we recognize the effects of cultural practices and social structures on services users' lives, and it makes these processes and structures a legitimate site of social service intervention.

Unlike earlier critical practice models, such as radical social work, anti-oppressive practice also values the contribution that local change processes can make to achieving social change. An anti-oppressive approach, then, would encourage us to consider how we can promote effective support for the Hayden family. It would also encourage us to constantly reflect on how our subjectivities shape our capacity to practise in an anti-oppressive way with all members of the Hayden family. For example, we would reflect on how our subjectivity as middle-class helping professionals limits our understanding of the dilemmas faced by Julia as the parent of five children living in public housing.

Anti-oppressive practice challenges social workers to recognize the cultural and structural context of their practice. In the case of the Hayden family, this allows us to move beyond a focus on family dynamics to recognize the cultural and structural dimensions of their situation. Thus, using an anti-oppressive approach, we might become involved in establishing support and advocacy services for families with parents affected by drug and alcohol use. In this way, we might prevent families, like the Hayden family, from reaching the crisis points that lead to statutory intervention.

Despite the growing popularity of anti-oppressive practice in the social work literature, we can also identify many limitations in this approach. We have serious concerns about the application of this model to 'high-risk' decision-making, that is, in situations where there is a significant risk of death or serious injury to a client. The strong critique of the 'psy' discourse underpinning this approach, accompanied by the prioritization of structural analysis of clients' experiences, can lead social workers to neglect individual psychological and personal factors that may contribute substantially to elevated risk in some contexts, such as child protection, mental health, and work in criminal justice. Social workers' capacity to act in high-

risk situations can be further limited by the principle of minimal intervention, which is based on insight into the oppressive effects of social work
intervention, but with the exception of the Dalrymple and Burke's (1995)
work on the topic, there is little acknowledgement of the importance and
helpfulness of the use of power in social service interventions. Indeed, in
situations involving spousal or child assault, what is experienced as oppressive social service intervention by one party, the assailant, may be experienced as the way out of an untenable situation by another, the victim of
violence. Even in less extreme situations, clients do not necessarily experience service intervention as oppressive; the anti-oppressive model fails to
take account of the diversity of clients' experiences of service provision,
especially the fact that some service users willingly seek out this form of
intervention to address a wide variety of needs (Wise, 1990).

Furthermore, the anti-oppressive principle of minimal intervention is
especially problematic in instances where service users present different and
conflicting needs, as it provides no way of prioritizing one set of service users'
needs over another. For example, the framework gives us no way of prioritizing the needs of Julia Hayden (the mother in our case study) and those of
her children, particularly Kathleen and Max (the two youngest children).

Another limitation of the anti-oppressive approach is its reliance on an
oppositional stance, in which the battle lines are clearly drawn even before
we enter specific sites of practice. Thompson (2006, p. 179), for example,
emphasizes that there 'can be no middle ground', meaning that our practice as social workers either challenges or reinforces discrimination and
oppression. The potential polarization between what is identified as anti-
oppressive practice and that which condones oppression is problematic in
many areas of social work practice where compromise and negotiation of
'grey areas' can be critical to negotiating a workable solution to a problem
at hand. If we arrive at these situations with preconceived notions of
'enemy and ally' and 'good and bad', our capacity to respectfully listen to,
and work with, a range of stakeholders will be constrained. In relation to
the Hayden family, we must also be careful about what is labelled as
'powerful and established' ideology and what is recognized as genuine
concerns. This case study raises some potentially painful issues, particularly for Julia, such as confronting the effects of her drug use on her
parenting, and we must be careful of the potential to dismiss these
concerns as evidence of a 'powerful and established' ideology, such as the
ideology of parenting.

A contradiction exists between anti-oppressive theorists' claim to
promote dialogue in practice and their assumptions that they hold a true
and correct analysis of the world. This is evident in the practice of
consciousness raising, in which the social worker, in a spirit of dialogue,
introduces a critical structural analysis of service users' experience. For

example, Mullaly (2002, p. 184), describes a three-stage model of consciousness raising, in which the service user develops an awareness of their shared oppression with other members of their oppressed category and gains a sense of identification, self-respect and pride with this category. The danger of consciousness-raising efforts is that those who do not conform to the truths presented by the anti-oppressive service provider may be dismissed as lacking critical consciousness or as conservative reactionaries. For example, Dominelli (2002b, p. 10) charges those who oppose anti-oppressive practice as fearful of losing 'the taken-for-granted privileges accorded to them through an inegalitarian social order'. The issue here is that by characterizing all those who oppose anti-oppressive practice 'insights' as self-interested or conservative, anti-oppressive theorists insulate their approach from the critical practical reflection required to understand the uses and the limits of the model for promoting critical practice in the diverse institutional contexts of social work activity.

The primary reliance on a structural analysis of power relations that underpins this theory leaves little room for recognizing different power relations at local levels. For example, in reflecting on a case scenario involving a young black woman, Burke and Harrison (2002, p. 232) contend that: 'A white male social worker brings to the situation a dynamic that will reproduce the patterns of oppression to which black women are subjected in the wider society.' The assumption here is that one's membership of certain identity categories associated with class, gender and race have direct and causative effects on local power relations. But other factors, such as organizational philosophy, current social policy and legislative dictates, and the valuing of different kinds of local knowledge, can also have profound effects on power relations (Featherstone and Fawcett, 1994; Healy, 2000). For example, while we should recognize the oppressions to which Julia has been subject by her father and her partner, we must also acknowledge and emphasize the kind of power that Julia exercises in relation to her children.

There is concern that anti-oppressive theorists do not adequately address the impact of institutional context on the development and application of anti-oppressive principles. While proponents of anti-oppressive practice urge workers to choose this model as the best, even the only, way for achieving social justice in social work practice, they fail to reflect on how this choice may be easier for service providers in some contexts than in others. Yet our understanding of client needs as well as our role and our options for intervention are profoundly shaped by context, including institutional context, client needs, and even our own capacities as social workers. For example, referring to the Hayden case study, statutory child protection workers have obligations to the application of statutory law, while other workers, such as drug and alcohol workers, have different obligations, in this case to advocate for the mother, Julia. These context-specific obligations will shape who we see as the primary service user and what will take priority in our practice and thus the extent to which we can apply key anti-oppressive principles. It may even be that, in some practice contexts, anti-oppressive practice may lead to harm by, for example, minimizing the recognition of risk (Healy, 1998). At the very least, greater recognition of the institutional limits to the application of anti-oppressive practice is needed for the critical and grounded development of this theory.

Conclusion

Anti-oppressive social work is a practice theory that stands on the cusp of modern and postmodern practice. We have categorized it as a modern critical approach because of its continuing reliance on notions of critical conscious-ness raising – which imply that there is a singular underlying truth to which service users should be exposed – and also because of its continuing emphasis on a structural analysis of oppression and its orientation to large-scale struc-tural reform, even though this is mediated by recognition of the personal and cultural dimensions of oppression. The postmodern elements of anti-oppressive practice, particularly the growing use of discourse analysis by anti-oppressive theorists (see Mullaly, 2002), also place it at the intersection of modern and postmodern practice. Yet, as we shall see in Chapter 10, post-modern approaches to critical social work urge social workers to adopt a sceptical attitude towards many of the claims on which modern forms of social work, including anti-oppressive practice, are founded.

Summary Questions

1   What are the key differences between anti-oppressive theory and other forms of critical social work, such as radical social work and feminist social work?

2   From the perspective of anti-oppressive theory, why is it important that social workers reflect on their personal biography?

3   What practical strategies do anti-oppressive social workers use to promote the empowerment of service users?

Recommended Reading

● Dalrymple, J. and Burke, B. (2006) *Anti-oppressive Practice: Social Care and the Law*, 2nd edn. (Maidenhead: Open University Press).

Essential reading for those keen to understand the history, application and emerging challenges for anti-oppressive practitioners. Has a strong practical focus and is especially helpful for those seeking to understand how they can apply anti-oppressive practice in practice.

- Jones, K., Cooper, B.T. and Ferguson, H. (eds) (2008) *Best Practice in Social Work: Critical Perspectives.* (Basingstoke: Palgrave Macmillan).
  Demonstrates how critical perspectives can inform direct practice in a broad range of service fields, including practice with children and families, professional supervision, mental health, and health and social care. Shows how modernist critical ideas can intersect with other modern theories, such as the strengths perspective, and critical postmodern theories. Excellent, grounded introduction to critically informed direct practice.

- Lavalette, M. (ed.) (2011) *Radical Social Work Today.* (Bristol: Polity Press).
  Researchers and practitioners from diverse fields of practice argue the case for radical social work.

- Mullaly, B. (2002) *Challenging Oppression: A Critical Social Work Approach.* (Ontario: Oxford University Press).
  Thorough introduction to the theoretical foundations of anti-oppressive practice. Explains the interactions across personal, cultural and structural dimensions of oppression.

Recommended Website

- **www.socialworkfuture.org**
  The UK's Social Work Action Network offers an international resource and network for social workers interested in radical approaches to practice.

10
POSTMODERN APPROACHES TO PRACTICE

Since the 1990s, postmodern theories have had a growing influence on the formal base of social work and have contributed to new understandings of, and approaches to, practice. In this chapter, we explain differences among 'post' theories, including postmodernism, poststructuralism and postcolonialism. These theories have been widely discussed in the social sciences and humanities since the 1960s, but their impact on the formal base of social work is relatively recent. Social workers need at least a basic acquaintance with these theories, given that they inform many of the disciplines on which our profession draws. While social work commentators debate the pros and cons of 'post' theories, a growing number of social workers apply these theories to a broad terrain of social work practices from casework to community work and policy practice. Indeed, despite some deserved bad press about the arcane language adopted by some postmodernists, we will see that social workers are already using many similar ideas to explain the complexities of power, identity and change processes.

In this chapter, we outline the key features of postmodernism in the human sciences and consider the historical development of postmodern ideas in social work practices. We discuss the core concepts underpinning 'post' theories and their implications for constructing service users' needs and practice responses. We consider a theory for practice, narrative therapy, that draws on postmodern ideas and use to a case study to consider the pros and cons of postmodernism in social work practice. We turn first to consider where postmodern theories fit in relation to the service discourses and the theories for practice we have discussed so far.

Postmodern theories draw on, but also disrupt, ideas from the discourses discussed in Part 1. In concert with the sociological discourse, postmodernists view all aspects of social work practice, particularly the concepts of client need and social work responses, as socially constructed. In contrast to the critical sociological discourse, which has focused our attention on how macro-processes associated with capitalism, patriarchy and imperialism produce client need and social work practice processes, postmodernists are attentive to the ways discourses construct these concepts. For example, postmodern perspectives urge us to recognize the different ways discourses, like biomedicine and citizen rights, construct 'client need', rather than view one of these perspectives as more accurate than the other. Like the anti-oppressive practice perspective, postmodern practices challenge some aspects of the 'psy' discourse, especially psychoanalytic ideas that seek the causes for the client's malaise in their past or in individual experience. Instead, as we shall see later in the chapter, some forms of postmodern practice seek to understand and, where necessary, disrupt the narratives that construct service users' self-understandings as well as the understandings of others. Postmodern perspectives challenge aspects of the alternative service discourses, such as the reliance of some new social movements on notions of shared and fixed identities (Healy, 2012). But, like the proponents of new social movements, social workers have drawn on postmodern perspectives to challenge traditional power relations and destabilize the privileged position of professional knowledge over other kinds of knowledge, particularly the lived experiences of service users (see Hanrahan, 2013).

As stated in Chapter 1, this book is written from a postmodern perspective, in that we seek to outline how key institutional and alternative discourses construct social work practices. You may be wondering why we have not positioned postmodernism as a separate, overarching discourse like the human science or alternative discourses considered in Part 1. The primary reason is that postmodernism remains a hotly contested discourse that is not widely accepted by either service providers or service users as a key frame of reference. Indeed, in my experience of conducting continuing professional education for social workers, I find that many workers consider 'post' theories as, at best, mysterious and, at worst, deeply alienating to them. Apart from debates among social workers in academia, practitioners express wariness about the arcane language within which postmodern debates are often couched and the seeming indifference to the realities of suffering and disadvantage to which social workers are daily exposed. However, once the core concepts are considered in a social work context, many practitioners find 'post' theories useful for articulating and developing their aspirations to recognize the local and diverse experiences and knowledge of service users.

First, we explain key themes in postmodern perspectives and how these can contribute to the formal base of social work. We then consider one practice approach, narrative therapy, emerging from postmodern perspectives. Figure 10.1 situates postmodern practice perspectives after the strengths perspective and anti-oppressive practice, to recognize their more recent influence on the formal base of social work practice. Indeed, while these three sets of practice perspectives have grown in influence since the 1990s, the strengths perspective and anti-oppressive theory are grounded in modernism assumptions. Postmodernism demands the critical interrogation of these assumptions.

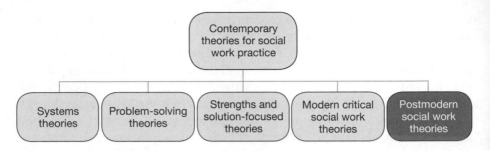

Figure 10.1 Postmodern practices in context

Differences among 'Post' Theories

The term 'postmodernism' is often used to describe the range of 'post' theories, but there are substantial differences among them. Here, we define three – postmodernism, poststructuralism and postcolonialism – and explore some differences among them; an understanding of these differences may be helpful to understanding their different applications to social work.

Postmodernism is concerned with theories of society, culture and history (Agger, 1991). Originating in the field of architecture, postmodernism has since extended into a range of social science and humanities disciplines (Weedon, 1997, p. 170). Postmodernists adopt a sceptical attitude to the truths of modernity, such as a faith in rationality, as the path to progress, on the grounds that these truths cannot help us understand, or respond to, the new cultural conditions of uncertainty and change (Lyotard, 1984, p. 5; Leonard, 1997, p. 25). Put simply, for postmodernists, the truths of modernity once made sense, but no longer do (Butler, 1993).

Poststructuralism, by contrast, is primarily focused on the influence of language on power, knowledge and identity (Agger, 1991). Poststructuralism derives, and deviates, from the work of Ferdinand de Saussure, a structural linguist (Weedon, 1997, p. 23). De Saussure showed that language is not merely a vehicle to reflect reality, rather, language helps to create the things it describes (Weedon, 1997, p. 23). Moving on from de Saussure's claims, poststructuralists argue that the relationship between language and the objects to which it refers is not fixed but shaped by the different meanings that discourses make available. For example, as we discussed in Part 1, different discourses offer us competing ways of understanding concepts such as 'need' as well as the roles of social workers and service users. In the mental health field, contests exist between traditional professional interpretation of needs, as being primarily the need for psychological and pharmaceutical intervention, and the recovery movement's focus on recognition of service users' needs to be heard and recognized as partners in the recovery process

(Gehart, 2012, p. 443). For poststructuralists, language is a key site of political struggle, as discourses shape how core concepts such as 'rights' and 'needs' are understood within any context. This has enormous implications for modern social work practice, because, as we have seen throughout this book, different discourses and theories for practice offer varying and sometimes conflicting ways of understanding and responding to client 'needs'.

Postcolonial theories are of increasing interest to social workers (see Payne and Askeland, 2008). Postcolonialism is a broad discipline committed to understanding, and responding to, the ongoing legacy of European colonization. Leela Gandhi (1998, p. 27) defines postcolonialism as a discipline 'devoted to the academic task of revisiting, remembering and, crucially, interrogating the colonial past … Postcolonial theory commits itself to a complex project of historical and psychological recovery.' Postcolonial approaches are well established in contemporary humanities and social sciences where they are used to analyse how the colonial legacy shapes contemporary understandings of, and responses to, a range of issues, such as migration, race, gender, slavery, and the representation of 'others'. Postcolonial perspectives have been used to confront, disturb and rewrite the narratives of settler societies, such as Canada and Australia, and in so doing 'make way for alternative (though not necessarily more valued) tales concerning a polity's history and culture' (Tuitt, 2011, p. 230). In contrast to critical histories within the modernist traditions, postcolonialists recognize that all accounts of the colonial legacy are politically situated and necessarily incomplete.

'Post' Theories and Social Work Practices

Since the late 1990s, a burgeoning literature has emerged on the applications of 'post' theories to social work (Leonard, 1997; Fook, 2002; Payne and Askeland, 2008; Fawcett, 2009; Healy, 2000, 2012; Hanrahan, 2013). In a collection of practice-based writings, Napier and Fook (2000) present a range of practitioners' reflections on the use of 'post' theory ideas for enabling social workers to critically reflect on the construction of social workers' and clients' 'identities' and narratives in practice. Similarly, Taylor and White (2000) use discourse analytic tools to show how truths – such as claims about child abuse or mental health diagnosis – are constructed, rather than discovered, in practice. The continuing debates about postmodernism (see Atherton and Bolland, 2002; Ferguson, 2008) contradict Noble and Henrickson's claim (2011, p. 129) that the postmodern challenge is 'losing its puff'.

Social workers associated with modern critical traditions of social work (see Chapter 9) have been especially divided in their responses to 'post' theories. Some critical social work commentators suggest that these theories failed to adequately recognize the structural origins of social oppression and, in so doing, undermine options for collective action (see Dominelli, 2002a; Fraser and Briskman, 2005; Ferguson, 2008). Yet, other critical social workers demonstrate their value for activist practices. Hanrahan (2013) outlines the application of postmodern ideas to destabilize power relations adhering to professional/service user identities in mental health services. Morley and MacFarlane (2012, pp. 701–2) advocate for the incorporation of feminist and postmodern ideas to critical social work on the grounds that: 'Postmodern critical thinking can assist us to reconstruct possibilities for agency, acknowledge complexity of context and identity, and value a range of knowledge systems.' Many critical social workers have argued that post-modern concepts allow for enhanced flexibility and responsiveness in the way they approach critical analysis and action (see Pease and Fook, 1999; Hanrahan, 2013). My own research has focused on using discourse analysis and deconstructive strategies to open the critical social work canon to a range of activisms in practice (see Healy, 2000, 2012). I am concerned that critical social work – radical, Marxist, feminist and anti-oppressive – has tended to privilege some forms and sites of activism and activist 'subjectivi-ties', usually nongovernmental services, while marginalizing critical prac-tice possibilities in other sites and other 'subjectivities' – such as government agencies and in practice by middle-aged or older practitioners (Healy, 2000, p. 4). I am also interested in using poststructural theories to show the complexities of local power in practice, as well as the macro-analyses that dominate modern critical social work approaches to power.

Many social work scholars have incorporated poststructural concepts, especially Foucault's work on governmentality, to interrogate the construc-tion of a variety of human services practices, policies and domains of work. For example, Saario and Stepney (2009, p. 41) examined how managerial auditing systems in Finnish mental health services 'began to reshape prac-tice by reinforcing certain modes of working and excluding others'. They found that the relational aspects of social work practice, often found to be so crucial to service user satisfaction (see Trotter, 2004; Sheldon and Macdonald, 2009), were rendered invisible in managerial systems for accounting for how workers' time is allocated and valued. By encouraging us to look for what has been made invisible in policy and managerial prac-tices, poststructural theories can assist our profession to advocate for the revaluation of some aspects of social work practice.

In recent years, a small body of social work literature has emerged debating the relevance and application of postcolonial perspectives to the discipline (Harrison and Melville, 2010; Crath, 2012; Lough, 2013). Postco-lonial perspectives demand that we recognize the ongoing legacy of coloni-zation in all aspects of social work practice, from the traumatic impact of the displacement of First Nations peoples through to the extension of 'First

World' social work knowledge and values into 'Third World' countries (Harrison and Melville, 2010, pp. 20–1). Sewpaul (2006) urges us to recognize the complexities of cultural identity, including acknowledgement of differences and also common aspirations among social workers from the global north and south, such as the aspiration for a more just world.

Postcolonial perspectives encourage critical analysis of how the colonial legacy is sustained in modern social work practices, even in anti-racist approaches. Postcolonial scholars problematize fixed racial identities and attack the dualism between European and non-European identities, while acknowledging the colonial legacies that contribute to experiences of oppression. In her analysis of Asian and black women's experiences as social workers, Lewis (2000) argues that social work scholars' continuing reliance on an opposition between European and non-European reinforces racialized social relations by ignoring substantial differences within identity groups such as 'Third World women', 'Europeans', 'Indigenous' people (see also Sewpaul, 2006). Overall, this criticism strikes at the heart of modern anti-racist social work (see Dominelli, 1988), insofar as this project accepts fixed identity categories such as 'European' and 'non-European' as the basis for analysis and social action. Using postcolonial perspectives, social work scholar Gail Lewis (2000, p. 119, emphasis added) argues that 'race/ethnicity needs to be understood and analysed as a major, *but only one*, axis of differentiations organizing a contingent set of social relations'. For example, we need to understand how other categories such as disability and sexuality as well as local differences differentiate racial and ethnic identifications and experiences.

Key Concepts

Here, we consider four key concepts in these theories – discourse, subjectivity, power and deconstruction. An understanding of these concepts is essential to understanding social workers' use and development of postmodern practice perspectives.

Discourse

Discourse is central to postmodern, poststructural and postcolonial theories as it is used to refer to the language practices through which knowledge, truth, our sense of selves and social relations are constructed. Throughout this book, we have used the term 'discourse' to analyse how key concepts such as client need and social work practices are constructed in health and welfare contexts and through different theories of practice. Thus, the term should now be familiar to you, but we will briefly recap this concept here.

Discourse refers to the language practices through which we understand 'reality' and act on it. Discourse constructs knowledge in practice, particularly what counts as true or sayable and what is considered false or unsayable (Foucault, 1980a, p. 131). Discourses have 'real' or material effects, in that they construct our understandings of key entities such as 'client need' and 'social work practice'. From a postmodern viewpoint, words are not simply vehicles as they constitute the phenomena social workers deal with in their practice, such as 'child abuse', 'ageing' and 'domestic violence'. This does not mean that experiences, such as child abuse, are made up by language, rather that we can only comprehend these phenomena through language, and language practices shape how we can understand and act. For example, while there can be little doubt that, throughout history, some children have experienced cruelty, the term 'child abuse' has emerged only relatively recently and has profoundly shaped the role of the state and the social work profession in relation to children and their families. The term has provided significant justification for the extension of state powers into previously private domains of family life, particularly for marginalized families. Of importance to social workers is that the term 'child abuse' is associated with the construction of parents or families as 'abusers' rather than as people in need, and deserving of, state support. The term privileges the concept of 'abuse' over other aspects of the vulnerable child's identity and experience, and in so doing can negate the possibility that, for some children, there is a strong desire to remain with their families or at least maintain contact with them.

From a postmodern viewpoint, discourses profoundly shape service users' experiences of, and social workers' responses to, experiences such as mental illness and disabilities. This point is well illustrated by Crossley and Crossley (2001), who undertook a comparative analysis of two anthologies written by people living with mental illness in the 1950s and the 1990s. Their analysis showed that the consumer rights discourse, which emerged during the 1970s (see Chapter 5), created new opportunities for (some) people living with mental illness to assert authority based on their expertise as survivors, rather than as patients, of psychiatric institutions (Crossley and Crossley, 2001, p. 1488). This transformed identity enabled some people living with mental illness the opportunities to critique and, in some instances, opt out of biomedical approaches to psychiatric care.

'Post' theorists draw attention to the way in which discourses operate within specific sites of social work practices. Fook (2002, p. 90) points out that: 'Because discourses are not fixed (that is, their meaning is relative to the situation and interpretation, and subject position), they may operate in different ways for different purposes at different times.' Focusing on the operations of discourse within specific practice contexts, we can see that even an apparently positive concept like 'citizen participation' can be used for a range of ends – from promoting client involvement in statutory decision-making through to facilitating the reduction of government involvement in the funding and provision of services (Healy, 1998). From a 'post' theory perspective, discourses shape our understandings of the rights, responsibilities, experiences of, and relationships between, service workers and services users. Moreover, social work and social services agencies are often sites of competing discourses. For example, child welfare services are the site of competing interpretations of, for example, the rights and needs of parents and children. Aged care services are sites of contest concerning public and private care in old age and disability services are sites of contest between social responsibility and self-realization.

Subjectivity

'Post' theorists use the term 'subjectivity', rather than 'identity', to refer to our sense of ourselves. They reject descriptions of 'identity' as fixed and unified, insisting instead that our identities are shaped by discourses and thus vary from context to context (Sawicki, 1991, p. 300). Because different discourses offer competing systems of social reality, we may experience different aspects of our 'identity' as fragmented and contradictory (Weedon, 1997, p. 33; Healy, 2000, p. 46). For example, as a young social worker working in a statutory child protection service, I exercised power and authority associated with my statutory role, but I also experienced powerlessness and vulnerability associated with my low status within the bureaucracy, my age, gender and (non)parenting status. All these subjectivities affected how I experienced my 'authority', and how I was seen by others, as well as the kinds of power and authority I was able to exercise. For instance, the professional assessments I was authorized and indeed required to undertake could be vetoed by others who were positioned more powerfully in these discursive fields of child protection, such as magistrates, doctors and institutional supervisors, even though these higher status professionals may have had little or no direct contact with the families in question. 'Post' theories suggest that these experiences of fragmentation and contradiction in our identities and our exercise of institutional power are an inevitable outcome of the clashes between different discourses that make up our practice contexts.

Just as we recognize the contradictions in the social work 'identity', from a poststructural perspective we must also acknowledge service users' multiple and often contradictory identifications For example, we may come to understand a 'violent offender' also as 'a victim of child abuse', 'an abusive parent', 'a loyal son', 'a person battling addiction' and so on. Indeed, in direct practice, practitioners often do recognize these multiple and sometimes competing identifications and, ironically, this probably contributes to the popular and derogatory image of social workers as 'bleeding hearts'.

Poststructural feminists challenge us to recognize ourselves and others as embodied beings. Poststructural feminists encourage us to recognize how bodily differences shape the way we inhabit different subjectivities (Healy, 2000, pp. 48–9). Consider the example of professional power. Critical social work theorists, including Marxist, radical and feminist, have drawn our attention to the authoritarian dimensions of professional power in social work practice. This has been an important critical insight into social work practice and has led to increased awareness of the oppressive effects of power and authority in practice. In addition, poststructural feminists invite us to consider how bodily differences associated with age, height, skin colour, ethnicity and gender complicate one's identifications and thus one's capacity to exercise professional power (see Healy, 2000, Ch. 7).

Critical social work commentators take particular exception to the notion of open and fluid subjectivity proposed by 'post' theorists (see Dominelli, 2002a). According to these commentators, the abandonment of fixed identities threatens progressive social movements that have relied on fixed and unified identifications such as 'women', 'people with disabilities' and so on (see Dominelli, 2002a, pp. 32–6). Critical poststructural commentators counter this criticism on a number of grounds.

Postmodernists argue that the unified notion of self, central to many critical social theories and progressive social movements, requires us to embrace identifications that are a source of oppression. Judith Butler (1993, p. 48) argues that:

> Surely there is caution offered here, that in the very struggle toward enfranchisement and democratization, we might adopt the very models of domination by which we were oppressed, not realizing that one way that domination works is through the regulation and production of subjects.

For postmodern critical social workers, the challenge seems to be that of recognizing how categories such as 'survivor', 'woman' or 'person with a disability' can explain our or service users' experiences, and form a basis for collaborative action, while also recognizing how these categories limit change activity. Instead, critical poststructural approaches assume that our identities are negotiated and provisional, rather than fixed. This can open up possibilities for recognizing differences within unified groups, such as 'women', 'European', 'people with disabilities', as well as opportunities to negotiate shared actions across groups (Sawicki, 1991; Butler, 1993; Weedon, 1997; Corker and Shakespeare, 2002). By recognizing and celebrating differences, 'post' theories can support respectful collaboration across differences.

Power

Power is a central concern of critical 'post' theorists, particularly Foucault and feminist poststructural authors, such as Cixous and Kristeva (see Healy, 1999, 2000). Foucault explicitly rejects the 'juridico-discursive' model of power, which represents power as the possession of individuals and a force that is imposed by one set of subjects, such as the ruling class, on others (Sawicki, 1991, p. 52; Healy, 2000, p. 43). In contrast to critical sociological discourse and anti-oppressive theory, which focus on minimizing power differences, critical poststructuralists see power as an ever-present and productive feature of social relations. Further, poststructuralists contend that power is a product of discourse rather than something that is attached to specific identities, such as 'male' or 'professional'. Thus, in this view, if we want to understand power in any context, we need to analyse how discourses operate to construct identity, knowledge and power within that specific context.

According to Sawicki (1991, p. 21), Foucault's approach to power rests on three axioms:

1 Power is exercised rather than possessed.

2 Power is not primarily repressive, but productive.

3 Power is analysed as coming from the bottom up.

We consider the implications of each of these principles for social workers.

Foucault invites us to shift our analysis from a focus on who possesses power to the consideration of how power is exercised from specific social locations and by specific people. Recognizing that power is exercised rather than possessed also allows us to acknowledge and expand the possibilities for relatively powerless groups to exercise power. A number of social work authors have used the Foucauldian notion of power to show how empowering discourses lead workers to ignore the ways in which marginalized groups, such as Indigenous people, homeless young women and young mothers, exercise power even though they do not 'possess' it (see Crinall, 1999; Healy, 2000). These commentators argue that a poststructural perspective can contribute to empowering practice by encouraging workers to recognize and support service users' capacities to exercise power, rather than focus on their relative powerlessness from a structural perspective.

In contrast to the view of power as something that oppresses and constrains, Foucault urges us to recognize the productivity of power. He argues that people submit to power because they gain something from their submission, in other words, a focus on power as oppressive ignores the positive dimensions of power. Foucault (1980a, p. 119) asserts that:

> What makes power hold good, what makes it accepted, is simply the fact that it doesn't only weigh on us as a force that says no, but that it traverses and produces things, it induces pleasure, forms of knowledge, produces discourse.

In contrast to the focus on the oppressive social work power that has dominated modern critical social workers' accounts of social work practice (see Chapter 9), Foucault's work encourages us to recognize the productivity of this power as well. This point is well illustrated by a number of critical studies of the micro-politics of practice, which have shown that some service users actively seek out social work services and gain something, such as improved capacities or sense of self, from the exercise of power in these practice contexts (see Wise, 1995; Healy, 2000).

Finally, in contrast to modern sociological discourse and anti-oppressive theories, Foucault urges us to analyse power from the local to the structural, rather than the other way around. Foucault (1980b, p. 99) argues that a focus on macro-processes of power is not particularly useful for understanding the micro-politics of power in local contexts. Rather than seeing power relations as merely an effect of macro-structures, such as capitalism or patriarchy, 'post' theorists recognize the micro-contexts of social work practice as sites where power is also produced. This recognition of the local production of power is particularly important in challenging the tendency towards structural determinism in some modern critical social work theories (see Chapter 9). It enables us to recognize the complex web of power relations within which service providers and service users are embedded and so guard against a tendency to see both as merely victims of social structures. For example, Featherstone and Fawcett (1994) have argued that, in child protection practice, a mother may be powerless in one context, say in relation to an abusive partner or the statutory authority, but powerful in others, such as in relation to her children. Thus, in one moment, a person may be 'both victim and victimizer and these positions themselves shift' (Featherstone and Fawcett, 1994, p. 134).

Deconstruction

'Deconstruction' is term commonly used by postmodernists and is associated with the work of Jacques Derrida, French literary theorist. The term describes the process of identifying and undermining oppositions through which discourses represent things such as knowledge, identity and other social phenomena (Weedon, 1997, p. 159). Some of the oppositions found in social work discourse include:

- normal/abnormal
- true/false
- powerful/powerless
- worker/service user
- middle class/working class
- male/female
- expert/layperson
- able bodied/disabled
- straight/gay or lesbian.

You can probably identify other oppositions within your practice domain. Derrida (1991) criticizes these oppositions because they create a hierarchy between the two opposed terms and hide the differences within and between each of them. For example, a 'middle-class' person may once have been 'working class' and even within the category of middle class, there are significant variations.

Deconstruction is aimed at breaking apart dualisms to show the range of positions that lie within and beyond opposed entities. For example, using a deconstructive approach, we would recognize that the states of 'powerful' and 'powerless' are two extremes on a continuum and that there are many positions of relative powerfulness and powerlessness in between. The process of deconstruction is endless, because the new forms of representation that deconstruction itself produces must themselves be subjected to deconstruction. In this sense, deconstruction involves ongoing interrogation of that which is excluded in the processes of representing anything. For example, people in the disability movement sometimes prefer the term 'differently abled' because the term 'disabled' only shows lack of ability, but from a deconstructive approach we would ask what the preferred term 'differently abled' also hides.

Narrative Therapy: A Postmodern Practice Approach

This chapter has outlined a variety of ways 'post' theories have been used to inform practice. A large body of work focuses on how these theories can assist social workers to transform their practice through critical interrogation of identity and power relations in practice. Various writers have pointed to opportunities for resistance and destabilizing of existing power relations from the 'front line' of statutory practices (see Napier and Fook, 2000) through to community practices (see Hanrahan, 2013) and to challenging managerial discourse (Saario and Stepney, 2009). By and large, a major contribution of 'post' theories has been to destabilizing and renewing existing forms of practice including critical modern practices.

However, some social workers have drawn on 'post' theories to create entirely new approaches to practice. Narrative therapy is among the most well-developed and celebrated illustration of the application of 'post' theory ideas to the development of social work practices. Michael White, Australian social worker, and his colleague David Epston, New Zealand-based therapist, are widely recognized as the leading proponents of these ideas (see White and Epston, 1990). Workers associated with the Dulwich Centre in Adelaide, Australia, a key centre for narrative therapy, have produced a wide body of work on the application of narrative ideas to a broad terrain of social services work, including group work and community development, and many fields of practice from mental health, family services, to grief in Indigenous communities (see Wingard, 1998). Social work theorists have also applied these ideas to direct social work practice (see Parton and O'Byrne, 2001).

Narrative therapy centres on the idea that the narratives we, and others, construct about us actively shape our experiences, our sense of selves, and our life options. According to this approach, service users' lives are constrained by the harmful narratives they and others have generated about them (Fook, 2002, p. 137). Often, these narratives have been produced in order to 'diagnose' and ultimately 'help' the person, but the effect is to imprison the person in a narrative that damages and constrains them. Narrative therapists contend that because narratives so powerfully shape our 'identities' and our life choices, these narratives should be the site of intervention. These narratives are used across a broad range of methods from interpersonal work through to community practice, where community development workers seek to assist communities to realize new narratives.

We turn now to the four key principles of the narrative approach.

1: Focus on the Narratives that Shape Service Users' Lives

In contrast to modernist forms of social service intervention, narrative therapy does not seek to uncover or construct a single truth about the causes of the service user's situation. Instead, narrative therapists seek to assess and transform the narratives that construct our lives. They seek to challenge the harmful narratives, that is, those that represent the service user in a negative and pathological frame, and instead seek to recognize and construct alternative narratives, that is, narratives that recognize and honour the person's capacities, including, for example, their capacity to take responsibility for violence (see Jenkins, 1990).

Narrative therapy requires the worker to adopt a curious and open, rather than truth-seeking, position towards the service user. An important feature of the initial engagement with the service user is that of exploring, with the service user, how they came to be 'recruited' into the dominant and harmful narrative about themselves. So, for example, rather than accepting the dominant narrative of Joan as schizophrenic, we might explore with her how this narrative was constructed, who constructed it, and how Joan herself has accepted or resisted this construction. In this way, the narrative about Joan's journey with schizophrenia separates her from the condition.

2: Separate the Person from the Problem

Another principle of narrative therapy is that the person is not the problem, rather the 'problem is the problem'. In line with this principle, narrative therapists use the strategy of 'externalizing conversations' to separate the person from the problem. A feature of these conversations includes giving a name to the problem that is separate from the person. For example, we might rename an apparently uncontrollable anger as 'the Dragon'. The use of the capital in Dragon is important for naming the problem. Narrative therapists often use magical and unusual terminology, like the term 'the Dragon' here, as a way of unlocking the service user's creative energies.

Let's say we are working with a young man, Peter, whose apparently uncontrollable anger is leading to conflict and unhappiness at home and at school. Using the technique of externalizing conversation, we might ask: 'When does the Dragon visit?' 'What sorts of events are likely to waken the Dragon?' 'When have you successfully fought the Dragon?' 'What would need to happen to banish the Dragon for good?' Through the use of externalizing conversations, we can facilitate the separation of the problem from individuals and communities, articulate the strategies they have already used effectively to address their problems, and offer hope that an alternative future is possible in which the problem does not control them. Recognition of moments in which the service user has effectively resisted the problem, sometimes referred to as 'news of difference', is especially important to the construction of alternative narratives about the self.

3: Reconstruct the Dominant Story of the Self

Narrative therapy aims to reconstruct the dominant narratives that shape the service user's life from those that emphasize pathology to those that highlight and support their capacities. This focus is similar to the strengths perspective and, indeed, some proponents of the strengths perspective draw on narrative practice techniques. This focus on the narrative construction of a problem is not to deny the existence of, say, serious mental illness or violent behaviour, rather it is an approach that illuminates and builds the service user's capacity to live a life of their choosing. For example, Jenkins (1990) uses narrative therapy approaches to invite men who are violent and abusive to take responsibility for their actions. The three-step strategy, outlined by Jenkins (1990, p. 62), involves:

- the worker declining 'invitations' by the man to attribute responsibili-ties for his actions to external factors, such as his partner's behaviour

- inviting the man to challenge the restraints on his acceptance of respon-sibility for his actions, such as sociocultural affirmations of male violence

- acknowledging and highlighting evidence of the man's acceptance of responsibility for his actions, by, for example, drawing attention to moments when the man contained his violent behaviour and showed his capacities for respectful and non-violent responses to others.

4: Co-constructing narratives through and with community

Proponents of narrative approaches recognize the importance of building communities that support affirming narratives of the self and community. Indeed, in the past decade, there has been a proliferation of literature by narrative therapists and others attesting to community narratives as a site of restoration and political activism (see Lessard et al., 2011). Michael White and his colleagues at the Dulwich Centre have written widely on the value of narrative work for assisting communities to recover from trauma. White (2003, p. 44) argues that through narrative practices in which community members are encouraged to articulate and deconstruct their community's experiences of trauma, people can 'find safe places in which to stand in the territory of memory ... that provide them with platforms for speaking of what hasn't been spoken about, for putting into more significant expres-sion their experiences of trauma'.

Narrative therapists recognize that the narratives others hold about the service user similarly shape the service user's capacities to live a life of their choosing. For this reason, narrative therapists often incorporate strategies aimed at building a supportive and life-affirming community around the service user. Narrative approaches sometimes incorporate ceremonies that mark the defeat of the pathological narrative and the emergence of alterna-tive narratives that affirm service users' capacities. For example, White and

Denborough (1998) presented a case study of a woman who invited her closest supporters to a ceremony at which they built a bonfire to destroy the psychiatric case files that contributed to the narrative of her life as a psychiatric patient.

Practice Exercise **Applying 'post' theories in practice**

Imagine you work in a community support centre in an area where there are many refugee families; several having fled areas of high conflict. In your role, you meet Jamilah, a 28-year-old woman with four children. Jamilah and her husband, Abroom (also 28), arrived from Somali three years ago. Jamilah has come to the community centre to ask for help in paying an electricity bill. Her two younger children (a baby and a 2 year old) are with her on the visit; the two older children (5 and 7) are at school. The children appeared content and calm in their mother's presence.

During the conversation, Jamilah becomes upset, and says she is struggling to cope with her life – she has frequent distressing memories of the fighting she and her family fled and her sleep is often disturbed. Six months ago, Jamilah's doctor prescribed tablets for her, but they made her feel drowsy so she did not complete the prescription. The family are struggling financially and are barely able to get by on the money Abroom earns from his work as a cleaner. Jamilah tells you that Abroom is a qualified secondary teacher and she is a qualified nurse in Somalia, but neither of their qualifications are recognized here. Jamilah often goes without meals so that her children and her husband are fed. Jamilah reveals that she is ashamed of asking for help.

● How would you apply narrative therapy concepts and other 'post' theory ideas to analyse and respond to the situation?

Uses and Limitations of 'Post' Theories for Social Work Practices

We now discuss the strengths and weaknesses of 'post' theories in social work, using the case of Jamilah. A postmodern approach to practice encourages practitioners to recognize and explore a range of perspectives about the problem facing the service user. When working with Jamilah, from a postmodern viewpoint, we would explore the multiple narratives shaping her situation. A focus on the narratives through which Jamilah and others construct her situation, including the professionals involved, would enable us to recognize its inherent complexities and ambiguities.

From a postcolonial perspective, we would analyse how cultural identifications and perspectives shape Jamilah's 'identity' and options. We would also recognize that 'cultural' subjectivity is only one of many identities that may be important to Jamilah's sense of self (see Lewis, 2000). For example, we can see that Jamilah is a refugee, a survivor of regional conflict, a mother and a wife. Jamilah may also refer to other subjectivities, such as those related to religious faith, which are important to her sense of self and the options available to her. From a postmodern perspective, it is important to explore how Jamilah defines herself and the nature of the challenges facing her, and consider how the discourses and narratives through which she and her problems are defined also shape the options available to her. For example, it may be that certain kinds of support, such as participating in a spiritual healing group, are more acceptable to her than seeking biomedical intervention for the trauma she is experiencing.

Postmodern theories also highlight the 'micro-politics' of practice. They draw attention to local contexts – including the institutional context – as key sites of analysis and action (Healy, 1998; Morley and MacFarlane, 2012). This contrasts with liberal humanist approaches to social work, such as task-centred practice, which have paid little attention to inequities between workers and service users. 'Post' theory approaches also differ from modern critical theories, including anti-oppressive practice, which have analysed local power relations as effects of structural processes (Healy, 1998, 2000, 2012). By recognizing complexity in local relations of power, 'post' theory would encourage us to explore how Jamilah and her family are able to exercise power in their lives, particularly in relation to the challenges they face. For example, it may be that Jamilah feels proud of her role as wife and mother and she may be reluctant to return to the paid workforce while her children are young and her husband is in low-paid work. Her preference may be to support her husband to achieve recognition of his qualifications, rather than to seek recognition of her qualifications. Such a perspective may, from a critical viewpoint, be understood as a lack of critical consciousness, while from the postmodern view, it may be interpreted as a different and equally valid approach to the way she and her family would prefer to live their lives.

From a postmodern perspective, we can recognize the oppressions faced by Jamilah and her family, while also acknowledging and supporting her capacity for agency (Crinall, 1999, p. 80; Healy, 2012). This could include acknowledging that Jamilah has resisted others' definitions and responses to the challenges facing her, such as her rejection of the biomedical intervention, and working with her to assist her to identify and work towards her preferred outcomes. In Jamilah's case, this does not necessarily mean that all biomedical approaches should be resisted but that any intervention, biomedical or otherwise, must take into account the specificities of Jamilah's context, such as her caring responsibilities for four young children.

Postmodernists also reject the notion that there is one desirable path for any individual or collective to follow and, instead, invite us to recognize and celebrate different paths and possibilities. In relation to the case study, this focus on differences would enable us to work with Jamilah to respect her decisions regarding Western healthcare and to consider other options, including possible ways of managing trauma and stress that are consistent with her cultural processes. This may include an exploration of how Jamilah's religious beliefs and spiritual life have shaped her understanding and ways of coping with her life experiences. Recognition of differences is also important for understanding that in some cultures, the wellbeing of the individual is not necessarily valued over collective responsibilities, such as Jamilah's responsibilities to her family.

Narrative strategies can be used to empower and energize service users by separating them from the perceived problem. This contrasts markedly with modernist forms of social work that have aimed to understand the service user's identity and issues and, in modern forms of critical social work, have encouraged individuals to embrace the oppressed identity (see Chapter 9). We could use narrative strategies to explore how Jamilah has already taken control of her situation and help her investigate how she has responded to the difficult situation. For example, we might help her name the characteristic, such as 'Determination', or the higher spiritual power that has helped her manage the challenges she faces.

So far we have considered the uses of 'post' theories for social work practices, now let's turn to their limitations. Again, we'll use the case study of Jamilah to ground these criticisms in social work. The focus of postmodernism on language practices can lead us to ignore the material realities of oppression and the extent to which these oppressions are shaped by macro-social structures, particularly capitalism, patriarchy and imperialism (see Ife, 1999; Dominelli, 2002a). In relation to Jamilah, we can argue that her situation, and her options for responding to it, are shaped by culture, gender and class. These categories represent social divisions that profoundly shape the life chances of disadvantaged people. For example, refugees and asylum seekers frequently suffer from post-traumatic stresses and often experience extreme material disadvantage and racism in the countries where they settle. Thus, a focus on the language practices that shape Jamilah's situation should not distract us from the pressing material needs of her situation or recognition of the broader contexts of oppression facing refugees and asylum seekers.

Many social workers question whether postmodern theories can provide a coherent framework for practice. The academic and often arcane language of most postmodern writing is alienating to many social workers. Agger (1991, p. 106) points out that most 'post' theory arguments are 'incredibly, extravagantly convoluted – to the point of disastrous absurdity'. But social workers' concerns go beyond issues about the inaccessibility of postmodern writings to concerns about the relativism inherent in this perspective and thus the loss of a moral and political framework for action (Peile and McCouat, 1997). Professional social workers often develop and legitimate their practice by appealing to universal social values, particularly social justice. For example, in working with Jamilah, many of the responses we've discussed so far are consistent with values of self-determination and social justice. Some critical social workers have responded to the concern about value relativism in postmodern approaches by combining these perspectives with other modernist frameworks such as human rights (Ife, 1999) or radical and feminist social work perspectives (see Leonard, 1997; Healy, 2000, 2012; Fook, 2002; Morley and MacFarlane, 2012).

Critical social workers, in particular, argue that 'post' theories can be used to support conservative policy agendas and practice approaches. While acknowledging their use for recognizing complexity and uncertainty, Ife (1999, p. 211) asserts that: 'a lingering doubt remains as to whether it [postmodernism] represents a 'sell-out' to the very ideologies of individualism, greed and exploitation against which social workers have claimed to stand' (see also Dominelli, 2002b; Ferguson, 2008). In Jamilah's situation, for example, we can see many grounds for political protest against the material realities of disadvantage facing this young woman and her family. The family's situation can be understood as directly linked to state policies that limit if not entirely exclude refugees and asylum seekers from the material supports available to citizens, and discriminatory employment practices that further marginalize and oppress them. 'Post' theories promote critically self-reflective practice by demanding that we, as social workers, interrogate all our assumptions about identity, power and values, but, in so doing, it also threatens to detract our attention and energies from much needed wide-ranging social change.

Conclusion

The burgeoning literature on postmodern theories in diverse fields and methods of social work and the growing popularity of narrative therapy have contributed to the legitimacy of these perspectives to the formal base of social work. In this chapter, we discussed how social workers can and do apply 'post' theory concepts to practice. For example, social workers often find themselves in the difficult situation of making sense of multiple and competing truth claims (Taylor and White, 2000) and in our contact with service users we often encounter multiple subjectivities in ourselves and in others. These theories can enrich our practice by providing a language through which we can understand and express the complexities and ambiguities we face, but an uncritical embrace of them also threatens our capacity to develop coherent ethical and political frameworks for practice.

Summary Questions

1   What are the common assumptions of the theories discussed in this chapter?

2   How does the postmodern view of 'subjectivity' challenge modern social work theories, such as the strengths perspective and anti-oppressive practice?

3   How might postcolonial perspectives assist social workers to understand the experiences of people who have been displaced from their own countries as a result of conflict?

4   Identify and discuss the practice principles of narrative therapy.

Recommended Reading

- Foucault, M. (1980) *Power/Knowledge: Selected Interviews and Other Writings 1972–1977*, ed. C. Gordon. (New York: Pantheon Books).
  Series of lectures, interviews and papers providing an accessible introduction to some of Foucault's most important ideas on power, subjectivity and change.

- Harrison, G. and Melville, R. (2010) *Rethinking Social Work in a Global World*. (Basingstoke: Palgrave Macmillan).
  Excellent introduction to international social work; clearly articulates the relevance of postcolonial theory for critical approaches to international social work practices.

- Healy, K. (2000) *Social Work Practices: Contemporary Perspectives on Change*. (London: Sage).
  Discusses the historical development, and application, of 'post' theory ideas to social work, emphasizing the implications for critical forms of social work practice.

- Lessard, H., Johnson, R. and Webber, J. (eds) (2011) *Storied Communities: Narratives of Contact and Arrival in Constituting Political Community*. (Vancouver: UBC Press).
  Collection of writings drawing on a range of perspectives, including poststructural and postcolonial ideas, to examine the political nature of narratives, including the possibilities for narratives to disrupt and rewrite dominant accounts of settler societies. Considers the potential of narratives to transform communities.

- Napier, L. and Fook, J. (eds) (2000) *Breakthroughs in Practice: Theorising Critical Moments in Social Work*. (London: Whiting & Birch).
  Collection of practice-based writings, where practitioners and academics working within a broad range of settings, including income security, mental health, child protection and services related to death and dying, using 'post' theory ideas to reflect on and develop their practice.

- White, C. and Denborough, D. (eds) (1998) *Introducing Narrative Therapy: A Collection of Practice-Based Writings*. (Adelaide: Dulwich Centre).

Beautiful collection of practice-based articles demonstrating a breadth of terrains for the application of narrative therapy ideas. Barbara Wingard's article on grief in indigenous communities is particularly recommended.

- White, M. (2003) Narrative practice and community assignments. *International Journal of Narrative Therapy and Community Practice*, 2, 17–55.
  Excellent paper outlining the theoretical ideas that inform White's approaches to narrative work in communities affected by trauma. Accessible introduction to how the application of Derrida's approach to deconstruction can be drawn on in assisting communities to value previously unheard and marginalized voices.

- White, M. and Epston, D. (1990) *Narrative Means to Therapeutic Ends*. (New York: WW Norton).
  Widely regarded as a classic in narrative therapy by two of the 'founding fathers' of the school. You are encouraged to read this text if you are interested in using narrative approaches to practice.

Recommended Website

- **www.dulwichcentre.com.au**
  The Dulwich Centre, based in Adelaide, Australia, is internationally recognized as a leading centre for narrative therapy education, writing and research. Includes recordings of narrative workshops and seminars on a wide range of topics, information about conferences and training opportunities, and online bookshop for Dulwich Centre publications.

11
CREATING FRAMEWORKS FOR PRACTICE

This book has introduced a contextually informed and dynamic approach to social work practice. Social work has been presented as a negotiated activity; in particular, our purpose and practices as social workers are negotiated through interactions between our institutional context, our 'formal' purpose, our professional base, service users and our frameworks for practice. It has been argued that the potential for social workers to influence the contexts and formal theory base of the profession is, as yet, underdeveloped. One of this book's intentions has been to enhance our capacities, as social workers, to actively use and influence the ideas that shape the institutional contexts of practice and the formal theory base of social work itself. In this chapter, we consider how we can use this knowledge of the ideas underpinning the institutions and formal theories for practice for constructing our framework for practice, which is the final component of the model introduced in Chapter 2.

Frameworks for Practice

In every practice encounter, we are drawing on, but also constructing, our framework for practice. In Chapter 2, the term 'framework for practice' was introduced to refer to the unique combination of formal and informal knowledge and skills developed by social workers in practice. This fusion includes formal theoretical and substantive knowledge as well as tacit, or difficult to articulate, knowledge, that can be built up through repeated exposure to practice situations. Ideally, our frameworks develop over time, through practice, and become increasingly useful to us for constructing unique responses in each practice encounter (see Fook et al., 2000).

The act of constructing our practice framework is creative, in that we draw on ideas from multiple sources, such as institutional context and formal theories, but we also transform these ideas through their application. For example, a social worker's application of the strengths perspective in one context, say with an older person with a mental health concern, is different to their use of this approach to support a young parent coping with the ongoing traumatic effects of childhood sexual abuse.

The processes through which we construct our practice frameworks involve the unique combination of the institutional contexts, out professional practice base and service users' needs, strengths and expectations. Part 1 outlined the discourses that underpin the institutional contexts of social service delivery in many contemporary contexts of practice. Other discourses may be influential, but those focused on in this book are dominant in major contexts of social work services in what might be termed 'wealthy' or 'Western' nations. Colleagues working in other contexts, such as in parts of Eastern Europe or Africa, have sometimes commented that other discourses are influential. For example, in some parts of Africa, discourses associated with traditional health practices, which differ substantially from the biomedical discourse, shape understanding of wellbeing and illness (Ross, 2008). Our intention has been to demonstrate a broad range of the major discourses shaping social work, while recognizing that this can never be entirely exhaustive. The analysis of the discursive construction of, and theoretical approaches to, social work practice contexts is to show that social work is practised *in* context but it is not *of* context. To put it differently, the key concepts of social work practice, such as ideas about client needs and social work responses, are constructed through discourses and theories for practice, but they are not merely products of these discourses and theories. By understanding the ideas that underpin health and welfare institutions and our formal professional base, we enhance our capacity to actively use and, where necessary, disrupt these ideas. For example, while our practice may be shaped and constrained by the new public management discourse, we can also use our understanding of this discourse to challenge it on its own terms. Drawing on this discourse, for instance, we might show how certain forms of practice, such as a risk-averse approach to child protection work, contribute to escalating economic (as well as social) costs by expanding certain types of service needs (such as the number of children in out-of-home care), while neglecting cost-effective approaches (such as community-based family support).

In this book, we have introduced five groups of theories for social work practice. We presented the historical, geographical and disciplinary origins of each group and considered some of the specific theories for practice that have emerged within each group. It is hoped that understanding the foundations of these theories will enhance your capacity to actively use and transform these theories within your practice context. Again, we have argued that social workers do not merely use theory but transform theory in our unique application of these ideas to address specific client needs within our practice contexts. Understanding the origins of these ideas is critical to their informed and creative use.

The creativity inherent in social workers' negotiation of their framework for practice is often unrecognized and undervalued. Over time, the frameworks we develop through a combination of knowledge, skills and experience become the 'commonsense' way of doing things and are rarely exposed to critical reflection, except in the context of a critical event that leads us to reconsider the foundations of our practice. One way of developing our frameworks for practice is to open these commonsense understandings of practice to critical scrutiny. Understanding the assumptions underpinning the discourses and theories that influence our practice provides one avenue for critical analysis and development of our practice.

This book has outlined how key entities such as 'need' and social work 'purpose' are constructed through various discourses and social work theories for practice. We can use this information to analyse how our practices are constructed in specific environments and how we might actively engage with these constructions. Some questions that may guide you in developing your framework for practice within a specific institutional context are:

- How do the institutional discourses construct service user needs and strengths?

- How do the institutional discourses construct my role as a worker?

- In what ways are these constructions consistent (or in tension) with my professional knowledge base and values?

- What opportunities do I have to resist or transform these constructions to be more consistent with issues of importance, such as clients' understanding of need and my professional values and ethics?

Our framework for practice can also be enriched by the informed and creative use of formal theories for practice. In this book we have introduced the historical, geographical and disciplinary origins of key contemporary social work theories for practice in order to promote critical reflection on how you might apply and transform these theories for use within your specific contexts of practice. Critical questions that can guide your analysis, use and transformation of these theories include:

- What are the historical, geographical and institutional contexts in which this theory was developed? How relevant is this to my context(s) of practice and my purposes within it?

- How does this theory of practice construct the purpose and process of social work practice? What constructions of practice does this theory make possible, and what possibilities does it marginalize?

Other components of our framework for practice include knowledge and skills that can be developed through action and critical reflection on our practice. The notion of building theory and knowledge through reflection on engagement is consistent with the reflective tradition espoused by Schön. From the reflexive approach (see Taylor and White, 2000), we understand the need to critically interrogate our reflections from practice to examine how they might be constructed through discourses and different stakeholders' viewpoints. Questions that can guide us in this analysis of knowledge in practice include:

- What elements of my practice experience might be helpful to understanding and responding to this situation?

- How do key stakeholders understand this situation and how does this fit with, enrich, or confound my understanding of events?

- What substantive or context-based knowledge is critical for understanding this event? Do I have access to this knowledge? If not, how do I gain access to relevant knowledge?

- What capacities do I, and the service user, bring to respond to this environment?

- What resources and opportunities does my practice context, including the institutional environment, offer for responding to the situation?

Through critical analysis of how we use and develop knowledge in practice, our embedded framework for practice is revealed. Being able to articulate our framework for practice enhances our capacity for collaboration in knowledge development with others, such as colleagues and service users. We are also in a position to understand the limitations of our framework for practice and this can provide directions for further development of our framework and future learning.

Formalizing Practitioner Contribution to Knowledge

Finally, we turn to the importance of social work practitioners using their framework for practice to influence the formal base of practice and the institutional contexts of our activity. In the dynamic model of social work practice introduced in Chapter 2, we emphasized that social workers actively create knowledge and theory in practice (see Taylor and White, 2000; White et al., 2006). Many social workers engage in theory building in a tacit and informal way as our understandings are expressed in our direct practice and, at best, shared among immediate colleagues (Fook et al., 2000). Unfortunately, these informal and localized knowledge production practices do little to create a bridge between the formal theoretical base of the profession and theoretical bases developed by practitioners.

Our profession is concerned with theory and knowledge for practice. Our professional mission and our value base mean that we must do more than understand the worlds in which we engage, we must seek to influence them. Yet despite the interest in applied theory and knowledge, much formal theory and knowledge development occurs within academic or specialist research institutions (Kirk and Reid, 2002). A significant challenge for the profession is that of promoting collaboration between social work and cognate disciplines as well as between academic and research institutions and the service agencies where social work is practised.

Truly involving practitioners in the development of the formal professional base requires those of us formally charged with knowledge building for the profession, that is, academic researchers and theorists, to be willing to open our ideas to practice-based scrutiny. Academic social workers must be willing to allow field-based workers to use their experiences of the messy and indeterminate nature of much social work practice to confound formal theories for practice. We also need to encourage practitioners, that is, those located in the direct delivery of social work services, to use the knowledge gained through practice to critically analyse and disrupt the formal base of social work practice and the discourses that underpin service delivery processes. Practitioners are encouraged to actively participate in formal theory development forums such as conferences and publication of their work.

Since the first edition of this book was published in 2005, I have seen some signs of hope for the flourishing of a diverse knowledge base in the profession. The increased participation of social workers in advanced degree-level programmes is developing a critical mass of social workers in practice, as well as in academia, equipped to contribute to the formal theory and knowledge base of practice. Various initiatives within social work associations and collaborations between social workers and service user communities may also provide new sites for theory and knowledge production. Notwithstanding the clear dangers posed by new public management, its emphasis on evidence and practice evaluation may also provide opportunities for social workers to improve the transparency and visibility of our practice. I am excited by the prospects offered by theoretical developments, particularly in relation to complex systems theories, environmental social work, and critical theories for assisting social workers to develop our theoretical bases in ways that honour the complex nature of our practice and the lives of the people with whom we work.

However, there are also signs of matters moving in directions that are harmful to the values of professional integrity, social justice and human rights that social workers champion. It is clear that new public management will continue to reshape services towards administratively defined categories of service provision (see Saario and Stepney, 2009). Social workers will struggle, perhaps more than we ever have, for the relational aspects and value base of our work to be recognized. For service users, the outlook will continue to be challenging, as governments retreat to a remedial, and in some instances punitive, approach to service provision. There can be little doubt that global warming will most damage poor and marginalized communities. In the context of government retreat from holistic service development and provision, it is likely these communities will find limited government support to address the effects of climate change on them. We must be sanguine about the capacity of social workers alone to turn around the significant challenges facing our profession and the communities with whom we work. While our profession can continue to advocate for quality services and, more broadly, for social justice, we must also recognize the need to collaborate with others – other disciplines and communities – to achieve the change we seek.

Over the coming decade, the influence of electronic information technology (IT) on social work practices is almost certain to be profound and is already the subject of intense debate (Gillingham, 2013). The use of electronic IT in social work is clearly not a neutral enterprise. On the one hand, it has the potential to extend our capacity to communicate with service users and improve service efficiency and effectiveness. Yet, if social workers do not actively participate in shaping how electronic IT is developed and used, it has the potential to render invisible and irrelevant the very core of social work, namely the relational aspects of our practices (Saario and Stephney, 2009; Gillingham, 2013).

Conclusion

Social work is a diverse and contextual activity. As social workers, we actively construct our purpose and our professional framework for practice by using, sometimes resisting, and changing aspects of our practice context and our formal professional base. Social workers face many barriers to formally influencing our contexts of practice and the formal base of the profession. This book has examined the ideas underpinning the institutional contexts and formal theories for social work practice in the hope that we will better understand them, as well as participate in transforming them.

BIBLIOGRAPHY

Addams, J. (1938) *Twenty Years at Hull-House*. (New York: Macmillan).
Agger, B. (1991) Critical theory, poststructuralism, postmodernism: their sociological relevance. *Annual Review of Sociology*, 17, 105–31.
Alston, M. and McKinnon, J. (2005) *Social Work: Fields of Practice*, 2nd edn. (Melbourne: Oxford University Press).
Anleu, S. (2000) *Law and Social Change*. (London: Sage).
Atherton, C.R. and Bolland, K.A. (2002) Postmodernism: a dangerous illusion for social work. *International Social Work*, 45(4), 421–33.
Bailey, R. and Brake, M. (1975) *Radical Social Work*. (London: Edward Arnold).
Baldwin, M. (2012) Participatory action research. In Gray, M., Midgley, J. and Webb, S. (eds) *The Sage Handbook of Social Work*. (Los Angeles, CA: Sage), pp. 467–81.
Ball, C. (1996) *Law for Social Workers*, 3rd edn. (Aldershot: Arena).
Banks, S. (2012) *Ethics and Values in Social Work*, 4th edn. (Basingstoke: Palgrave Macmillan).
Barnes, C. (1996) Institutional discrimination against disabled people and the campaign for anti-discrimination legislation. In Taylor, D. (ed.) *Critical Social Policy: A Reader*. (London: Sage), pp. 95–112.
Bartlett, H. (1970) *The Common Base of Social Work Practice*. (Washington: NASW).
Bennett, B., Green, S., Gilbert, S. and Bessarab, D. (2013) *Our Voices: Aboriginal and Torres Strait Islander Social Work*. (South Yarra: Palgrave Macmillan).
Berg, E., Barry, J. and Chandler, J. (2008) New public management and social work in Sweden: challenges and opportunities for staff in predominantly female organizations. *International Journal of Sociology and Social Policy*, 28(3/4), 114–28.
Berg, I.K. (1992) *Family Based Service*. (Milwaukee, WI: Brief Family Therapy Press).
Berg, I.K. (2000) *Brief Therapy for Addictions*. (Alexandria, VA: Alexander Street Press).
Berg, I.K. and Kelly, S. (2000) *Building Solutions in Child Protection Services*. (New York: WW Norton).
Bessarab, D. and Crawford, F. (2013) Trauma, grief and loss: the vulnerability of Aboriginal families in the child protection system. In Bennett, B., Green, S., Gilbert S. and Bessarab, D. (eds) *Our Voices: Aboriginal and Torres Strait Islander Social Work*. (South Yarra: Palgrave Macmillan), pp. 93–113.
Besthorn, F. (2001) Transpersonal psychology and deep ecological philosophy: exploring linkages and applications for social work. In Canda, E. and Smith,

E. (eds) *Transpersonal Perspectives on Spirituality in Social Work*. (New York: Hawthorn Press), pp. 23–44.

Besthorn, F. (2012) Deep ecology's contributions to social work: a ten-year retrospective. *International Journal of Social Welfare*, 21(3), 248–59.

Bishop, A. (2002) *Becoming an Ally*. (Crows Nest, NSW: Allen & Unwin).

Bland, R., Renouf, N. and Tullgren, A. (2009) *Social Work Practice in Mental Health: An Introduction*. (Crows Nest, NSW: Allen & Unwin).

Bloom, S. (2000) Social work and the behavioural sciences: past history, future prospects. *Social Work in Health*, 31(3), 25–37.

Boas, P. and Crawley, J. (1975) *Explorations in Teaching Generic Social Work Theory*. (Bundoora, Victoria: Preston Institute of Technology Press).

Bolland, K. and Atheron, C. (1999) Chaos theory: an alternative approach to social work practice and research. *Families in Society*, 80(4), 367–73.

Borden, W. (2000) The relational paradigm in contemporary psychoanalysis: toward a psychodynamically informed social work perspective. *Social Service Review*, 74(3), 352–79.

Bourdieu, P. (1987) The force of law: toward a sociology of the juridical field. *Hastings Law Journal*, 38(5), 805–54.

Brady, S. (1998) The sterilization of children with intellectual disabilities: defective law, unlawful activity and the need for a service oriented approach. *Australian Journal of Social Issues*, 33(2), 155–77.

Braye, S. and Preston-Shoot, M. (1997) *Practising Social Work Law*, 2nd edn. (Basingstoke: Macmillan – now Palgrave Macmillan).

Brayne, H. and Carr, H. (2010) *Law for Social Workers*, 11th edn. (Oxford: Oxford University Press).

Brewster, B. and Whiteford, J. (1976) *Sociology and Social Work: New Perspectives for Practitioners*. (Hatfield: Organisation of Sociologists in Polytechnics and Cognate Institutions).

Bricker-Jenkins, M., Hooyman, N.K. and Gottlieb, N. (1991) *Feminist Social Work Practice in Clinical Settings*. (Newbury Park, CA: Sage).

Bronfenbrenner, U. (1979) *The Ecology of Human Development: Experiments by Nature and Design*. (Cambridge, MA: Harvard University Press).

Bruer, J. (1999) *The Myth of the First Three Years: A New Understanding of Early Brain Development and Lifelong Learning*. (New York: Free Press).

Burke, B. and Harrison, P. (2002) Anti-oppressive practice. In Adams, R., Dominelli, L. and Payne, M. (eds) *Social Work: Themes, Issues and Critical Debates*, 2nd edn. (Basingstoke: Palgrave – now Palgrave Macmillan), pp. 227–36.

Butler, J. (1993) *Bodies That Matter: On the Discursive Limits of 'Sex'*. (New York: Routledge).

Byrne, D. (1998) *Complexity and the Social Sciences*. (London: Routledge).

Campbell, J. and Oliver, M. (1996) *Disability Politics: Understanding Our Past, Changing Our Future*. (London: Routledge).

Canda, E. (1988) Conceptualizing spirituality for social work: insights from diverse perspectives. *Social Thought*, 14(1), 30–46.

Capra, F. (1996) *The Web of Life*. (New York: Anchor & Doubleday).

Carlson, G. and Wilson, J. (1998) A model of substitute decision-making. *Australian Social Work*, 51(3), 17–23.

Carmichael, A. and Brown, L. (2002) The future challenge for direct payments. *Disability and Society*, 17(7), 797–808.

Carniol, B. (1992) Structural social work: Maurice Moreau's challenge to social work practice. *Journal of Progressive Human Services*, 3(1), 1–20.

Carpenter, J. (2002) Mental health recovery paradigm: implications for social work. *Health and Social Work*, 27(2), 86–92.

Carpiano, R., Lloyd, J. and Hertzmann, C. (2009) Concentrated affluence, concentrated disadvantage and children's readiness for school: a population-based, multi-level investigation. *Social Science and Medicine*, 69(3), 420–32.

Catholic Care (Diocese of Leeds) and Charity Commission for England and Wales, In an Appeal to the Upper Tribunal (Tax and Chancery), November 3, 2012, http://www.judiciary.gov.uk/Resources/JCO/Documents/Judgments/catholic-care-charity-commission-judgment-02112012.pdf, retrieved 18/08/13.

Chapin, R. (1995) Social policy development: the strengths perspective. *Social Work*, 40(4), 506–14.

Clarke, J. (2004) Dissolving the public realm? The logics and limits of neo-liberalism. *Journal of Social Policy*, 33(1), 27–48.

Coleman, J. and Leiter, B. (1996) Legal positivism. In Patterson, D. (ed.) *A Companion to the Philosophy of Law and Legal Theory*. (Malden: Blackwell), pp. 241–60.

Connolly, M, and Morris, K. (2012) *Understanding Child and Family Welfare: Statutory Responses to Children at Risk*. (Basingstoke: Palgrave Macmillan).

Corker, M. and Shakespeare, T. (eds) (2002) *Disability/Postmodernity: Embodying Disability Theory*. (London: Continuum).

Corrigan, P. and Leonard, P. (1978) *Social Work Practice under Capitalism: A Marxist Approach*. (London: Macmillan).

Cournoyer, B. (2012) Crisis intervention. In Gray, M., Midgley, J. and Webb, S. (eds) *The Sage Handbook of Social Work*. (Los Angeles, CA: Sage), pp. 248–63.

Cowger, C. (1998) Clientism and clientification: impediments to strengths based social work practice. *Journal of Sociology and Social Welfare*, 25(1), 25–37.

Crath, R. (2012) Belonging as a mode of interpretive in-between: image, place and space in the video works of racialised and homeless youth. *British Journal of Social Work*, 42(1), 42–57.

Cree, V. (2010) *Sociology for Social Workers and Probation Officers*, 2nd edn. (London: Routledge).

Cree, V. and Davis, A. (2006) *Social Work: Voices from the Inside*. (New York: Routledge).

Crompton, M. (1998) *Children, Spirituality, Religion and Social Work*. (Aldershot: Ashgate).

Crossley, M. and Crossley, N. (2001) 'Patient' voices, social movements and the habitus: how psychiatric survivors 'speak out'. *Social Science and Medicine*, 52, 1477–89.

Crotty, M. (1998) *The Foundations of Social Research: Meaning and Perspective in the Research Process.* (St Leonards, NSW: Allen & Unwin).

Crowther, N. (2007) Nothing without us or nothing about us. *Disability and Society,* 22(7), 791–4.

Daly, J., Gullemin, M. and Hill, S. (2001) Introduction: the need for critical compromise. In Daly, J., Gullemin M. and Hill, S. (eds) *Technologies and Health: Critical Compromises.* (Melbourne: Oxford University Press), pp. xii–xx.

Dalrymple, J. and Burke, B. (1995) *Anti-oppressive Practice: Social Care and the Law.* (Buckingham: Open University Press).

Dalrymple, J. and Burke, B. (2006) *Anti-oppressive Practice: Social Care and the Law,* 2nd edn. (Maidenhead: Open University Press).

Darley, V. (1994) Emergent phenomena and complexity, available at http://cadia. ru.is/wiki/_media/public:vincedarely-emergence_alife.pdf, accessed 10/1/14.

Davis, A. and George, J. (1993) *States of Health: Health and Illness in Australia,* 2nd edn. (Pymble, NSW: Harper).

Day, P. (1987) *Sociology in Social Work Practice.* (Basingstoke: Macmillan).

DeAngelis, D. and Monahan, M.J. (2012) Professional credentials and professional regulations: social work professional development. In Dulmus, C. and Sowers, K. (eds) *The Profession of Social Work: Guided by History, Led by Evidence.* (Hoboken, NJ: Wiley), pp. 91–103.

Decker, J. and Redhorse, J. (1979) The principles of general systems theory applied to the medical model. *Journal of Sociology and Social Welfare,* 6(2), 144–53.

Derrida, J. (1991) Différance. In Kamuf, P. (ed.) *A Derrida Reader: Between the Blinds.* (New York: Columbia University Press), pp. 59–79.

De Shazer, S. (1985) *Keys to Solution in Brief Therapy.* (New York: WW Norton).

De Shazer, S. (1988) *Clues: Investigating Solutions in Brief Therapy.* (New York: WW Norton).

De Shazer, S. and Berg, I.K. (1992) Doing therapy: a post-structural re-vision. *Journal of Marital and Family Therapy,* 18(1), 71–81.

De Shazer, S., Berg, I.K., Lipchick, E. et al. (1986) Brief therapy: focused solution development. *Family Process,* 25, 207–21.

Doel, M. (1998) Task-centred work. In Adams, R., Dominelli, L. and Payne, M. (eds) *Social Work: Themes, Issues and Critical Debates.* (Basingstoke: Macmillan – now Palgrave Macmillan), pp. 196–206.

Doel, M. and Marsh, P. (1992) *Task-centred Social Work.* (Aldershot: Ashgate).

Doll, W.E. and Trueit, D. (2010) Complexity and the health care professions. *Journal of Evaluation in Clinical Practice,* 16(4), 841–8.

Dominelli, L. (1988) *Anti-racist Social Work: A Challenge for White Practitioners and Educators.* (Basingstoke: Macmillan).

Dominelli, L. (1996) De-professionalizing social work: anti-oppressive practices, competencies and postmodernism. *British Journal of Social Work,* 26, 153–75.

Dominelli, L. (1997) *Sociology for Social Work.* (Basingstoke: Macmillan – now Palgrave Macmillan).

Dominelli, L. (2002a) *Feminist Social Work: Theory and Practice.* (Basingstoke: Palgrave – now Palgrave Macmillan).

Dominelli, L. (2002b) Anti-oppressive practice in context. In Adams, R., Dominelli, L. and Payne, M. (eds) *Social Work: Themes, Issues and Critical Debates*, 2nd edn. (Basingstoke: Palgrave – now Palgrave Macmillan), pp. 3–19.

Dominelli, L. (2012) *Green Social Work: From Environmental Crises to Environmental Justice*. (Cambridge: Polity Press).

Dominelli, L. and Hoogvelt, A. (1996) Globalization and technocratization of social work. *Critical Social Policy*, 16(2), 45–62.

Dominelli, L. and McLeod, E. (1989) *Feminist Social Work*. (Basingstoke: Macmillan).

Donnellan, H. and Jack, G. (2010) *The Survival Guide for Newly Qualified Child and Family Social Workers: Hitting the Ground Running*. (London: Jessica Kingsley).

Dziegielewski, S. (2013) *The Changing Face of Health Care Social Work: Opportunities and Challenges for Professional Practice*. (New York: Springer).

Edwards, L. (2007) *How to Argue with an Economist: Reopening Political Debate in Australia*, 2nd edn. (Cambridge: Cambridge University Press).

Edwards, P. (2002) Spiritual themes in social work counselling: facilitating the search for meaning. *Australian Social Work*, 55(1), 78–87.

Ellison, M. (2007) Contested terrains within the neo-liberal project: the re-organisation of services for children in Europe: gender, citizenship and the forging of new public management within professional child care social work practice in Europe. *Equal Opportunities International*, 26(4), 331–51.

Epstein, L. and Brown, L. (2002) *Brief Treatment and a New Look at the Task-centered Approach*, 4th edn. (Boston, MA: Allyn & Bacon).

Erickson, M. (1954) Special techniques of brief hypnotherapy. *Journal of Clinical and Experimental Hypnosis*, 2, 109–29.

Fairclough, N. (1992) *Discourse and Social Change*. (Cambridge: Polity Press).

Fawcett, B. (2009) Postmodernism. In Gray, M. and Webb, S. (eds) *Social Work Theories and Methods*. (Los Angeles, CA: Sage), pp. 119–28.

Fawcett, B., Goodwin, S., Meagher, G. and Phillips, R. (2010) *Social Policy for Social Change*. (Basingstoke: Palgrave Macmillan).

Fay, B. (1987) *Critical Social Science: Liberation and its Limits*. (Ithaca, NY: Cornell University Press).

Featherstone, B. and Fawcett, B. (1994) Feminism and child abuse: Opening up some possibilities? *Critical Social Policy*, 14(3), 61–80.

Ferguson, I. (2008) *Reclaiming Social Work: Challenging Neo-Liberalism and Promoting Social Justice*. (London: Sage).

Ferguson, I. (2011) Why class (still) matters. In Lavalette, M. (ed.) *Radical Social Work Today: Social Work at the Crossroads*. (Bristol: Policy Press), pp. 115–34.

Fook, J. (1993) *Radical Casework: A Theory of Practice*. (Sydney: Allen & Unwin).

Fook, J. (2002) *Social Work: Critical Theory and Practice*. (London: Sage).

Fook, J., Ryan, M. and Hawkins, L. (2000) *Professional Expertise: Practice, Theory and Education for Working in Uncertainty*. (London: Whiting & Birch).

Ford, P. and Postle, K. (2000) Task-centred practice and care management. In Stepney, P. and Ford, D. (eds) *Social Work Models, Methods and Theories: A Framework for Practice*. (Lyme Regis: Russell House), pp. 52–64.

Foucault, M. (1980a) Truth and power. In Gordon, C. (ed.) *Power/Knowledge: Selected Interviews and Other Writings 1972–1977*. (New York: Pantheon Books), pp. 109–33.

Foucault, M. (1980b) Two lectures. In Gordon, C. (ed.) *Power/Knowledge: Selected Interviews and Other Writings 1972–1977*. (New York: Pantheon Books), pp. 78–108.

France, E.F., Locock, L., Hunt, K. et al. (2012) Imagined futures: how experiential knowledge of disability affects parents' decision making about fetal abnormality. *Health Expectations*, 15(2), 139–56.

Fraser, H. and Briskman, L. (2005) Through the eye of a needle: the challenge of getting justice in Australia if you're Indigenous or seeking asylum. In Ferguson, I., Lavalette, M. and Whitmore, E. (eds) *Globalisation, Global Justice and Social Work*. (London: Routledge), pp. 109–24.

Fraser, N. (1997) *Justice Interruptus: Critical Reflections on the 'Postsocialist' Condition*. (New York: Routledge).

Friedman, M. (1982) *Capitalism and Freedom*. (Chicago: University of Chicago Press).

Galper, J. (1980) *Social Work Practice: A Radical Perspective*. (Englewood Cliffs, NJ: Prentice Hall).

Friedman, M. and Friedman, R. (1980) *Free to Choose: A Personal Statement*. (Melbourne: Macmillan).

Gambrill, E. (1994) What's in a name? Task-centered, empirical and behavioral practice. *Social Service Review*, 68(4), 578–99.

Gandhi, L. (1998) *Postcolonial Theory: A Critical Introduction*. (St Leonards, NSW: Allen & Unwin).

Garrett, A. (1958) The worker-client relationship. In Parad, H. (ed.) *Ego Psychology and Dynamic Casework: Papers from the Smith College School for Social Work*. (New York: Family Service Association of America), pp. 53–72.

Garrett, P.M. (2009) Questioning Habermasian social work: a note on some alternative theoretical resources. *British Journal of Social Work*, 39(5), 867–83.

Garvin, C.D. (2003) *Generalist Practice: A Task-centred Approach*. (New York: Columbia University Press).

Gehart, D. (2012) The mental health recovery movement and family therapy, part 1: consumer-led reform of services to persons diagnosed with severe mental illness. *Journal of Marital and Family Therapy*, 38(3), 429–42.

Germain, C. and Gitterman, A. (1996) *The Life Model of Social Work Practice: Advances in Theory and Practice*. (New York: Columbia University Press).

Gibelman, M. (1995) *What Social Workers Do*. (Washington: NASW Press).

Gibelman, M. and Demone, H. (2002) The commercialization of health and human services: natural phenomenon or cause for concern. *Families in Society: Journal of Contemporary Human Services*, 83(4), 387–97.

Gillingham, P. (2013) The development of electronic information systems for the future: practitioners, 'embodied structures' and 'technologies-in-practice'. *British Journal of Social Work*, 43(3), 430–45.

Goffman, E. (1991) *Asylums: Essays on the Social Situation of Mental Patients and Other Inmates*. (Harmondsworth: Penguin).

Golan, N. (1978) *Treatment in Crisis Situations*. (New York: Free Press).

Golan, N. (1986) Crisis theory. In Turner, F. (ed.) *Social Work Treatment: Interlocking Theoretical Approaches*. (New York: Free Press), pp. 296–340.

Goldberg, E.M., Walker, D. and Robinson, J. (1977) Exploring the task-centred casework method. *Social Work Today*, 9(2), 9–14.

Golstein, H. (1973) *Social Work Practice: A Unitary Approach*. (Columbia, SC: University of South Carolina Press).

Gomory, T., Wong, S.E., Cohen, D. and Lacasse, J.R. (2011) Clinical social work and the biomedical industrial complex. *Journal of Sociology and Social Welfare*, 38(4), 135–65.

Gordon, W. (1969) Basic constructs for an integrative and generative conception of social work. In Hearn, G. (ed.) *The General Systems Approach: Contributions Toward a Holistic Conception of Social Work*. (New York: Council on Social Work Education), pp. 5–11.

Gorman, K. (2001) Cognitive behaviourism and the Holy Grail: the quest for a universal means of managing offender risk. *Probation Journal*, 48(1), 3–9.

Gray, M. and Lovat, T. (2007) Horse and carriage: why Habermas's discourse ethics gives virtue a praxis in social work. *Ethics and Social Welfare*, 1(3), 310–28.

Gray, M. and Lovat, T. (2008) Practical mysticism, Habermas and social work praxis. *Journal of Social Work*, 8(2), 149–63.

Gray, M. and Webb, S. (eds) (2009) *Social Work Theories and Methods*. (London: Sage).

Gray, M., Coates, J. and Hetherington, T. (eds) (2013) *Environmental Social Work*. (New York: Routledge).

Green, G. and Haines, A. (2002) *Asset Building and Community Development*. (London: Sage).

Green, D. and McDermott, F. (2010) Social work from inside and between complex systems: perspectives on person-in-environment for today's social work. *British Journal of Social Work*, 40(8), 2414–30.

Hall, C. and Slembrouck, S. (2010) Categorisations of child 'in need' and child 'in need of protection' and implications for the formulation of 'deficit' parenting. In Candlin, C. and Crichton, J. (eds) *Discourses of Deficit*. (Basingstoke: Palgrave Macmillan), pp. 63–81.

Hall, C., Slembrouck, S. and Sarangi, S. (2006) *Language Practices in Social Work: Categorization and Accountability in Child Welfare*. (London: Routledge).

Hamilton, G. (1951) *Theory and Practice of Social Case Work*, 2nd edn. (New York: Columbia University Press).

Hamilton, G. (1958) A theory of personality: Freud's contribution to social work. In Parad, H. (ed.) *Ego Psychology and Dynamic Casework: Papers from the Smith College School for Social Work*. (New York: Family Service Association of America), pp. 11–37.

Hanmer, J. and Statham, D. (1999) *Women and Social Work: Towards a Woman-Centred Practice*, 2nd edn. (Basingstoke: Macmillan).

Hanrahan, C. (2013) Critical social theory and the politics of narrative in the mental health professions: the mental health film festival as an emerging postmodern praxis. *British Journal of Social Work*, 43(6), 1150–69.

Harris, M., Halfpenny, P. and Rochester, C. (2003) A social policy role for faith-based organizations? Lessons from the UK Jewish voluntary sector. *Journal of Social Policy*, 32(1), 93–112.

Harrison, G. and Melville, R. (2010) *Rethinking Social Work in a Global World*. (Basingstoke: Palgrave Macmillan).

Healy, J. (1998) *Welfare Options: Delivering Social Services*. (St Leonards, NSW: Allen & Unwin).

Healy, K. (1998) Participation and child protection: the importance of context. *British Journal of Social Work*, 28, 897–914.

Healy, K. (1999) Power and activist social work. In Pease, B. and Fook, J. (eds) *Transforming Social Work Practice: Critical Postmodern Perspectives*. (St Leonards, NSW: Allen & Unwin), pp. 115–34.

Healy, K. (2000) *Social Work Practices: Contemporary Perspectives on Change*. (London: Sage).

Healy, K. (2002) Managing human services in a market environment: What role for social workers? *British Journal of Social Work*, 32, 527–40.

Healy, K. (2009) A case of mistaken identity: the social welfare professions and new public management. *Journal of Sociology*, 45(4), 401–18.

Healy, K. (2012) Critical perspectives. In Gray, M., Midgley, J. and Webb, S. (eds) *The Sage Handbook of Social Work*. (London: Sage), pp. 191–206.

Healy, K. and Meagher, G. (2001) Practitioner perspectives on performance assessment in family support services. *Children Australia*, 26(4), 22–8.

Healy, K. and Meagher, G. (2004) The reprofessionalization of social work: collaborative approaches for achieving professional recognition. *British Journal of Social Work*, 34, 157–74.

Healy, K. and Walsh, K. (1997) Making participatory processes visible: practice issues in the development of a peer support network. *Australian Social Work*, 50(3), 45–52.

Healy, K. and Young Mothers for Young Women (1996) Valuing young families: child protection and family support strategies with young mothers. *Children Australia*, 21(2), 23–30.

Hearn, G. (1969) Progress toward a holistic conception of social work. In Hearn, G. (ed.) *The General Systems Approach: Contributions Toward a Holistic Conception of Social Work*. (New York: Council on Social Work Education), pp. 63–70.

Heffernan, K. (2006) Social work, new public management and the language of 'service user'. *British Journal of Social Work*, 36(1), 139–47.

Hohman, M. (2012) *Motivational Interviewing in Social Work Practice*. (New York: Guilford Press).

Holloway, M. and Moss, B. (2010) *Spirituality and Social Work*. (Basingstoke: Palgrave Macmillan).

Houston, S. (2009) Jürgen Habermas. In Gray, M. and Webb, S. (eds) *Social Work: Theories and Methods*. (London: Sage), pp. 13–22.

Howe, D. (1987) *An Introduction to Social Work Theory: Making Sense in Practice*. (Aldershot: Arena).

Hudson, C. (2000) The edge of chaos: A new paradigm for social work? *Journal of Social Work Education*, 36(2), 215–30.

Humphrey, J. (1999) Disabled people and the politics of difference. *Disability and Society*, 14(2), 173–88.

Hunter, M., O'Dea, I. and Britten, N. (1997) Decision-making and hormone replacement therapy: a qualitative analysis. *Social Science and Medicine*, 45(10), 1465–603.

Hutchinson-Reis, M. (1989) And for those of us who are black? Black politics in social work. In Langan, M. and Lee, M. (eds) *Radical Social Work Today*. (London: Unwin & Hyman), pp. 165–77.

Hutchinson, G., Lund, L., Lyngstad, R. and Oltedal, S. (eds) (2001) *Social Work in Five Countries: A Report*. (Bodo: University of Bodo).

Hutchison, W. (1998) The role of religious auspiced agencies in the postmodern era. In Meinert, R., Pardeck, J. and Murphy, J. (eds) *Postmodernism, Religion and the Future of Social Work*. (New York: Haworth Press), pp. 55–69.

Hyde, M. and Power, D. (2000) Informed parental consent for cochlear implantation of young deaf children: social and other considerations in the use of the 'bionic ear'. *Australian Journal of Social Issues*, 35(2), 117–20.

Ife, J. (1999) Postmodern, critical theory and social work. In Pease, B. and Fook, J. (eds) *Transforming Social Work Practice: Critical Postmodern Perspectives*. (St Leonards, NSW: Allen & Unwin), pp. 211–23.

Industry Commission (1995) *Charitable Organisations in Australia*, Report 45. (Melbourne: Australian Government Publishing Service).

Jenkins, A. (1990) *Invitations to Responsibility: The Therapeutic Engagement of Men who are Violent and Abusive*. (Adelaide: Dulwich Centre).

Jenkins, J. and Barrett, R. (2004) Introduction. In Jenkins, J. and Barrett, R. (eds) *Schizophrenia, Culture, and Subjectivity: The Edge of Experience*. (Cambridge: Cambridge University Press).

Johnson, P. (1994) *Feminism as Radical Humanism*. (St Leonards, NSW: Allen & Unwin).

Jones, P. (2010) Responding to the ecological crisis: transformative pathways for social work education. *Journal of Social Work Education*, 46(1), 67–84.

Kanel, K. (2003) *A Guide to Crisis Intervention*. (Pacific Grove, CA: Brooks/Cole).

Kanter, J. (1983) Reevaluation of task-centred social work practice. *Clinical Social Work Journal*, 11(3), 228–44.

Kaplan, C. (2002) An early example of brief strengths based practice: Bertha Reynolds at the National Maritime Union. *Smith College Studies in Social Work*, 72(3), 403–16.

Kemp, S., Whittaker, J. and Tracy, E. (1997) *Person in Environment Practice: The Social Ecology of Interpersonal Helping*. (New York: Aldine de Gruyter).

Kenen, R. (1996) The at-risk health status and technology: a diagnostic invitation and the gift of knowing. *Social Science and Medicine*, 42(11), 1533–45.

Killen, K. (1996) How far have we come in dealing with the emotional challenge of abuse and neglect? *Child Abuse and Neglect*, 20, 791–5.

Kirk, S. and Reid, W. (2002) *Science and Social Work: A Critical Appraisal*. (New York: Columbia University Press).

Kirkpatrick, I., Ackroyd, S. and Walker, R. (2005) *The New Managerialism and Public Service Professions*. (Basingstoke: Palgrave Macmillan).

Kissman, K. and Maurer, L. (2002) East meets west: therapeutic aspects of spirituality in health, mental health and addiction recovery. *International Social Work*, 45(1), 35–43.

Kretzmann, J. and McKnight, J. (1993) *Building Communities from the Inside Out.* (Chicago: Center for Urban Affairs and Policy Research).

Krumer-Nevo, M., Weiss-Gal, I. and Levin, L. (2011) Searching for poverty-aware social work: discourse analysis of job descriptions. *Journal of Social Policy*, 40(2), 313–32.

Lavalette, M. (ed.) (2011) *Radical Social Work Today.* (Bristol: Polity Press).

Lavalette, M. and Ferguson, I. (eds) (2007) *International Social Work and the Radical Tradition.* (London: Venture Press).

Lees, R. (1972) *Politics and Social Work.* (London: Routledge & Kegan Paul).

Leighninger, R. (1978) Systems theory. *Journal of Sociology and Social Welfare*, 5, 446–66.

Leonard, P. (1966) *Sociology in Social Work.* (London: Routledge & Kegan Paul).

Leonard, P. (1994) Knowledge/power and postmodernism: implications for the practice of a critical social work education. *Canadian Social Work Review*, 11(1), 11–26.

Leonard, P. (1995) Postmodernism, socialism and social welfare. *Journal of Progressive Human Services*, 6(2), 3–19.

Leonard, P. (1997) *Postmodern Welfare: Reconstructing an Emancipatory Project.* (London: Sage).

Lessard, H., Johnson, R. and Webber, J. (eds) (2011) *Storied Communities: Narratives of Contact and Arrival in Constituting a Political Community.* (Vancouver: UBC Press).

Levine, E. (1998) Church, state and social welfare: purchase of service and the sectarian agency. In Gibelman, M. and Demone, H. (eds) *The Privatization of Human Services: Policy and Practice Issues.* (New York: Springer), pp. 117–53.

Levy, R. (2010) New public management: End of an era? *Public Policy and Administration*, 25(2), 234–40.

Lewis, G. (2000) *'Race', Gender, Social Welfare: Encounters in a Postcolonial Society.* (Cambridge: Polity Press).

Lindsay, R. (2002) *Recognising Spirituality: The Interface between Faith and Social Work.* (Crawley, WA: University of Western Australia Press).

Lough, B.J. (2013) Social work perspectives on international volunteer service. *British Journal of Social Work*, doi:10.1093/bjsw/bct001.

Lyall, D. (2001) Spiritual institutions? In Orchard, H. (ed.) *Spirituality in Health Care Contexts.* (London: Jessica Kingsley), pp. 47–56.

Lyons, M. (2001) *The Contribution of Nonprofit and Cooperative Enterprises in Australia.* (St Leonards, NSW: Allen & Unwin).

Lyotard, J. (1984) *The Postmodern Condition: A Report on Knowledge*, trans. G. Bennington and B. Massumi. (Minneapolis: University of Minnesota Press).

McCarthy, M. (2009) 'I have the jab so I can't be blamed for getting pregnant': contraception and women with learning disabilities. *Women's Studies International Forum*, 32(3), 198–208.

McDonald, C. (2006) *Challenging Social Work: The Institutional Context of Practice.* (Basingstoke: Palgrave Macmillan).

McGrath, P. (1997) Chemotherapy, bioethics and social work: forging the link. *Australian Social Work*, 50(4), 53–60.

McKinnon, J. (2013) The environment: A private concern or a professional practice issue for Australian social workers? *Australian Social Work*, 66(2), 156–70.

McLeod, F. and Bywaters, P. (2000) *Social Work, Health, and Equality.* (London: Routledge).

McMillen, J.C. (1999) Better for it: how people benefit from adversity. *Social Work*, 44(5), 455–68.

Maidment, J. and Egan, R. (eds) (2004) *Practice Skills in Social Work and Welfare: More than Just Common Sense* (Crows Nest, NSW: Allen & Unwin).

Mainzer, K. (1996) *Thinking in Complexity: The Complex Dynamics of Matter, Mind, and Mankind.* (Berlin: Springer).

Marsh, P. and Doel, M. (2005) *The Task-centred Book.* (London: Routledge).

Martin, J. (2003) Historical development of critical social work practice. In Allan, J., Pease, B. and Briskman, L. (eds) *Critical Social Work: An Introduction to Theories and Practice.* (Crows Nest, NSW: Allen & Unwin), pp. 17–31.

Mary, N.L. (2008) *Social Work in a Sustainable World.* (Chicago: Lyceum).

Mattaini, M. and Meyer, C. (2002) The ecosystems perspective: implications for practice. In Mattaini, M., Lowery, C. and Meyer, C. (eds) *The Foundations of Social Work Practice: A Graduate Text.* (Washington: NASW Press), pp. 3–24.

Matto, H. and Strolin-Golzman, J. (2010) Integrating social neuroscience and social work: innovations for advancing practice-based research. *Social Work*, 55(2), 147–56.

Matto, H., Strolin-Golzman, J. and Ballan, M. (2014) *Neuroscience for Social Work: Current Research and Practice.* (New York: Springer).

Meyer, C. (1976) *Social Work Practice.* (New York: Free Press).

Middleman, R.R. and Goldberg, G. (1974) *Social Service Delivery: A Structural Approach to Social Work Practice.* (New York: Columbia University Press).

Miller, W.R. and Rollnick, S. (2002) *Motivational Interviewing: Preparing People for Change,* 2nd edn. (New York: Guilford Press).

Mishler, E. (1989) Critical perspectives on the biomedical model. In Brown, P. (ed.) *Perspectives in Medical Sociology.* (Belmont, CA: Wadsworth), pp. 153–65.

Moreau, M. (1979) A structural approach to social work practice. *Canadian Journal of Social Work Education*, 5(1), 78–94.

Moreau, M. (1990) Empowerment through advocacy and consciousness-raising: implications of a structural approach. *Journal of Sociology and Social Welfare*, 17(2), 53–67.

Morley, C. and Macfarlane, S. (2012) The nexus between feminism and postmodernism: still a central concern for critical social work. *British Journal of Social Work*, 42(4), 687–705.

Mullaly, B. (2002) *Challenging Oppression: A Critical Social Work Approach.* (Ontario: Oxford University Press).

Mullaly, B. (2007) *The New Structural Social Work*, 3rd edn. (Ontario: Oxford University Press).

Mullaly, R. (1993) *Structural Social Work: Ideology, Theory, and Practice.* (Toronto: McClelland and Stewart).

Mune, M. (1979) Exploring the utility of the general systems approach. In Pavlin, F., Crawley, J. and Boas, P. (eds) *Perspectives in Australian Social Work.* (Bundoora, Victoria: PIT), pp. 61–77.

Munro, E. (1996) Avoidable and unavoidable mistakes in child protection work. *British Journal of Social Work*, 26(6), 793–808.

Munro, E. (1998) *Understanding Social Work: An Empirical Approach.* (London: Althlone Press).

Napier, L. and Fook, J. (eds) (2000) *Breakthroughs in Practice: Theorising Critical Moments in Social Work.* (London: Whiting & Birch).

National Secular Society (2012) *Catholic Adoption Agency Loses Fight Over Gay Adoption*, www.secularism.org.uk/news/2012/11/catholic-adoption-agency-loses-fight-over-gay-adoption, accessed 18/08/13.

Nicolson, P., Bayne, R. and Owen, J. (2006) *Applied Psychology for Social Workers*, 3rd edn. (Basingstoke: Palgrave Macmillan).

Noble, C. and Henrickson, M. (2011) Editorial: After neo-liberalism, new managerialism and postmodernism, what next for social work? *Journal of Social Work*, 11(2), 128–31.

O'Connell, B. (2005) *Solution-Focused Therapy*, 2nd edn. (London: Sage).

Oliver, M. (2001) Disability issues in the postmodern world. In Barton, L. (ed.) *Disability, Politics and the Struggle for Change.* (London: David Fulton), pp. 149–59.

Olsen, K. (ed.) (2008) *Adding Insult to Injury: Nancy Fraser Debates her Critics.* (London: Verso).

Opie, A. (1995) *Beyond Good Intentions: Support Work with Older People.* (Wellington, New Zealand: Institute of Policy Studies).

Osborne, D. and Gaebler, T. (1993) *Reinventing Government: How the Entrepreneurial Spirit is Transforming the Public Sector.* (New York: Plume).

Parad, H. (1965) *Crisis Intervention: Selected Readings.* (New York: Family Service Association of America).

Parad, H. and Parad, L. (1968) A study of crisis-oriented planned short-term treatment: Part 1. *Social Casework*, 49, 346–55.

Parker, N. (1969) Speaking about human rights. In Lawrence, R. (ed.) *Norma Parker's Record of Service.* (Sydney: Australian Association of Social Work/ Department of Social Work at Sydney University/Department of Social Work at the University of New South Wales), pp. 209–11.

Parsons, R., Gutiérrez, L. and Cox, E. (1998) A model for empowerment practice. In Gutiérrez, L., Parsons, R. and Cox, E. (eds) *Empowerment in Social Work Practice: A Sourcebook.* (Pacific Grove, CA: Brooks/Cole), pp. 3–23.

Parton, N. (1994) 'Problematics of government', (post) modernity and social work. *British Journal of Social Work*, 24, 9–32.

Parton, N. (2000) Some thoughts on the relationship between theory and practice in and for social work. *British Journal of Social Work*, 30, 449–63.

Parton, N. (2003) Rethinking professional practice: the contributions of social constructionism and the feminist 'ethics of care'. *British Journal of Social Work*, 33, 1–16.

Parton, N. and O'Byrne, P. (2001) *Constructive Social Work: Towards a New Practice.* (Basingstoke: Macmillan – now Palgrave Macmillan).

Payne, C. (1994) Systems theory. In Philpot, T. and Hanvey, C. (eds) *Practising Social Work.* (London: Routledge), pp. 8–21.

Payne, M. (1997) *Modern Social Work Theory*, 2nd edn. (Basingstoke: Macmillan – now Palgrave Macmillan).

Payne, M. (2005) *Modern Social Work Theory*, 3rd edn. (Basingstoke: Palgrave Macmillan).

Payne, M. and Askeland, G.A. (2008) *Globalization and International Social Work: Postmodern Change and Challenge.* (Aldershot: Ashgate).

Pearman, J. (1973) *Social Science and Social Work: Applications of Social Science in the Helping Professions* (Metuchen, NJ: Scarecrow Press).

Pearman, J. and Stewart, B. (1973) The social and behavioural science input to social work practice. In Pearman, J. (ed.) *Social Science and Social Work: Applications of Social Science in the Helping Professions.* (Metuchen, NJ: Scarecrow Press), pp. 9–22.

Pease, B. and Fook, J. (eds) (1999) *Transforming Social Work Practice: Postmodern Critical Perspectives.* (St Leonards, NSW: Allen & Unwin).

Peile, C. (1988) Research paradigms in social work: from stalemate to creative synthesis. *Social Service Review*, 62(1), 1–19.

Peile, C. (1993) Determinism versus creativity: Which way for social work? *Social Work*, 38(2), 127–34.

Peile, C. (1994) *The Creative Paradigm: Insight, Synthesis and Knowledge Development.* (Aldershot: Avebury).

Peile, C. and McCouat, M. (1997) The rise of relativism: the future of theory and knowledge development in social work. *British Journal of Social Work*, 27(3), 343–60.

Perlman, H. (1957) *Social Casework: A Problem-Solving Process.* (Chicago: University of Chicago Press).

Perry, B.D. (2002) Childhood experience and the expression of genetic potential: what childhood neglect tells us about nature and nuture. *Brain and Mind*, 13(1), 79–100.

Perry, B.D. (2009) Examining child maltreatment through a neurodevelopmental lens: clinical applications of the neurosequential model of therapeutics. *Journal of Loss and Trauma*, 14(40), 240–55.

Pichot, T. and Dolan, T. (2003) *Solution-focused Brief Therapy: Its Effective Use in Agency Settings.* (Binghamton, NY: Haworth Clinical Practice Press).

Pincus, A. and Minahan, A. (1973) *Social Work Practice: Model and Method.* (Madison, WI: University of Wisconsin).

Plath, D. (2006) Evidence-based practice: current issues and future directions. *Australian Social Work*, 59(1), 56–72.

Puddifoot, J. (2000) Some problems and possibilities in the study of dynamical social processes. *Journal for the Theory of Social Behaviour*, 30(1), 79–95.

Quinn, P. (1998) *Understanding Disability: A Lifespan Approach.* (Thousand Oaks, CA: Sage).

Rapp, C. (1998) *The Strengths Model: Case Management with People Suffering from Severe and Persistent Mental Illness.* (New York: Oxford University Press).

Reid, W. (1977) Task-centered treatment and trends in clinical social work. In Reid, W. and Eptsein, L. (eds) *Task-Centered Practice.* (New York: Columbia University Press), pp. 1–18.

Reid, W. (1992) *Task-Strategies: An Empirical Approach to Clinical Social Work.* (New York: Columbia University Press).

Reid, W. (1994) The empirical practice movement. *Social Service Review*, 68(2), 165–84.

Reid, W. and Epstein, L. (1972) *Task-Centered Casework.* (New York: Columbia University Press).

Reid, W. and Shyne, A. (1969) *Brief and Extended Casework.* (New York: Columbia University Press).

Reisch, M. and Andrews, J. (2001) *The Road Not Taken: A History of Radical Social Work in the United States.* (Philadelphia, PA: Brunner-Routledge).

Reynolds, B. (1951) *Social Work and Social Living: Exploration in Philosophy and Practice.* (New York: Citadel Press).

Richmond, M. (1917) *Social Diagnosis.* (New York: Russell Sage Foundation).

Rojek, C., Peacock, G. and Collins, S. (1988) *Social Work and Received Ideas.* (London: Routledge).

Rose, N. (1999) *Governing the Soul: The Shaping of the Private Self.* (London: Free Association Books).

Rosenberg, L. and Rosenberg, D. (2012) *Human Genes and Genomes: Science, Health and Society.* (Amsterdam: Academic Press).

Rosenman, L., O'Connor, I. and Healy, K. (1998) Social work. In The Academy of Social Sciences in Australia. *Challenges for the Social Sciences in Australia* (Canberra: Australian Government Publishing Service), pp. 215–21.

Ross, E. (2008) The intersection of cultural practices and ethics in a rights based society: implications for South African social workers. *International Social Work*, 51(3), 384–95.

Saario, S. and Stepney, P. (2009) Managerial audit and community mental health: a study of rationalising practices in Finnish psychiatric outpatient clinics. *European Journal of Social Work*, 12(1), 41–56.

Saleebey, D. (1996) The strengths perspective in social work practice: extensions and cautions. *Social Work*, 41(3), 296–305.

Saleebey, D. (2012a) Introduction: power in the people. In Saleebey, D. (ed.) *The Strengths Perspective in Social Work Practice*, 6th edn. (Boston, MA: Pearson), pp. 1–24.

Saleebey, D. (2012b) The strengths perspective: possibilities and problems. In Saleebey, D. (ed.) *The Strengths Perspective in Social Work Practice*, 6th edn. (Boston, MA: Pearson), pp. 278–304.

Sandler, T. (2001) *Economic Concepts for the Social Sciences.* (Cambridge: Cambridge University Press).

Sawicki, J. (1991) *Disciplining Foucault: Feminism, Power, and the Body.* (New York: Routledge).

Shlonsky, A. and Wagner, D. (2005) The next step: integrating actuarial risk assessment and clinical judgment into an evidence-based practice framework in CPS case management. *Children and Youth Services Review*, 27(3), 409–27.

Schön, D. (1983) *The Reflective Practitioner.* (New York: Basic Books).

Schön, D. (1995) Reflective inquiry in social work practice. In McCartt-Hess, P. and Mullen, F. (eds) *Practitioner-Researcher Partnerships: Building Knowledge From, In, and For Practice.* (Washington DC: NASW), pp. 31–55.

Semidei, J., Radel, L.F. and Nolan, C. (2001) Substance abuse and child welfare: clear linkages and promising responses. *Child Welfare*, 80(2), 109–27.

Sewpaul, V. (2006) The global–local dialectic: challenges for African scholarship and social work in a post-colonial world. *British Journal of Social Work*, 36(3), 419–34.

Shah, H. (1989) 'It's up to you sisters': black women and radical social work. In Langan, M. and Lee, M. (eds) *Radical Social Work Today.* (London: Unwin Hyman), pp. 178–91.

Shakespeare, T. (2003) Rights, risks and responsibilities: new genetics and disabled people. In Williams, S., Birke, L. and Bendelow, G. (2003) *Debating Biology: Sociological Reflections on Health, Medicine and Society.* (London: Routledge), pp. 198–209.

Shakespeare, T. (2006) *Disability Rights and Wrongs.* (Hoboken, NJ: Taylor & Francis).

Shardland, E. (2012) Systematic review. In Gray, M., Midgley, J. and Webb, S. (eds) *The Sage Handbook of Social Work.* (Los Angeles, CA: Sage), pp. 482–98.

Sharry, J. (2007) *Solution-focused Groupwork.* (London: Sage).

Sheldon, B. (2000) Cognitive behavioural methods in social care: looking at the evidence. In Stepney, P. and Ford, D. (eds) *Social Work Models, Methods and Theories.* (Dorset: Russell House), pp. 65–83.

Sheldon, B. and Macdonald, G. (2009) *A Textbook of Social Work.* (New York: Taylor & Francis).

Shoemaker, L. (1998) Early conflicts in social work education. *Social Service Review*, 72(2), 182–92.

Simpkin, M. (1979) *Trapped Within Welfare: Surviving Social Work.* (London: Macmillan).

Slater, L. and Finck, K. (2011) *Social Work Practice and the Law.* (New York: Springer).

Smith, A. (2010) The third sector, regeneration and sustainable communities: 'rolling' with the new Labour agenda. *International Journal of Sociology and Social Policy*, 30(1/2), 48–65.

Smith, C. (2001) Trust and confidence: possibilities for social work in 'high modernity. *British Journal of Social Work*, 31(2), 287–305.

Smith, D. and Vanstone, M. (2002) Probation and social justice. *British Journal of Social Work*, 32(6), 815–30.

Sparrow, R. (2005) Defending deaf culture: the case of cochlear implants. *Journal of Political Philosophy*, 13(2), 135–52.

Specht, H. and Vickery, A. (eds) (1977) *Integrating Social Work Methods*. (London: George Allen and Unwin).

Spolander, G., Pullen-Sansfacon, A., Brown, M. and Engelbrecht, L. (2011) Social work education in Canada, England and South Africa: a critical comparison of undergraduate programmes. *International Social Work*, 54(6), 816–31.

Stansfield, A.J, Holland, A.J. and Clare, I.C. (2007) The sterilisation of people with intellectual disabilities in England and Wales during the period 1988 to 1999. *Journal of Intellectual Disability Research*, 51(8), 569–79.

Stein, H.D. (1958) Social science in social work practice and education. In Parad, H. (ed.) *Ego Psychology and Dynamic Casework: Papers from the Smith College School for Social Work*. (New York: Family Service Association of America), pp. 226–40.

Stein, H. (2003) Social science and social work education. In Aronoff, N. (ed.) *Challenge and Change in Social Work Education: Toward a World View, Selected Papers by Herman D. Stein*. (Alexandria, VA: Council on Social Work Education), pp. 101–18.

Stevens, I. and Cox, P. (2008) Complexity theory: developing new understandings of child protection in field settings and in residential child care. *British Journal of Social Work*, 38(7), 1320–36.

Stillwell, F. (1996) Neoclassical economics: a long cul-de-sac. In Stillwell, F. and Argyrous, G. (eds) *Economics as a Social Science: Readings in Political Economy*. (Sydney: Pluto Press), pp. 94–7.

Stoesz, D. (2000) Renaissance: families in society. *Journal of Contemporary Human Services*, 81(6), 621–8.

Sullivan, M. (1987) *Sociology and Social Welfare*. (London: Unwin Hyman).

Summers, N. (2003) *Fundamentals for Practice with High-Risk Populations*. (Pacific Grove, CA: Thompson Brooks/Cole).

Swain, P. (2002) A critical alliance? Some concluding thoughts. In Swain, P. (ed.) *In the Shadow of the Law: The Legal Context of Social Work Practice*. (Annandale, Sydney: Federation Press), pp. 266–8.

Swift, A.L. (1956) The church and social welfare. In Johnson, F.E. (ed.) *Religion and Social Work*. (New York: Harper and Brothers), pp. 1–15.

Taylor, C. and White, S. (2000) *Practising Reflexivity in Health and Welfare: Making Knowledge*. (Buckingham: Open University Press).

Taylor, S. (1998) A case of genetic discrimination: social work advocacy within a new context. *Australian Social Work*, 51(1), 51–7.

Taylor, S. (2001) The new quest for genetic knowledge: the need for critique and compromise in predictive technologies. In Daly, J., Gullemin, M. and Hill, S. (eds) *Technologies and Health: Critical Compromises*. (Melbourne: Oxford University Press), pp. 2–15.

Taylor, S. (2013) *What is Discourse Analysis?* (London: Bloomsbury).

The Royal Society (2011) *Brain Waves, Module 1: Neuroscience, Society and Policy*. (London: The Royal Society).

Taylor, S., Treloar, S., Barlow-Stewart, K. et al. (2008) Investigating genetic discrimination in Australia: a large-scale survey of clinical genetics clients. *Clinical Genetics*, 74(1), 20–30.

Thompson, N. (1995) *Theory and Practice in Health and Social Welfare*. (Buckingham: Open University Press).

Thompson, N. (2006) *Anti-discriminatory Practice*, 4th edn. (Basingstoke: Palgrave Macmillan).

Thornton, M. (2000) Neo-liberalism, discrimination and the politics of ressentiment. In Jones, M. and Basser Marks, L. (eds) *Explorations on Law and Disability in Australia*. (Annandale, Sydney: Federal Press), pp. 8–27.

Throssell, H. (1975) Social work overview. In Throssell, H. (ed.) *Social Work: Radical Essays*. (Brisbane, Queensland: Queensland University Press), pp. 3–25.

Tilley, E., Walmsley, J., Earle, S. and Atkinson, S. (2012) The silence is roaring: sterilization, reproductive rights and women with intellectual disabilities. *Disability and Society*, 27(3), 413–26.

Trinder, L. (2000) Evidence-based practice in social work and probation. In Trinder, L. and Reynolds, S. (eds) *Evidence-Based Practice: A Critical Appraisal*. (Oxford: Blackwell Science), pp. 138–62.

Trotter, C. (1999) *Working with Involuntary Clients: A Guide to Practice* (St Leonards, NSW: Allen & Unwin).

Trotter, C. (2004) *Helping Abused Children and their Families: Towards an Evidence-based Practice Model*. (Crows Nest, NSW: Allen & Unwin).

Trotter, C. (2006) *Working with Involuntary Clients: A Guide to Practice*, 2nd edn. (London: Sage).

Trotter, C. (2013) *Collaborative Family Work: A Practical Guide to Working with Families in the Human Services*. (Crows Nest, NSW: Allen & Unwin).

Tuitt, P. (2011) Narratives of origins and the emergence of the European Union. In Lessard, H., Johnson, R. and Webber, J. (eds) *Storied Communities: Narratives of Contact and Arrival in Constituting a Political Community*. (Vancouver: UBC Press), pp. 229–44.

Turnell, A. and Edwards, S. (1999) *Signs of Safety: A Solution and Safety Oriented Approach to Child Protection Casework*. (New York: Norton).

Vallacher, R. and Nowak, A. (1997) The emergence of dynamical social psychology. *Psychological Enquiry*, 8(2), 73–99.

Van Heugten, K. (2011) Registration and social work education: A golden opportunity or a Trojan horse? *Journal of Social Work*, 11(2), 174–90.

Van Wormer, K. (2001) *Counselling Female Offenders and Victims: A Strengths-Restorative Approach*. (New York: Springer).

Van Wormer, K. and Davis, R. (2003) *Addiction Treatment: A Strengths Perspective*. (Pacific Grove, CA: Brooks/Cole).

Von Bertalanffy, L. (1968) *General System Theory: Foundations, Development, Applications*. (New York: George Braziller).

Wakefield, J. (1996a) Does social work need the eco-systems perspective? Part 1: Is the perspective clinically useful? *Social Service Review*, 70(1), 1–32.

Wakefield, J. (1996b) Does social work need the eco-systems perspective? Part 2: Does the perspective save social work from incoherence? *Social Service Review*, 70(2), 183–213.

Warren, K., Franklin, C. and Streeter, C. (1998) New directions in systems theory: chaos and complexity. *Social Work*, 43(4), 357–72.

Wastell, D. and White, S. (2012) Blinded by neuroscience: social policy, the family and the infant brain. *Families, Relationships and Societies*, 1(3), 397–414.

Weakland, J., Fisch, R., Watzlawick, P. and Bodin, A. (1974) Brief therapy: focused problem resolution. *Family Process*, 13, 141–68.

Weedon, C. (1997) *Feminist Practice and Poststructuralist Theory*. (Oxford: Blackwell).

Weeks, W. (ed.) (1994) *Women Working Together: Lessons from Feminist Women's Services*. (Melbourne: Longman Cheshire).

Weick, A., Rapp, C., Sullivan, P. and Kisthardt, W. (1989) A strengths perspective for social work practice. *Social Work*, 34(4), 350–4.

White, C. and Denborough, D. (eds) (1998) *Introducing Narrative Therapy: A Collection of Practice-Based Writings*. (Adelaide: Dulwich Centre).

White, M. (2003) Narrative practice and community assignments. *International Journal of Narrative Therapy and Community Practice*, 2, 17–55.

White, M. and Epston, D. (1990) *Narrative Means to Therapeutic Ends*. (New York: WW Norton).

White, S. (2009) Discourse analysis and reflexivity. In Gray, M. and Webb, S. (eds) *Social Work: Theories and Methods*. (London: Sage), pp. 161–71.

White, S. and Wastell, D. (2013) *A Response to Brown and Ward, 'Decision-Making within the Child's Timeframe'*. Available at SSRN: http://papers.ssrn.com/sol3/papers.cfm?abstract_id=2325357.

White, S., Fook, J. and Gardiner, F. (eds) (2006) *Critical Reflection in Health and Social Care*. (Buckingham: Open University Press).

White, V. (2006) *The State of Feminist Social Work*. (London: Routledge).

Williams, S. (2003) *Medicine and the Body*. (London: Sage).

Wingard, B. (1998) Introducing 'sugar'. In White, C. and Denborough, D. (eds) *Introducing Narrative Therapy: A Collection of Practice Based Writings*. (Adelaide: Dulwich Centre), pp. 157–64.

Wise, S. (1990) Becoming a feminist social worker. In Stanley, L. (ed.) *Feminist Praxis: Research, Theory and Epistemology in Feminist Sociology*. (London: Routledge).

Wise, S. (1995) Feminist ethics in practice. In Hugman, R. and Smith, D. (eds) *Ethical Issues in Social Work*. (London: Routledge), pp. 104–19.

Wolf-Branigin, M. (2009) Applying complexity and emergence in social work education. *Social Work Education: The International Journal*, 28(2), 115–27.

Wolf-Branigin, M., Schuyler, V. and White, P. (2007) Improving quality of life and career attitudes of youth with disabilities. *Research on Social Work Practice*, 17(3), 324–33.

Woods, M.E. and Hollis, F. (1990) *Casework: A Psychosocial Therapy*, 4th edn. (New York: McGraw-Hill).

Zahl, M. (2003) Spirituality and social work: a Norwegian reflection. *Social Thought*, 21, 77–90.

INDEX